Northern Forest Canoe Trail

Northern Forest Canoe Trail

THE OFFICIAL GUIDEBOOK

KATINA DAANEN
& The Northern Forest Canoe Trail

2ND EDITION

Enjoy 740 miles of canoe, kayak, and SUP destinations in New York, Vermont, Québec, New Hampshire, and Maine.

MOUNTAINEERS BOOKS

MOUNTAINEERS BOOKS is dedicated to the exploration, preservation, and enjoyment of outdoor and wilderness areas.

1001 SW Klickitat Way, Suite 201, Seattle, WA 98134
800-553-4453, www.mountaineersbooks.org

Printed in China

First edition, 2010. Second edition, 2024.
Design and layout: McKenzie Long, Cardinal Innovative
Cartographer: Pease Press Cartography
Cover photographs, clockwise from top left: *Moose are a common sight on the NFCT in Maine* (iStock/KJMPhotography); *The town of Rangeley, Maine is the center of the Rangeley Lakes region* (Photo courtesy of Nick Leadley Nature Photography); *Paddlers on the Saranac River, New York* (Photo by Nancie Battaglia) Frontispiece: *Sharing time on the water with friends and family is an unparalleled experience.* (Photo courtesy of Due West Photography)

LNT Seven Principles © Leave No Trace, www.LNT.org

Library of Congress Cataloging-in-Publication Data is available at https://lccn.loc.gov/2024004609. The LC ebook record is available at https://lccn.loc.gov/2024004610.

Mountaineers Books titles may be purchased for corporate, educational, or other promotional sales, and our authors are available for a wide range of events. For information on special discounts or booking an author, contact our customer service at 800-553-4453 or mbooks@mountaineersbooks.org.

Printed on FSC-certified materials

MIX
Paper from
responsible sources
FSC
www.fsc.org   FSC® C189328

ISBN (paperback): 978-1-68051-638-8
ISBN (ebook): 978-1-68051-639-5

An independent nonprofit publisher since 1960

Contents

Thru-Paddler's Overview   257

Suggested Trips   268

Points of Interest   288

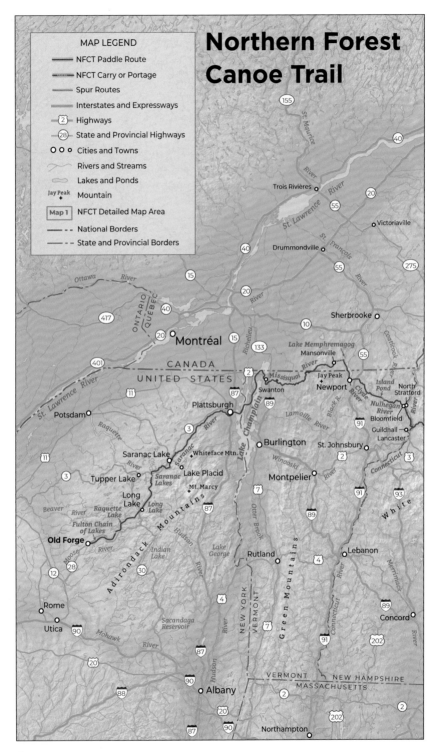

Northern Forest Canoe Trail

MAP LEGEND

———— NFCT Paddle Route

·····+ NFCT Carry or Portage

———— Spur Routes

———— Interstates and Expressways

—(2)— Highways

—(28)— State and Provincial Highways

O O o Cities and Towns

∿∿ Rivers and Streams

⌒⌒ Lakes and Ponds

Jay Peak
  +   Mountain

| Map 1 | NFCT Detailed Map Area

—— - - National Borders

—— - - State and Provincial Borders

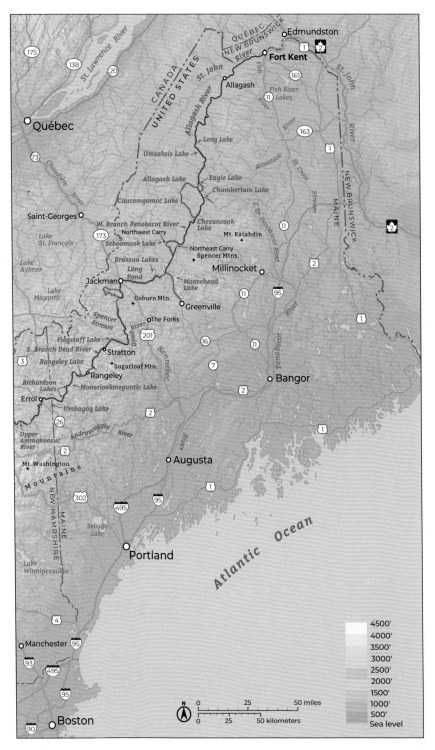

175
138
20
QUÉBEC
NEW BRUNSWICK
St. John River
Edmundston
1
2
Fort Kent
161
St. Lawrence River
Allagash
CANADA
UNITED STATES
St. John
Allagash River
Fish River
Fish River Lakes
Québec
73
Long Lake
River
163
1
Chaudière River
Umsaksis Lake
Aroostook
St. Croix
MAINE
NEW BRUNSWICK
Saint-Georges
Allagash Lake
Eagle Lake
Chamberlain Lake
E. Br. Penobscot River
River
Stream
Lake St. François
Caucomgomoc Lake
Chesuncook Lake
W. Branch Penobscot River
173
Northwest Carry
Mt. Katahdin
Lake Aylmer
Seboomook Lake
Northeast Carry
Spencer Mtns.
11
2
Lake Mégantic
Brassua Lakes
Long Pond
Millinocket
Jackman
Moosehead Lake
11
95
River
1
Coburn Mtn.
Greenville
Spencer Stream
Dead River
The Forks
201
Flagstaff Lake
16
11
Penobscot River
S. Branch Dead River
Stratton
Kennebec River
7
3
Rangeley Lake
Sugarloaf Mtn.
Rangeley
Richardson Lakes
Mooselookmeguntic Lake
2
Bangor
Errol
Umbagog Lake
26
2
River
1
Upper Ammonoosuc River
Androscoggin River
2
Mt. Washington
Augusta
River
Mountains
1
NEW HAMPSHIRE
302
95
MAINE
495
Sebago Lake
Portland
Lake Winnipesaukee
Atlantic Ocean
4
Manchester
95
93
495
95
Boston
90

N
0   25   50 miles
0   25   50 kilometers

4500'
4000'
3500'
3000'
2500'
2000'
1500'
1000'
500'
Sea level

Elevation Profile of the Northern Forest Canoe Trail

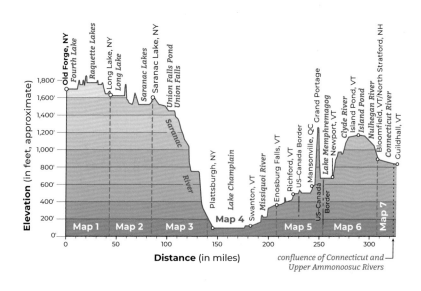

confluence of Connecticut and Upper Ammonoosuc Rivers

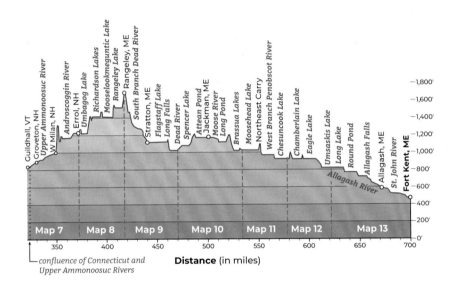

Guildhall, VT
Groveton, NH
Upper Ammonoosuc River
W. Milan, NH
Androscoggin River
Errol, NH
Umbagog Lake
Richardson Lakes
Mooselookmeguntic Lake
Rangeley Lake
Rangeley, ME
South Branch Dead River
Stratton, ME
Flagstaff Lake
Long Falls
Dead River
Spencer Lake
Attean Pond
Jackman, ME
Moose River
Long Pond
Brassua Lakes
Moosehead Lake
Northeast Carry
West Branch Penobscot River
Chesuncook Lake
Chamberlain Lake
Eagle Lake
Umsaskis Lake
Long Lake
Round Pond
Allagash Falls
Allagash River
Allagash, ME
St. John River
Fort Kent, ME

—1,800'
—1,600'
—1,400'
—1,200'
—1,000'
—800'
—600'
—400'
—200'
—0'

Map 7   Map 8   Map 9   Map 10   Map 11   Map 12   Map 13

350   400   450   500   550   600   650   700

Distance (in miles)

confluence of Connecticut and
Upper Ammonoosuc Rivers

Introduction

The Northern Forest Canoe Trail (NFCT) is a chain of possibilities as well as physical places, a string of beautiful waterways across 740 miles of northern New England and New York. The variety of paddling experiences along the Trail offers countless options to explore forests, villages, and farmlands from the unique perspective of a paddler. Serpentine streams, such as Brown Tract Inlet and the upper Nulhegan, transport paddlers through bogs full of wildlife that would be difficult or impossible to see on foot. Broad lakes such as Champlain, Flagstaff, and Chesuncook provide breathtaking vistas of mountain ranges. Rivers vary from the leisurely curves of the Raquette and Connecticut to the quickwater of the Upper Ammonoosuc to the rapid sections of the Saranac, Missisquoi, and Moose.

This guidebook is one of several resources that will help you explore the waters and communities of the NFCT. It complements the online Trip Planner, thirteen-map series, and the Northern Forest Canoe Trail FarOut app. The NFCT website and store offer additional information and books inspiring day trips, weekend getaways, weeklong vacations, or even an end-to-end Thru-Paddling expedition.

TRAIL FACTS
Rivers and Streams: 23
Lakes and Ponds: 59
Carries or Portages: 65, totaling 70-plus miles
Skills Needed: Novice to expert, canoes and kayaks. The route includes flat- and whitewater paddling, poling, lining, and portaging.
National Wildlife Refuges: 3
Communities: 45
States and Provinces: 5
Flow of the Trail: Downstream and upstream. Water levels fluctuate due to spring runoff, drought, and dam releases.

Opposite: *Section paddlers, like this family, experience the Trail a little at a time, often paddling a new stretch each year.* (Photo by Chris Harris)

Even if you know where you are, there's always something to learn when you consult your NFCT map. (Photo courtesy of Northstar Canoes)

Direction to Paddle: All maps describe waterways in a downstream direction. Destination and Section-Paddlers typically choose to paddle downstream. Thru-Paddlers paddle west to east to minimize upstream paddling.

Lodging Options: Depending on the section, choices range from primitive campsites to bed-and-breakfast inns and historic hotels, to motels and cabins, with overnight options roughly every 15 miles.

Landscape: The Trail passes through hills and mountains, forests, farmlands, and village centers.

Guidebook: This book is where you launch your next paddling adventure—perhaps while still standing in the bookstore aisle or enjoying a cozy winter evening by the fire. It will help you get a feel for what each section of the Trail looks like, what kind of paddling you will encounter, and what the towns and surrounding landscapes have to offer when you're not on the water. The guidebook is the place to go with questions like: What's a good section to paddle with young kids? What is camping like in this area? Where can I find a remote paddling trip where I'll see more moose than people? Which area will let me paddle from inn to inn so I don't have to sleep on the ground? How many rapids and portages are there on this river? Where can I combine paddling and hiking? For those considering paddling the Trail in its entirety from Old Forge, New York, to Fort Kent, Maine, as a single journey, the Thru-Paddler's Overview—found at the end of this book—provides general information and tips written by one of the first paddlers to accomplish this feat. Whatever your skills and interests, the guidebook will familiarize you with the character of each section of the Trail so you can plan a fun adventure.

Trip Planner: The Trip Planner tool found on the Northern Forest Canoe Trail website is an interactive map to help you design your trip, and displays features like portages, campsites, and points of interest. Load a map section or zoom right in. This online resource will also help you connect with local services, including outfitters, lodging, and shuttles. Throughout this book you will notice that a private business may occasionally be referenced as part of a section description. The nature of the NFCT is such that in some areas a general store or a remote private campsite, for example, operates as a public landmark or natural section starting or stopping point. When looking for service contact information, you will be directed to use the Trip Planner.

NFCT Maps: NFCT publishes a set of thirteen sturdy, waterproof, topographical maps, each showing a 40- to 60-mile section of the Trail with precise locations of portages, access areas, and campsites. Despite the convenience of other helpful navigation tools, having the physical NFCT maps that correlate to your route is crucial to a successful NFCT journey. The route is shown in numbered points across the map, and each point is accompanied by a written description and the mileage to that spot. On each body of water, the route is numbered and described in the downstream direction for ease of navigation. Paddlers attempting to traverse the whole Trail from west to east will need to paddle upstream on some rivers; consult the Thru-Paddler's Overview in the back of this guidebook for helpful tips. The regulations and land use specific to each area are included on the maps, as well as some interesting history, flora and fauna information, photographs, and a list of recommended books, guides, and other maps to augment your trip. The NFCT map is the final planning piece you will use and the resource you will keep available for reference while you're on the water. Periodically, the organization makes edits to the maps. Visit the NFCT website's "Trail Updates" page to learn about any recent changes to the Trail. The page provides information about route alterations that have occurred since the NFCT maps were printed, such as a dam that was removed, a portage that was rerouted,

NFCT medallions mark the Trail where it meets land at campsites, portages, and access areas. (Photo by NFCT)

A NOTE REGARDING TOTAL TRAIL MILEAGE

Since its inception, the Northern Forest Canoe Trail (NFCT) has been billed as a 740-mile water trail. Unlike land-based hiking trails, getting from point A to point B following a water trail does not necessarily mean you are always taking the most direct route. For example, paddlers may choose to hug shorelines instead of cutting across a large lake. Anyone tracking their paddling trips using GPS will likely discover mileage discrepancies. Thru-Paddlers in particular will find that their total trip mileage adds up to about 700 miles. Likewise, the NFCT FarOut app plots a route following a single line that also reflects a 700-mile total. However, the NFCT includes options connecting a few water bodies that ultimately encompass 740 mapped miles. Additional miles are attributed to the inclusion of the Northwest Carry, which, like the Northeast Carry, originates out of Moosehead Lake in Maine (NFCT Map 11) and connects to the West Branch Penobscot. Paddlers can also choose between taking the inner or outer passages around North Hero Island on Lake Champlain (NFCT Map 4), a bifurcation that is also included as part of the total mapped NFCT mileage.

or the installation of a new campsite. Maps are available for purchase individually or as a set from the NFCT website and outdoor supply stores.

FarOut App: This app doesn't replace the need to carry maps (devices can lose power or fall overboard), but the app is helpful for navigating the NFCT once your trip is planned. The GPS-enabled guide includes over 1400 waypoints, site photos, and several base maps, which can also be downloaded for offline use. You can see user comments about site conditions, locate yourself on a portage, and quickly determine distance to the next site of interest. The app contains real-time updates and changes to the Trail. Purchase a guide for the whole trail or for individual sections.

NFCT Website and Other Resources: In addition to the online Trip Planner, visit the NFCT website to keep informed of news, events, and the most recent updates and changes to the Trail. You'll also discover itineraries and special packages to direct you to the unique attractions along each section of the Trail. The online NFCT store is where one can purchase maps, the FarOut app, and NFCT memoirs and books, including *The Northern Forest Canoe Trail Through-Paddler's Companion*, a standalone guidebook specific for aspiring Thru-Paddlers.

ORIGINS OF THE NORTHERN FOREST CANOE TRAIL

The idea for the Northern Forest Canoe Trail (NFCT) as a contiguous route was brought to life in the 1990s. Ron Canter, Mike Krepner, and Randy Mardres of Native Trails, Inc., researched the many traditional east–west water routes used by Native Americans and early settlers as they explored, sought food and building supplies, waged war, and otherwise navigated throughout the mountainous Northern Forest region. Canter, Krepner, and Mardres proposed linking several of the regional east–west routes in order to create a long, single path to traverse the Northern Forest. Kay Henry and Rob Center, former management principals of the Mad River Canoe company, formed the Northern Forest Canoe Trail organization in 2000 as a way to translate this research into a recreational, community, and regional resource.

Water trails are similar to hiking or other land-based trails in that they provide a designated route for recreational use and are cared for by volunteers or an organization. They differ from terrestrial trails in that they are often a reincarnation of ancient travel routes, and as their travel surface already exists, people may travel the route without realizing they are on an established trail.

Stewarding a water trail means, among other things, maintaining the places where the route comes into contact with land: access areas, campsites, and portage trails. The NFCT owns no land and thus is wholly reliant on local, state, and federal agencies—and the generosity of landowners—to create paddling access in the Northern Forest. To maintain these areas, the NFCT organization coordinates with many landowners, volunteers, government agencies, and other organizations whose work overlaps with the mission of the Trail.

CONNECTING PEOPLE TO PLACES

The Northern Forest Canoe Trail (NFCT) entices experienced Thru-Paddlers, weekend adventurers, and first-time paddlers alike. Those who travel its waters experience beauty and the incredible hospitality of the people and communities the trail strings together. Stories celebrate the joys and challenges of exploring our waterways, and the important role that individuals, businesses, and community partners play in ensuring that our route is maintained and accessible. By providing access to wild places, people's lives are improved, communities are strengthened, and care for our natural world increases.

The NFCT stewards and promotes an unrivaled network of diverse paddling opportunities across the Northern Forest through organized waterway work trips, youth paddling, and events including symposiums, regattas, community paddles, and races. Details about events hosted by the NFCT can be found at the website.

A team in a wooden voyageur canoe competes in the annual Adirondack Canoe Classic. (Photo by NFCT)

WATERWAYS AND SMALL BOATS: ANCIENT PARTNERS IN THE NORTHERN FOREST

The Northern Forest is a region of craggy mountains, deep forests, and webs of waterways. Comprising 80 million acres in northern New York, Vermont, New Hampshire, and Maine, and arcing into southern Canada, the Northern Forest is the largest intact ecosystem east of the Mississippi. Until relatively recently—the nineteenth or twentieth century in most cases—the simplest way to travel through this rumpled landscape was by water. In some places, such as northern Maine, water may still provide the most direct route. While big boats can navigate the region's many large lakes and wide north–south rivers, small boats are the only way to follow the east–west rivers and streams. Foot travel remains more challenging and less efficient than water travel through the mountainous terrain, and road building came late to this sparsely populated area.

People have been using small boats in the Northern Forest since the wane of the last ice age over 12,000 years ago. Ancestors of today's Wabanaki and Iroquois hunted, gathered, fished, traded, and traveled in paddle craft dug out from logs or framed with wood and covered with tree bark or animal skins. European immigrants and their descendants copied these designs as they trapped, logged, and settled in the Northern Forest. Guideboats, a broader, more stable paddle craft that could accommodate several passengers and their gear on hunting and fishing trips, evolved in the Adirondacks and the Rangeley Lakes region as tourism became a popular activity. Artists, writers, and philosophers ventured into the region seeking inspiration and documented the changes as natural resources—primarily logs and animal pelts—were sent downstream to serve the needs and desires of growing populations to the south.

Waterways have always been central to life in the Northern Forest, and today is no different. The regional economy is slowly shifting from one based largely on resource extraction to a diverse economic future that includes more recreation and tourism. Traveling across the NFCT today is a journey through changing human and natural landscapes, through forests and towns, farmlands and working woodlands. Along the way, alert paddlers will spot relics from each post–ice age era and will notice that some traditions of the past are resurfacing and strengthening, while others are being replaced by new ways of living in this rugged and beautiful place.

FLORA AND FAUNA

The Northern Forest ecosystem is a transition zone between the more temperate forests to the south and the boreal forests and tundra to the north. As such, it supports a rich variety of flora and fauna from both of those regions, and it provides important seasonal habitat for migrating animals. Spruce, fir, and tamarack line swamps and top ridgelines, while white and red pines inhabit sandier soils. Hillside hardwood forests are primarily birch, beech, maple, and

Moose feed on aquatic plants and are frequently spotted wading and eating along the more remote sections of the Trail. (Photo by Clyde Smith)

ash. Cedars and silver maples sink their roots in the floodplains along rivers, helping to stabilize the soil and absorb high waters.

Moose are a common symbol of the Northern Forest, but their historic range has been sharply limited in the last century due to development and overhunting. While these pressures caused the moose to disappear entirely from the Adirondacks of New York, the past several decades have seen a slow return of moose into the High Peaks region. Moose are most frequently seen along the eastern half of the NFCT, in New Hampshire and Maine, where their numbers have traditionally remained strong. However, the moose population now faces new pressures due to a changing environment. As the climate continues to warm, parasites like winter (moose) ticks are able to remain attached to moose throughout the year, oftentimes by the thousands, causing life-threatening blood loss and other afflictions. Moose are also susceptible to liver flukes and the brain worms responsible for brain-wasting disease, parasites transmitted through white-tailed deer.

Traveling the valleys of the Trail, paddlers may see beavers, otters, foxes, and a wide variety of waterfowl, including loons, herons, and many types of ducks, geese, and mergansers. Along the entire route, osprey are frequently spotted overhead or perched in large, stick-built nests and nesting platforms. Bald eagles and peregrine falcons are making a comeback after pesticides

BEAVERS

Throughout the various watersheds traversed by the Northern Forest Canoe Trail (NFCT) beavers cut down trees and dam up the little mountain streams (and sometimes the bigger valley streams as well), creating impoundments that retain the region's fast-flowing water through dry times and wet times, releasing it gradually, thus keeping the streams flowing and viable as canoe waterways for most of the year. Only when winter locks the streams in ice does canoeing have to stop. Historically, beavers were an important part of the region's nineteenth-century economy. . . . They were trapped and their fur sold for beaver top hats, coats, and other uses, drawing explorers, trappers, and traders to the region. Once trapped relentlessly, beavers have made a major comeback and are once again part of the forest ecology of the North Country.

—Tom Slayton,
excerpted from the introduction of
*Northeast Passage: A Photographer's Journey Along the
Historic Northern Forest Canoe Trail* by Clyde H. Smith

threatened their survival, and fisheries are also improving as the quality of waterways is restored.

The wooded mountainsides above the Trail are home to black bears, coyotes, white-tailed deer, lynx, and martens. Barred owls swoop to grab moles, voles, mice, and snowshoe hares. Chickadees, blue and gray jays, thrushes, and woodpeckers range from the hillsides through the wetlands, where vegetation like Labrador tea, sundew, and bog rosemary surround the floating water lilies and shelter a variety of frogs, salamanders, and turtles.

Significant plant and animal populations are noted throughout the guidebook's trail descriptions, but field guides published by expert sources such as Audubon, National Geographic, and Appalachian Mountain Club will help sharpen your eyes and identification skills while paddling the Northern Forest.

CHANGING TIMES IN THE NORTHERN FOREST

The Northern Forest, an 80-million-acre forested ecosystem straddling the Canadian border and extending from northern New York to Nova Scotia, has been a source of subsistence, wealth, recreation, and renewal for centuries. Native peoples traversed watersheds and mountain ranges in annual cycles of hunting, gathering, and trade. With the arrival of Europeans, the waterways of the region became pathways of settlement, battle, and cultural exchange. Beginning in the 1800s, the landscape came to serve as both a refuge from the city and a working resource, producing primarily timber but also providing farmland, mining, and hydropower for growing European settlements.

At the end of the twentieth century, as economies began shifting from a local to a more global orientation, the natural resource functions of the Northern Forest shifted to play a different role in the overall economy. Today, trees are still harvested, but numerous timber and pulp mills have closed across the region, and family farms are in decline. Large tracts of land once dedicated to timber production or farming have, in some cases, been sold and sometimes broken into smaller parcels or developed.

Today, government agencies, private companies, local communities, nonprofit organizations, and numerous individuals are working together with renewed levels of collaboration to protect the diversity of interests in the region during this current transitional time. NFCT's role supports the linkage between a community of paddlers and outdoor recreation and environmental tourism industries. It helps provide a connection to the trailside communities where they paddle. This fits with a broader regional effort to build more diverse local and regional economies, including a tourism economy linked to the region's spectacular natural resources and traditional North Woods or agrarian culture. NFCT works actively with local communities, chambers of commerce, and state and regional tourism groups to leverage the power of the Trail to connect people and places in ways that sustain and support a wide array of community and regional partners and natural habitats. Links to NFCT's various business members, local service providers, and other partner organizations can be found on the NFCT website and Trip Planner.

The Northern Forest region is at once a working landscape, a conserved landscape, and a recreational destination. In some cases, access and tourism opportunities are linked directly to the generosity of private landowners who recognize the recreational value of their lands. In other cases, landscape conservation plays a role in the changing use of natural resources. The Trail passes through three federally managed refuges and countless areas conserved by private citizens, municipalities, states, and land trusts. Conservation policies range from maintaining wildlife habitat without any human development to the Silvio O. Conte National Fish and Wildlife Refuge's innovative work to conserve the entire 7.2 million acres of the Connecticut River watershed in four states by working with various landowners on management strategies for the resources and uses within the watershed. Most conservation efforts fall somewhere between these two extremes, allowing for specific activities such as recreation, hunting, or logging, while limiting development of roads and buildings.

Plus ça change, plus c'est la même chose— "the more things change, the more they stay the same." The Northern Forest region has fostered and withstood change for centuries; throughout, the waterways of the NFCT have and will continue to flow, connecting communities to each other and paddlers to special landscapes and a unique heritage.

How to Use This Guide

The Northern Forest Canoe Trail (NFCT) spans four states and one province, encompassing 740 miles as it meanders from Old Forge, New York, to Fort Kent, Maine. The route is broken into thirteen sections, each detailed on a separate NFCT map. This guidebook matches the maps' breakdown by state and section, with the exception that we've given Québec its own guidebook section, immediately following Vermont (on the maps, Québec and Vermont share space).

Just as each NFCT map's route is described in a downstream direction, this guidebook follows the geography of the rivers from their upper ends to their lower ends. This sounds elementary, as few people choose to paddle upstream (and those who do can reference the Thru-Paddler's Overview at the end of this book), but what this means is that in some places, such as on the Missisquoi River in Vermont, the river route will be described east to west, as the river flows, even though the overall NFCT is described from its western end in New York to its eastern end in Maine. The NFCT is not one long, continuous downstream current from New York to Maine, of course, and the flow of rivers, and thus of the route, varies from section to section, and even within the sections of the Trail. Most visitors experience the Trail as Section-Paddlers, meaning that they choose manageable segments, and the ability to avoid upstream travel, portages, and other difficulties as much as possible. A Thru-Paddler undertaking the route in its entirety encounters more than 160 miles of upstream travel when following each map sequentially.

Each section is described in this book and includes relevant information for the trip, including put-ins and take-outs. Note that most NFCT put-ins and take-outs are accessible by car, but not all of them use physical addresses. For example, some boat launches, like Axton Landing in the Adirondacks or the Thoroughfare in the Allagash, are remote and located at the end of backcountry roads. Others are associated by a geographic feature like an NFCT kiosk or a dam, or are known by name like Davis Park. This book includes GPS coordinates to identify every access point, but physical addresses have only been included where put-ins and take-outs are located in or near towns, or when associated with improved boat launches. All GPS coordinates are in decimal degrees, following the World Geodetic System of 1984 (WGS 84).

Bunji is one of many dogs who have experienced the wonders of the Trail with paddling families. (Photo by Cole Gosner and Ashley Hyatt)

ROUTE INFORMATION

The book is divided into state/province, maps, and sections of the Trail. Each state or province begins with an overall introduction that includes information about the area's waterways, geology, human history, and recreational opportunities. A summary of services is also listed by community.

Individual NFCT maps cover between 40 and 60 miles, which this book then subdivides into consecutive paddling sections that may be a half day, a full day, or several days long, depending on the access available and the wisdom and experience of the original team of writer-paddlers. Sections begin with quick-reference info blocks followed by short summaries providing additional navigational details. Physical addresses are included, where they exist, for each access point. However, some section put-ins and take-outs, like those found in Maine, connect remote sections using backcountry roads where GPS coordinates are essential. When businesses or services are mentioned, always be sure to contact any that you plan to use. The NFCT website, Trip Planner tool, and the NFCT FarOut app will contain the most up-to-date listings of available services or changes to the Trail that may have occurred since this book was printed.

Kiosks, like this one in Long Lake, NY, provide information about local communities and waterways and are located in most towns along the Trail. (Photo by NFCT)

Information blocks for each section contain the following information:

Section Name

Each section has an overview, which includes water type/river rating. (See Water Terms and River Ratings in the next section, Planning a Trip, for definitions.)

TRIP DISTANCE: Number of miles covered in the section

TRIP DURATION: An approximation of how long it will take to paddle the section

FLOW/SEASON: Indicating the best paddling conditions and recommended cubic feet per second (CFS) ranges

DIRECTION OF CURRENT: The direction a river flows, such as west to east or south to north, and any gauge information

PUT-IN(S): The starting point for the section, including GPS coordinates (in decimal degrees) and physical address, where possible

TAKE-OUT(S): The ending point for the trip section, including GPS coordinates and physical address, where possible

MAP: Official NFCT map corresponding to the section

PORTAGES: Total number of portages or carries per section, named with noted distance and usefulness of portage wheels

HAZARDS: Wind, rapids, waterfalls, breached dams, and so on

OTHER ACCESS: Breaking the section into a shorter paddle and/or alternative access areas

CONTACT: Name of applicable land and water managers (contact details listed in Resources)

SERVICES: General information of restaurants, lodging, outfitters, groceries, and/or shuttles available within the section (see NFCT Trip Planner for contact information)

CAMPING: Available options such as primitive sites or campgrounds (public or private), and/or whether a fee is charged or reservation is needed

Looking for a recommended trip in a specific area? Check out the Suggested Trips chapter. These curated itineraries will acquaint you not only with the waterways of the NFCT but also with the landscapes and communities that define this northern region. The itineraries contain some extra information in the info blocks such as cell service coverage and opportunities to see and do more that will help you make the most of a visit to the NFCT.

TO PORTAGE OR TO CARRY?

On most sections of the NFCT, paddlers *portage* their boats on portage trails around obstacles or between bodies of water. But in the Adirondacks, paddlers *carry* their boats on carry trails. This regional difference in terminology doesn't indicate any difference in practice: walking across land, lugging your boat and gear to the next stretch of paddleable water. While the words are interchangeable, most NFCT portages have been named "carry," while signs tend to use the term "portage."

Portage Distances and Portage Carts

In order to experience many of the sections in their entirety, portaging will be part of your paddling adventure. The NFCT includes about 70 miles of mapped and signed portages. These carries help paddlers avoid hazards or are used as the means of connecting water bodies. Some portage distances measure only a few hundred yards, and paddlers need only carry their gear for short durations around obstacles such as Buttermilk Falls along the Raquette River in New York, or the Weston Dam outside of Groteton, New Hampshire. Longer

Not all portages follow roads, but where they do, a good set of portage wheels may come in handy. (Photo courtesy of Northstar Canoes)

The NFCT works with local landowners to create riverside campsites along the Trail in Vermont where there is little public land. (Photo by NFCT)

portages will require more persever-ance and perhaps the use of a portage cart (wheels). Although many por-tages follow maintained trails and roads where carts are helpful, some carries follow rough trails where wheeling is impractical or impos-sible. The mile-long Raquette Falls Carry in New York or the 2.5-mile (or longer!) Rapid River Carry in Maine are examples of rugged portages required for remote paddling travel where wheeling becomes challeng-ing. With mindful trip planning, pad-dlers can choose sections that avoid many of the portages.

PRIVATE LANDS AND PUBLIC ACCESS

The NFCT is the longest inland water trail connecting numerous rivers, lakes, and watersheds in the nation. It relies on local volunteer trail stewards to help maintain aspects of the Trail, including many of the free first-come, first-served campsites. But unlike a park system, campsites are not always moni-tored on a regular basis. While campsites are expected to be occupied only for a night or two, it is possible that paddlers may encounter non-paddling folks who have settled in a site for a less-than-temporary duration. In this situation, paddlers are advised to stay elsewhere and to let the NFCT know of any con-cerns they may have with campsite occupancy.

Much of the Trail is also dependent on private landowners who provide pub-lic recreational access. We also credit the governments of each state—New York, Vermont, New Hampshire, and Maine—for creating laws that protect these landowners from liability.

Outdoor opportunities, like the canoe trail, are part of a long tradition of private landowners allowing for recreational activities such as angling, pad-dling, hunting, and hiking. Hundreds of private landowners give individuals and families lifelong memories through the relatively simple act of supporting paddlers and other outdoor enthusiasts as they venture through private lands along the canoe trail and throughout the northeast.

Some private landowners permit paddlers to camp for free on their prop-erty, while others may change a small fee for parking or boat launching.

Please be respectful of this access. Obey signs and leave as little trace of your visit as possible. It's a privilege, and one that we must not take for granted.

Planning a Trip

Waterways are dynamic systems, and even the most detailed route descriptions cannot account for seasonal changes due to fluctuations in water level, down trees, recent floods, geological disturbances, or storms and rainfall. For a complete list of changes, see the "Trail Updates" page at the Northern Forest Canoe Trail website. Be smart: plan for unexpected situations, and stay alert while on the water.

The American Canoe Association provides the following information to help you plan and carry out a fun paddle trip. For more details, consult their website or the excellent information provided by many other paddling and trail organizations listed in the Resources.

PRETRIP CONSIDERATIONS

Know what you are paddling. River guidebooks and topographic maps are valuable references in trip planning. Plan alternate routes in case of winds, changing weather, or unexpected paddler limitations.

Plan each day's itinerary. Set up locations for put-ins and take-outs along with possible lunch break stops. Consider time, distance, and the abilities of your group. Arrange for a shuttle.

Be prepared for anything. Make sure the equipment you take is appropriate to help you survive and rescue yourself, because once you are on the water, it will be all that you have. Refer to the Paddler's Checklist below.

File a float plan with someone who will notify others if you don't return on time. This is especially important in the Northern Forest, where cell phone coverage is spotty and you cannot rely on being able to phone for help.

Clarify participant responsibilities with paddlers before getting on the water. Unless you are instructing or commercially guiding the group, your trip is likely a "common adventure" trip format, in which each participant takes responsibility for the decision to participate, the selection of appropriate equipment, and the decision to run, scout, or portage rapids. More experienced paddlers should assist those with less experience in making proper decisions on the trip.

Don't overreach. Paddle within both your own and your group's limits.

INTERNATIONAL BORDER CROSSINGS

Paddlers passing through international waters will encounter border protection stations (customs) along the Missisquoi River at East Richford, Vermont, and on Lake Memphremagog—either at Leadville Pier in Québec (Canadian citizens) or Newport, Vermont (US citizens). Be aware that laws governing guns, knives, and bear spray differ between the United States and Canada. There are also regulations about crossing the border with pets.

A passport is necessary for all border crossings. For entering the United States, CBP ROAM is a free mobile application that provides an option for pleasure boaters to report their US entry to US Customs and Border Protection (CPB) via their personal smart device. You should still carry your passport even when using the mobile app. For more information about US Customs rules, regulations, and the ROAM app, visit cbp.gov.

A passport or passport card will be needed for entering Canada. For more information about Canadian restrictions, visit the government website at cbsa-asfc.gc.ca.

THE TEN ESSENTIALS

The point of the Ten Essentials, originated by the Mountaineers, has always been to answer two basic questions: Can you prevent emergencies and respond positively should one occur (items 1–5)? And can you safely spend a night—or more—outside (items 6–10)? Use this list as a guide and tailor it to the needs of your outing.

1. **Navigation:** The five fundamentals are a map, altimeter, compass, GPS device, and a personal locator beacon or other device to contact emergency first responders.
2. **Headlamp:** Include spare batteries.
3. **Sun protection:** Wear sunglasses, sun-protective clothes, and broad-spectrum sunscreen rated at least SPF 30.
4. **First aid:** Basics include bandages; skin closures; gauze pads and dressings; roller bandage or wrap; tape; antiseptic; blister prevention and treatment supplies; nitrile gloves; tweezers; needle; nonprescription painkillers; anti-inflammatory, anti-diarrheal, and antihistamine tablets; topical antibiotic; and any important personal prescriptions, including an EpiPen if you are allergic to bee or hornet venom.
5. **Knife:** Also consider a multitool, strong tape, some cordage, and gear repair supplies.
6. **Fire:** Carry at least one butane lighter (or waterproof matches) and firestarter, such as chemical heat tabs, cotton balls soaked in petroleum jelly, or commercially prepared firestarter.

Opposite: *Whether you are an avid paddler looking for a wilderness experience or a novice looking to get started close to town, the NFCT has a trip for you.* (Photo by Aaron Black-Schmidt)

7. **Shelter:** In addition to a rain shell, carry a single-use bivy sack, plastic tube tent, or jumbo plastic trash bag.
8. **Extra food:** For shorter trips a one-day supply is reasonable.
9. **Extra water:** Carry sufficient water and have the skills and tools required to obtain and purify additional water.
10. **Extra clothes:** Pack additional layers needed to survive the night in the worst conditions that your party may realistically encounter.

PADDLER'S CHECKLIST

In addition to the Ten Essentials, which are necessary for any outdoor trip, paddlers also need the following gear and supplies for the safety of the group:

- Personal flotation device (PFD) for every paddler
- Spare paddle
- Whistle or sound-signaling device
- Helmet (whitewater)
- Spray skirt or other way to shed water (kayak, optional for canoe)
- Throw bags and other self-rescue gear such as a paddle float, slings, and tow rope
- River knife for cutting ropes or rigging, including throw ropes
- Bilge pump and/or bailer, especially important on open water
- Light or signal, such as a flashlight or light sticks
- Straps, tie-downs, or some other means to attach essential gear to the boat
- UV eye protection with a strap
- Hat with a brim
- Dry bags for clothing, emergency gear, cameras, and cell phones (although service is unreliable)
- Clothing that can be layered for changing conditions and that dries quickly or keeps you warm when wet
- Footwear that will stay on when swimming and preferably with a closed toe
- Insect repellent
- Duct tape/small repair kit
- VHF radio and personal locator beacon (PLB) if venturing away from shore on a large lake or wilderness area, or a solid plan for how to manage communication in case of emergency
- Portage yoke
- Portage cart (optional, but recommended for long wheelable carries)
- CBP ROAM mobile app and passport (for international border crossing)

WATER SAFETY

Paddling carries inherent risks, which can be mitigated by exercising caution, using common sense, and following these tips:

More than a tasty means of replenishing calories and satisfying an appetite, the meals you eat are a highlight of any trip. (Photo by Jim Sausville)

Wear a PFD. Have a properly fitted life jacket (personal flotation device, or PFD) and *wear it*. Most recreational boating fatalities are due in part to the absence of PFDs.

Prepare and provide a float plan to someone who will notify others if you don't return on time. Let them know which waterbodies you expect to travel on and where you plan to camp or stay.

Be a competent swimmer with the ability to handle yourself underwater and in moving water, waves, or current.

Don't drink the water without treating. Although many sections of the NFCT traverse areas of exceptional water quality, always treat or boil any water drawn from lakes, streams, or rivers for consumption.

Keep the craft under control. Do not enter a rapid unless reasonably sure you can navigate or swim the entire rapid.

Be sure to keep an appropriate distance between craft (a good general rule is to keep the craft behind you in view) Normally, stay behind the lead boat and in front of the sweep boat. Both the lead and sweep boats should be experienced boaters.

Know what hazards to expect on your route, and watch for unexpected hazards—and avoid them. Consult maps, river guides, and experienced paddlers to learn about the known hazards along your route, such as dams, rapids, holes, strainers, logjams, and debris from old mills or other riverside structures. Keep an eye out for unexpected hazards and direct your group in avoiding them.

Cruising along one of the twenty-three Northern Forest Canoe Trail rivers and streams. (Photo courtesy of Matt Burnett Guiding)

Know your emotional and physical limitations. Group members need to constantly assess the behavior of others in their group.

Respect others along the route. Respect the rights of anglers and landowners when paddling.

On Flatwater:
- Remember to watch for water and weather changes.
- Keep an eye out for other boat traffic and keep your group together when traffic is heavy.
- Pay attention to all safety warnings.
- Be sure you are visible to other boaters.
- Have emergency lights.
- Keep your shoes on.
- Be prepared for an unanticipated swim.

On Large Lakes:
- Stay close to shore. Follow the shore that is most protected from wind and waves.
- Do not paddle during a lightning storm or when large wind-driven waves are present.
- As you travel away from shelter, make sure you have the necessary skills to travel back.
- Watch conditions for developing winds and fog.

- Understand wave height, wind speed (Beaufort scale), and fetch, and how they will affect your travel.
- Be sure to use adequate flotation in your craft. Flotation bags not only keep the boat from sinking and aid in self-rescue, but they also help cut down on windage, which makes it easier to control the boat.
- Stay aware of all boat traffic and keep yourself visible using flags, brightly colored gear, and lights, and by keeping your group close together.
- Attach essential gear to the boat so as to avoid loss in the event of capsize.
- Learn boat-righting and other self-rescue techniques before you need them.
- Know how to reenter your boat from the water and how to assist others back into their craft.

On Whitewater and Rivers:

- Use adequate flotation in your craft.
- Walk around all low-head dams, even if they look harmless—they are often extremely dangerous.
- Watch for hydraulics (holes) and know how to read them from your boat.
- Looking downstream, if a hole is "smiling" (meaning the ends of the hole are facing downstream, which tends to feed a paddler out) it is probably friendly. If it's "frowning" (meaning the ends are facing upstream, which could trap a paddler) it is probably unfriendly.
- Beware of strainers! Strainers are fallen trees, bridge pilings, undercut rocks, or anything else that allows the current to flow through it while holding you. Strainers are deadly.
- If in doubt, get out and scout.
- Avoid loose-line entanglement.
- Keep your group together and determine how you will signal each other (whistles, paddle signals) to eddy out and wait.

WATER TERMS

The following terms are used throughout this guidebook to describe NFCT waterways. Be aware that some variation in these terms and their definitions may be in use locally or regionally. Also, as water levels rise and fall, waterways will change in character. Paddlers should be prepared for water conditions that differ from the guidebook description.

Bog or marsh: Places where water may be obstructed by vegetation, making the route difficult to navigate; current, when noticeable, is slow

Bony: River sections containing many rocks or boulders requiring a good deal of maneuverability

Many segments of the Trail are ideal for introducing the next generation of paddlers to the waterways. (Photo courtesy of the Harris family)

Class: Classification of rapids according to the international ratings described below

Confluence: The point where two or more rivers meet

Deadwater: Standing or still water in situations where flow is weak and a pool forms within a river or stream

Eddy: An area of calm(er) water downstream of an obstruction, such as a boulder

Flatwater: Water with little or no discernible current

Gauge (Gage): Instrument that measures river volume in feet (physical height of the water) and flow (cubic feet per second, or CFS) at a specific point in the river

Lake or pond: Water with no discernible current

Lining: The process of maneuvering a boat downstream through whitewater by means of painters (ropes), allowing the paddler to walk rather than run the vessel through current

Painters: 25- to 30-foot rope lengths (made of braided polypropylene that floats) attached to the bow and stern of a boat and used for lining and tracking through strong current

Put-in: The starting point of a paddling trip

Quickwater: Moving water with a distinct, fast current

Rips: A term more often associated with ocean currents but also used to describe swift-moving waves or strong Class I riffles

River: Moving water with higher volume than a stream; current may be slow or quick and may include rapids

River-right/river-left: The side of the river as seen looking downstream

Strainer: A fallen tree, bridge piling, or anything else in which water flows through but where a boat or person cannot; this is a serious river hazard

Stream: Moving water with lower volume than a river, usually narrow and shallow; current may be slow or quick and may include rapids

Take-out: The finishing point of a paddling trip

Tracking: The process of maneuvering a boat upstream through shallow water or current by means of painters (ropes)

Whitewater: Swift-moving water whose surface has become wavy and turbulent due to obstacles or a constriction of the flow; whitewater is classified as Class I through Class VI, from least difficult to most difficult (see below)

RIVER DIFFICULTY RATINGS

The not-for-profit American Whitewater (see Resources) provides the following definitions of the international river difficulty ratings and reminds paddlers that this system is not exact; rivers do not always fit easily into one category, and regional or individual interpretations may cause misunderstandings.

Class I: Fast-moving water with riffles and small waves. Few obstructions, all obvious and easily missed with little training. Risk to swimmers is slight; self-rescue is easy.

Class II–Novice: Straightforward rapids with wide, clear channels, which are evident without scouting. Occasional maneuvering may be required, but rocks and medium-sized waves are easily missed by trained paddlers. Swimmers are seldom injured and group assistance, while helpful, is seldom needed.

Some sections of the Trail require whitewater paddling skills, although portaging any rapid is always an option. (Photo by Mike Lynch)

Class III–Intermediate: Rapids with moderate, irregular waves, which may be difficult to avoid and which can swamp an open canoe. Complex maneuvers in fast current and good boat control in tight passages or around ledges are often required; large waves or strainers may be present but are easily avoided. Strong eddies and powerful current effects can be found, particularly on large-volume rivers. Scouting is advisable for inexperienced parties. Injuries while swimming are rare; self-rescue is usually easy but group assistance may be required to avoid long swims.

Class IV–Advanced: Intense, powerful, but predictable rapids requiring precise boat handling in turbulent water. Depending on the character of the river, it may feature large, unavoidable waves and holes or constricted passages demanding fast maneuvers under pressure. A fast, reliable eddy turn may be needed to initiate maneuvers, scout rapids, or rest. Rapids may require "must" moves above dangerous hazards. Scouting may be necessary the first time down. Risk of injury to swimmers is moderate to high, and water conditions may make self-rescue difficult. Group assistance for rescue is often essential but requires practiced skills. Expert kayak rolling skills are highly recommended.

Class V–Expert: Extremely long, obstructed, or very violent rapids which expose a paddler to added risk. Drops may contain large, unavoidable waves and holes or steep, congested chutes with complex, demanding routes. Rapids may continue for long distances between pools, demanding a high level of fitness. What eddies exist may be small, turbulent, or difficult to reach. At the high end of the scale, several of these factors may be combined. Scouting is recommended but may be difficult. Swims are dangerous, and self-rescue is often difficult even for experts. A very reliable kayak roll, proper equipment, extensive experience, and practiced rescue skills are essential.

CLEAN, DRAIN, DRY

Aquatic invasive species threaten the evolved integrity of our waters as well as the quality of our recreational experience. Play your part in preventing their spread. Follow these guidelines any time you transition from one waterbody to another to ensure you are not the carrier for these aquatic pests.

Clean

Remove mud, plants, fish, and organisms from your boat. Dispose of them in a proper container or on dry land.

- Clean the inside and outside of your boat.
- Clean your paddles and any other gear, including your shoes, if they have come in contact with the water.
- If a hose is available for use before heading into the next waterbody, rinse your boat and gear to help ensure they are properly cleaned.

Drain

Drain all water from hatches, boat wells, bags, bailers, and containers while still at the river or lake you are leaving.

- Avoid using sponges as bailers because it is hard to get all the water out of them between quick (same-day) transitions.

Dry

Dry your boat and gear. Aquatic invasives need moisture to survive. If you use a towel, stow it to be cleaned and dried later.

- Quick-dry towels can be very useful. Make sure that any towel you use to dry your boat and gear is completely dry before using it again on another waterbody.
- If possible, alternate two pair of shoes to give footwear time to dry when making quick (same-day) transitions. Research available shoes and find types that allow for quick drainage and dry time.

LEAVE NO TRACE

In order to maintain the beauty and health of the places where we recreate, as well as the ability to access them, the following principles were developed by

Follow "Clean, Drain, Dry" guidelines every time you transition between NFCT water bodies. (Photo by NFCT)

the Leave No Trace Center for Outdoor Ethics (lnt.org). NFCT is a Leave No Trace member and encourages all paddlers to familiarize themselves with these principles, practice them along the Trail, and help others learn to tread lightly.

Plan Ahead and Prepare

- Know the regulations and special concerns for the area you'll visit.
- Prepare for extreme weather, hazards, and emergencies.
- Schedule your trip to avoid times of high use.

- Visit in small groups. Split larger parties into smaller groups.
- Repackage food to minimize waste.
- Use a map and compass to eliminate the use of marking paint, rock cairns, or flagging.

Travel and Camp on Durable Surfaces

- Durable surfaces include established trails and campsites, rock, gravel, dry grasses, or snow.
- Protect riparian areas by camping at least 200 feet from lakes and streams.
- Good campsites are found, not made.
- Altering a site is not necessary.
- In popular areas, concentrate use on existing trails and campsites.
- Walk single file in the middle of the trail, even when it is wet or muddy.

Dispose of Waste Properly

- Pack it in, pack it out.
- Inspect your campsite and rest areas for trash or spilled foods.
- Pack out all trash, leftover food, and litter.
- If there is no established outhouse, deposit solid human waste in cat holes dug 6 to 8 inches deep at least 200 feet from water, camp, and trails.
- Cover and disguise the cat hole when finished.
- Pack out toilet paper and hygiene products.
- To wash yourself or your dishes, carry water 200 feet away from streams or lakes and use small amounts of biodegradable soap.
- Scatter strained dishwater.

Leave What You Find

- Preserve the past: observe, but do not touch, cultural or historic structures and artifacts.
- Leave rocks, plants, and other natural objects as you find them.
- Avoid introducing or transporting nonnative species.
- Do not build structures or furniture, or dig in pristine areas.
- Disperse camping areas to prevent the creation of campsites and trails.
- Avoid places where human impact is becoming evident.

Minimize Campfire Impacts

- Be aware that campfires can cause lasting impacts to the backcountry.
- Use a lightweight stove for cooking and enjoy a candle lantern for light.

- Where fires are permitted, use established fire rings, fire pans, or mound fires.
- Keep fires small.
- Only use sticks from the ground that can be broken by hand.
- Burn all wood and coals to ash, put out campfires completely, then scatter cool ashes.

Respect Wildlife

- Observe wildlife from a distance. Do not follow or approach them.
- Never feed animals. Feeding wildlife damages their health, alters natural behaviors, and exposes them to predators and other dangers.
- Protect wildlife and your food by storing rations and trash securely.
- Control pets at all times, or leave them at home.
- Avoid wildlife during sensitive times: when mating, nesting, raising young, or in winter.

Be Considerate of Other Visitors

- Respect other visitors and protect the quality of their experience.
- Be courteous. Yield to other users on the trail.

A peaceful morning dawns in the Allagash Wilderness Waterway.
(Photo by John S. Read)

A NOTE ABOUT SAFETY

Safety is an important concern in all outdoor activities. No guidebook can alert you to every hazard or anticipate the limitations of every reader. Therefore, the descriptions of waterways, roads, trails, routes, and natural features in this book are not representations that a particular place or excursion will be safe for your party. When you follow any of the routes described in this book, you assume responsibility for your own safety. Under normal conditions, such excursions require the usual attention to traffic, water, road, equipment, and trail conditions, weather, terrain, the capabilities of your party, and other factors. Keeping informed on current conditions and exercising common sense are the keys to a safe, enjoyable outing.

—Mountaineers Books

- Step to the downhill side of the trail when encountering pack stock.
- Take breaks and camp away from trails and other visitors.
- Let nature's sounds prevail. Avoid loud voices and noises.

Think Before You Post

When you post on social media about a place you visited, consider your potential communications through a leave-no-trace lens by modeling responsible outdoor recreation in your posts. Consider removing location tags, particularly for areas that are already popular or very easy to access, to help prevent overuse.

Whether you seek a day trip, a weekend adventure, a weeklong journey, or an expedition paddling the entire distance, the NFCT has something for everyone. Use this guidebook to begin, and enrich your exploration of the waters, communities, and landscapes that make the Northern Forest such a treasured place. Happy paddling!

Next page: *Adirondack guideboats, designed to ferry another era's tourists and hunters to remote camps and lodges, are still used as recreational boats today.* (Photo by NFCT)

New York

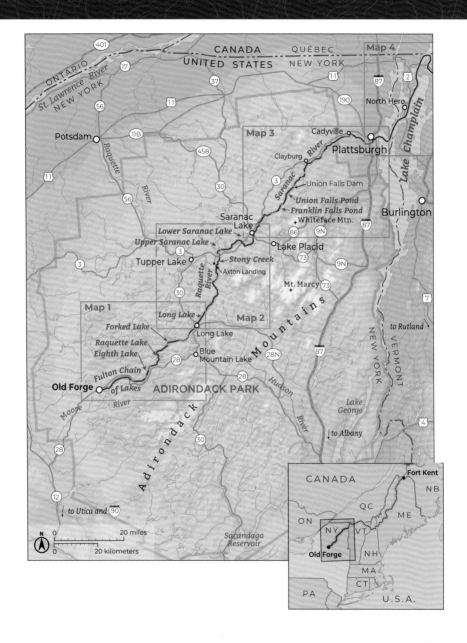

The Adirondacks region of northern New York includes the Adirondack Park and surrounding countryside, and the western shore of Lake Champlain.

Over time, the Adirondack Park has grown from 2 million acres when it was created in 1892 to more than 6 million acres of public and private land. The 2.5 million acres of state land is the largest publicly protected area in the continental United States—greater in size than Yellowstone, Everglades, Glacier, and Grand Canyon National Parks combined. The western terminus of the Northern Forest Canoe Trail (NFCT) is in Old Forge, in the Central Adirondacks. From there, the Trail traverses 145 miles along the Adirondacks' scenic rivers, lakes, and ponds.

The Adirondack Mountains are a geologic island formed from billion-year-old bedrock and surrounded by a sea of younger, gentler terrain. Pressure from deep within the Earth's crust pushed this prehistoric rock up into a giant

Numerous fish species can be found in the lakes, rivers, and streams of the NFCT. Check state-specific rules and regulations on each state's Fish and Game website. (Photo courtesy of Matt Burnett Guiding)

dome. During the past million years, continental ice sheets swept over this area at least four times, gouging valleys, damming waterways, and distributing 2900 lakes and ponds throughout the forested valleys. The uplift is the center of about 30,000 miles of streams and rivers flowing in all directions. This complex drainage system provides many interconnected waterways, making it one of the best paddling regions in North America. The NFCT weaves through this region of seemingly infinite paddling possibilities, and some well-loved routes off the Trail are also described.

The lakes in the Adirondacks provide abundant game fish: northern pike, lake trout, rainbow trout, brook trout, landlocked salmon, largemouth bass, smallmouth bass, yellow perch, brown bullhead, and tiger muskie (muskellunge). All anglers sixteen and older require a New York State fishing license.

Mallard ducks and Canada geese are typical paddling companions, as are hooded and common mergansers. Blue herons, bitterns, deer, and beavers are frequently sighted along the shores. Loons, bald eagles, broad-winged hawks, and turkey vultures are less frequently sighted. Songbirds such as vireos and thrushes are more likely to be heard before their perch is seen. Brown Tract Inlet's swampy forests provide habitat for boreal birds such as black-backed woodpeckers, gray jays, and boreal chickadees.

The word *Adirondack* probably derives from the Iroquois *ha-de-ron-da*, meaning "bark-eater," referring to a subsistence practice of eating bark and buds during long, lean winters. The Iroquois used the mountainous region seasonally to hunt and fish, as did the Algonquins, but they did not live here year-round. The rough terrain and challenging climate doomed white settlers' initial attempts to develop permanent residence here, leaving the area relatively isolated long after surrounding lands had been settled.

Some of the first permanent settlers in the Adirondacks were Abenaki who migrated from Vermont following the American Revolution. The Sabattis family was one of three Abenaki families who settled here, and their name is still attached to local landmarks. Mitchell Sabattis lived near Long Lake during the mid-1800s when guiding became a commercial activity in the Adirondacks. He became known as a trusted guide and one of the first developers of the Adirondack guideboat (see "Adirondack Guideboats" sidebar, this section).

The NFCT from Old Forge to Saranac Lake follows what is probably the oldest Native American water trail through the Adirondacks, as well as the shortest and most direct west-to-east paddling route. This "traditional highway of the Adirondacks" is celebrated as an annual race held the weekend after Labor Day. The Adirondack Canoe Classic, or 90-Miler, tests the skill and endurance of both serious racers and recreational paddlers amid splendid mountain and forest vistas. The course also shares the same mileage with the first two maps of the NFCT. The Saranac Lake Area Chamber of Commerce began the event in 1983, and the Adirondack Watershed Alliance operated it from 1999 to 2019. In 2020, NFCT took over management of the 90-Miler.

As paddlers approach Saranac Lake, they may spot a couple of the town's many antique "cure cottages" with porches. These cottages were built starting in 1885 when Dr. Edward L. Trudeau established the Adirondack Cottage Sanitarium, which would become a world-renowned center for the treatment of pulmonary tuberculosis, or "consumption." Patients were exposed to as much cold, healthy air as they could stand, even being bundled for up to eight hours on a porch in midwinter. Robert Louis Stevenson lived in a cottage at the end of Stevenson Lane in 1887–88. He survived the so-called cure, and the cottage is now maintained as a museum dedicated to the author of *Treasure Island*. Although an antibiotic to treat pulmonary tuberculosis was developed in 1921, the sanitarium treatment was not phased out until 1954. The cure cottages were transformed for use by tourists. Some are bed-and-breakfasts today.

From Saranac Lake, the NFCT descends from the Adirondack Plateau to the Lake Champlain Valley via the sometimes calm, sometimes wild Saranac River. In 1846 the Saranac River became an official public highway—for logs. With 200,000 logs sluiced down it per year, it was one of the great log drive rivers of the East, with busy pulp mills located between Cadyville and Kent Falls. Since the Saranac River connects to Lake Champlain, a major north–south highway from colonial days, its water power was tapped early on for industrial purposes. In addition to pulp production, ore and minerals mined near Clayburg and Redford spurred local ironworks and glass production.

Marketable softwood trees ran out in the 1920s. For a time, the big mills brought in logs by rail. Railroads were more expensive than river drives, though, and with the start of the Great Depression, they became uneconomical. Dams, sluices, and some buildings were converted to generate electricity. Along the river, beside New York Route 22B in Morrisonville, is a monument to logging days made from three great millstones.

There's always something to see along the Trail: sometimes it's majestic and sometimes it's a brood of common mergansers. (Photo by Mike Lynch)

ADIRONDACK GUIDEBOATS

Pointed at both ends and quickly propelled by oars, the Adirondack guideboat is a cross between a rowboat and a canoe, and it's light enough for one person to carry over muddy and slippery trails between lakes. Guideboats were designed to hold a guide, the sport (the guide's client), and his duffel. They were used for hunting and trapping, carrying freight, and general transportation. Early guideboats could be difficult to control in high winds, so builders, who were often guides, adapted the design to increase seaworthiness and volume while reducing weight. Modern guideboats are lighter, faster craft than the original lapstrake version and on a windy lake can be more seaworthy than a canoe.

The Saranac River flowed freely down Indian Rapids on its final five miles to the lake before Zephaniah Platt founded Plattsburgh and built his first dam in 1786. By the middle of the nineteenth century, this stretch became a chain of six millponds, with each pond's dam powering four or more factories. Treadwell Mills Dam and Imperial Mill Dam create the last two remaining impoundments. The river again flows in rapids and enlivens the heart of a city.

The past spreads an elegiac quality over a cruise on the lower Saranac. It is a river of ruins. Remains of the muscled industries that once drank from the river now lie broken in the woods. The valley reflects a regional progression, common along the NFCT, from wilderness, through farmland, to towns and industry, and in some places, back to farmland.

The present is kinder to the river and the land, but propriety has not always flourished. The land and water degradation caused by the logging practices of the nineteenth century were a major reason the Adirondack Park was established by the State of New York. While responsible logging on private land is still an important part of the local economy, shoreline cutting is now prohibited, and public lands are protected from development and logging under the New York State constitution as "forever wild lands."

From the Adirondacks to Lake Champlain, from open vistas to wild rivers, you'll discover a full range of paddling opportunities throughout this section. New York's many public boat launches, state campgrounds, and plentiful shoreline campsites and lean-tos, managed by the New York State Department of Conservation (NYSDEC), make it easy to plan day, weekend, weeklong, or longer trips. Whether you want to camp under towering pines, or stay the night in one of the latticed villages steeped in gilded-age history, or simply spend a few hours fishing impoundment backwaters or running a bit of whitewater, this living reminder of when waterways were both highways and routes of communication is sure to inspire adventure.

NFCT MAP 1: ADIRONDACK NORTH COUNTRY (WEST)

Fulton Chain of Lakes to Long Lake

Steeped in history, geologic interest, and abundant wildlife, this 41-mile lake-to-lake trip through the Central Adirondacks passes shoreline camps, stretches of quiet forest, and small towns where hot meals, supplies, and lodging can be found. Views of both near and distant peaks are spectacular, the paddling is generally easy (unless it is windy), and campsites are plentiful.

Initially a gathering place for local trappers, guides, hunters, and sportsmen, Old Forge got its name when iron ore was discovered in the late eighteenth century and a forge was established. Today, Old Forge is a premier vacation and travel destination, attracting over a million visitors each summer. There are a variety of lodging, dining, and recreational opportunities. Old Forge Hardware is a great place to browse, providing a lot more than just hardware.

The dam on Old Forge Pond was built around 1798 to control water flow through the Fulton Chain of Lakes and to expand the lake chain from 2762 to 3481 acres. In the fall, the dam lowers the water level upstream to protect docks and boathouses from freeze-thaw damage. The picturesque red mill house on the dam is a reminder of the gristmill that was built in 1805 and operated until 1825, when it was determined that the soil of the western Adirondacks was too thin and poor in quality to profitably grow grain.

The Fulton Chain comprises a variety of small ponds and broad lakes, ringed by camps and never far from the services of town. On Fourth Lake, lakeside dining and lodging establishments offer dock access to boaters. In Inlet, boardwalk mooring is provided at Arrowhead Park along the channel between Fourth and Fifth Lakes for short trips to shops, an outfitter, and restaurants. Arrowhead Park provides day parking (overnight parking is not allowed), limited toilet facilities, and access to Fifth Lake. Long-term parking is permitted at Fern Park, located 1 mile outside of Inlet, when special events are not being held.

By Sixth Lake, the shoreline camps become sparse, and Seventh and Eighth Lakes are characterized by a mixed forest of beech, birch, red maple, red spruce, white pine, balsam fir, and tamarack.

The Fulton Chain of Lakes is popular with paddlers who are learning long-distance tripping skills or who prefer to sleep in shoreline inns. (Photo courtesy of Northstar Canoes)

The Seventh Lake boat launch and fishing access, 4.3 miles east of downtown Inlet on NY 28, provides day-use-only parking, limited toilet facilities, and access to Sixth and Seventh Lakes. North of the boat launch, look for the stand of old growth called Cathedral Pines, where a marked foot trail will lead you on a short loop through these massive trees. Seventh Lake is stocked annually with salmon; smallmouth bass, rainbow, and lake trout are also plentiful. The best fishing is along the rocky shorelines, especially on the north shore. Eighth Lake is stocked with rainbow and lake trout and salmon. Fish the rocky areas for smallmouth bass.

Brown Tract Inlet rewards paddlers who make the effort to carry to its start; its quiet, meandering path through wetlands feels like a world apart from the wide lakes more characteristic of this section of the Trail. The stream's boggy shoreline is markedly different from the drier, tree-lined shores of the lakes and ponds. The carry used to involve sinking bog bridges and slippery, half-submerged docks, but now the boardwalk over the wetland has been rebuilt to protect fragile plant life. As you cruise over beaver dams through this unique area, you'll spot Labrador tea, mountain holly, bog rosemary, sweet gale, and the insectivorous pitcher plants and sundew along the banks. Your bow will slide past pickerelweed, white water lilies, and yellow pond lilies.

BALD (RONDAXE) MOUNTAIN FIRE TOWER

A scenic hike to the top of 2350-foot Bald Mountain provides panoramic views of the Fulton Chain and surrounding wilderness. The popular trail ascends 1 mile up to the summit and fire tower through a mix of trees and beautiful rock formations. There are plenty of views along the way. The trail is rooty and uneven, and sturdy hiking shoes are recommended. Vehicles can travel 4.5 miles past the Town of Webb Visitor Information Center on New York Route 28 to turn left on Rondaxe Road 0.2 mile to the parking area on the left and the trailhead.

Raquette Lake (*Papolpoga'mak*, meaning "full of bays") has many points and coves hosting a variety of lodges, including Adirondack Great Camps and historic churches. South Inlet is navigable for 2 miles to a pool under a waterfall, and old-growth forests can be glimpsed on the shores of Sucker Brook Bay.

The lake has three basins. Smallmouth bass can be found along the rocky shoreline in any basin. The northern basin near Beecher Island has a high catch rate for lake trout. The middle basin has largemouth bass in its back bays, as do the other basins. Brook trout fishing is good in May at the mouth of the Marion River in the southern basin.

Forked Lake is 7 miles long with three arms. The shores are wooded and provide shelter from the wind. Forked Lake has good populations of smallmouth and largemouth bass; the south end has the best habitat. You are apt to find smallmouth bass in rocky areas, while largemouth bass prefer shallow, stump-infested habitat. Fish for brook trout in the spring. Landlocked salmon are also stocked. Fishing is not allowed near the privately owned shoreline at the north end of the lake.

The serenity of Forked Lake is followed by the whitewater and waterfalls of the Raquette River (*Masta'qua*, meaning "largest river"), which drops 116 feet on its 4-mile descent to Long Lake (*Kwenogamak*, meaning "long lake").

This section of the Trail ends one-third of the way up the narrow finger of Long Lake, where the town of Long Lake sits on the slopes above the water. Each September, the NFCT partners with Long Lake Recreation and Tourism to host the Long Lake Long Boat Regatta. The event features the North American Voyageur Canoe Championships, the Adirondack Kayak Championship, and other 10-mile figure-eight-course races. Lodging, dining, and a seasonal market are available in this quintessential Adirondack village.

This entire section can be paddled in three to four days or enjoyed as a series of day and overnight trips. Campsites and lean-tos are plentiful. Side trips include exploring the distant fingers of Forked Lake, poking up the small streams that wind into Raquette Lake's many coves, and following the historic and lovely Marion River route to Blue Mountain Lake. See NFCT Map 1 and the NFCT website for additional trip planning and navigational details.

SECTION 1

Fulton Chain of Lakes

This paddle follows a series of lakes through classic Adirondack scenery: forested mountains rising above lakeside cottages, Adirondack Great Camps, small towns, and tree-lined shores. Flatwater ponds and small, sometimes shallow lakes are connected by portages.

TRIP DISTANCE: 15.5–18 miles

TRIP DURATION: Allow 1–2 days

FLOW/SEASON: Old Forge Pond Dam maintains a navigable water level from April ice-out to November freeze-up.

DIRECTION OF CURRENT: n/a

PUT-IN: Western terminus of the NFCT at the Old Forge Visitor Information Center, 3140 New York Route 28, Old Forge. Overnight parking. GPS: 43.712483°, –74.969401°

TAKE-OUT: Eighth Lake state campground boat launch on Seventh Lake, 1353 NY 28, Inlet. Overnight parking. Day-use fee. GPS: 43.758172°, –74.715883°

MAP: NFCT Map 1, Adirondack North Country (West)

PORTAGES (1–2): Fifth Lake Carry, 0.5 mile (wheelable); **Eighth Lake state campground Carry,** 0.9 mile (wheelable; only necessary if continuing beyond the take-out to Eighth Lake)

HAZARDS: Fourth Lake and Seventh Lake are shallow, and late-morning winds can create rolling waves.

OTHER ACCESS: Fourth Lake: Alger Island access at South Shore Rd./County Rd. 118. Day-use and overnight parking fees. GPS: 43.737193°, –74.892207°; Fourth Lake New York State Department of Environmental Conservation (NYSDEC) boat launch, Inlet. Vehicles may not be left for more than 24 hours. GPS: 43.75518°, –74.79432°; **Sixth Lake:** Hand carry canoe and kayak access below dam. Small parking area. GPS: 43.745241°, –74.782508°; **Seventh Lake:** NYSDEC boat launch on NY 28. Overnight parking. GPS: 43.744188°, –74.725108°

CONTACT: Town of Webb Visitor Information Center in Old Forge; Inlet Information Office; NYSDEC,Regions 5 and 6; NFCT Trip Planner

SERVICES: Restaurants, groceries, lodging, and outfitting in Old Forge and Inlet

CAMPING: Free first-come, first-served primitive NYSDEC campsites and lean-tos are plentiful; Alger Island and Eighth Lake state campgrounds charge a fee and may require reservations.

Launch at the dock behind the Visitor Information Center in Old Forge, the location of the charming red mill house dam and NFCT western terminus kiosk. Paddle 1.5 miles east on this impounded stretch of the middle branch of the Moose River, a winding stream with docks and boathouses lining the shore. Many of the cabins are hidden in the dense trees, but if the weather's nice, you're bound to get waves and greetings from folks sitting on their docks.

First, Second, Third, and Fourth Lakes are essentially one long lake separated by narrow straits. Although this part of the Trail may have more lakeside cabins than any other segment, you'll still see mostly trees along the shores as you paddle the curves through the first three small lakes. The cliff band of Bald (Rondaxe) Mountain slides by on your left. A marked channel leads to Second Lake and will pass by DeCamps Island (Treasure Island), which is owned by New York State.

From Third Lake, you'll see the Bald Mountain fire tower perched high above the left shore. At the end of the lake, enter a narrow, shallow, winding channel connecting to Fourth Lake. Give large tour boats a wide berth—they need the whole channel.

Fourth Lake is lined with cabins and camps and is by far the largest of the Fulton Chain. A public boat access—and the permit station for NYSDEC's Alger Island Campground—is located on the south shore, at a picnic area within the lake's west end. If you follow Fourth Lake's north shore, you'll paddle by the unique Shoal Point lighthouse. Either way, after you pass Alger Island, the lake

Fall is a spectacular time to visit Adirondack waters, frequently offering clear skies as well as brilliant foliage. (Photo by Joe Geronimo)

ADIRONDACK STYLE AND THE GREAT CAMPS

Examples of Adirondack architecture are on display along this section of the NFCT, in everything from small cabins to hotels to the Great Camps where the tradition began. Adirondack style, or Great Camp style, is characterized by harmonious woodland architecture featuring log construction, native stonework, and decorative rustic woodwork and furnishings made of twigs, branches, and birchbark.

This style of architecture and decorating probably began at Camp Pine Knot, or Huntington Memorial Camp, which was built in 1877 on the southwest tip of Long Point on Raquette Lake by William West Durant, son of railroad tycoon Thomas C. Durant. President Benjamin Harrison built his Great Camp, Berkeley Lodge, in 1895 on Second Lake. Great Camp Sagamore, built in 1897 by Durant on Sagamore Lake, is today the only publicly accessible Great Camp. It is located south of Raquette Lake, on a dirt road that meets NY 28 opposite the Raquette Lake Village Road.

Durant's Great Camp style spread throughout the Adirondacks and beyond. President Theodore Roosevelt is said to have been influenced by the Adirondack architecture he saw as a child and to have incorporated it into plans for national park buildings. The Old Faithful Inn in Yellowstone National Park is a classic example of Adirondack style that spread far beyond these northern lands.

opens in front of you. When it curves to the east, you'll approach Arrowhead Park and the hamlet of Inlet, marked by a boardwalk on the left side of the channel to Fifth Lake.

Paddling away from Arrowhead Park, enter a winding stream to access Fifth Lake, a very small pond. Cross Fifth Lake and enter another winding stream, past a rustic private lean-to/boathouse, to the dock, and the start of the first carry. This 0.5-mile carry gets you to the other side of NY 28, where you put in on Sixth Lake (hand carry access only) by a dam similar in age and design to the one at Old Forge. Sixth Lake is only 1 mile long and is surrounded by cottages. You will soon be paddling under Seventh Lake Road (NY 13) into Seventh Lake, where NYSDEC campsites and lean-tos dot the north shore.

A winding, stump-strewn channel leads to the take-out at NYSDEC's Eighth Lake state campground, marked by two floating docks and a steel boat ramp at a sandy beach. End your section trip here or carry 0.9 mile on a flat road through the campground to add Eighth Lake to the day's paddle (see Section 2 below). After exploring Eighth Lake, you then return to the campground to take out. Toilets and drinking water are available at this popular campground. A day-use permit is required if you park a vehicle here.

SECTION 2

Eighth Lake, Brown Tract Inlet, Raquette Lake, and Forked Lake

Eighth Lake is 1.5 miles long with undeveloped shorelines and no formal access at the north end. Brown Tract Inlet (also known as Browns Tract) is a low-gradient, winding paddle through a scenic bog, which leads to the wide expanses of Raquette Lake. While also large, Forked Lake's narrow fingers make it feel more intimate.

TRIP DISTANCE: 15–16.5 miles

TRIP DURATION: Allow 1–2 days

FLOW/SEASON: A navigable water level is maintained from April ice-out through November freeze-up.

DIRECTION OF CURRENT: Brown Tract, west to east

PUT-IN: Eighth Lake state campground boat launch on Eighth Lake, 1353 New York Route 28, Inlet. Day-use fee. GPS: 43.769237°, −74.711076°

TAKE-OUT: Forked Lake state campground boat launch, 381 Forked Lake Campsite Rd., Long Lake. Day-use fee. GPS: 43.90483°, −74.527997°

MAP: NFCT Map 1, Adirondack North Country (West)

PORTAGES (2): Brown Tract Carry, 1.2 miles (mostly wheelable); **Forked Lake Carry**, 0.5 mile (wheelable)

HAZARDS: Afternoon winds can create rolling waves on Raquette Lake.

OTHER ACCESS: Brown Tract: Informal access where the carry comes close to the road on NY 28. No overnight parking.

GPS: 43.796539°, −74.695098°;

Raquette Lake: Town of Raquette Lake. Overnight parking. GPS: 43.81315°, −74.656495°; South Inlet canoe and kayak access, GPS: 43.807056°, −74.609580°; Golden Beach state campground. Day-use fee. GPS: 43.815825°, −74.597892°;

Forked Lake: Forked Lake Carry Rd. boat launch. GPS: 43.892593°, −74.592887°

CONTACT: Town of Long Lake Parks & Recreation (includes Raquette Lake); New York State Department of Environmental Conservation (NYSDEC) Region 5; NFCT Trip Planner

SERVICES: Restaurant and general store in the town of Raquette Lake

CAMPING: Free first-come, first-served primitive NYSDEC campsites and lean-tos are plentiful; Eighth Lake, Brown Tract Pond, Golden Beach, Tioga Point, and Forked Lake state campgrounds charge a fee and may require reservations.

Adventure abounds on the Northern Forest Canoe Trail. (Photo courtesy of Matt Burnett Guiding)

If you've begun your trip from the boat launch on Eighth Lake, after paddling its length, you will next portage the 1.2-mile Brown Tract carry. The carry crosses an 1825-foot-high divide (though you don't feel like you're climbing anything steep) to the 500-foot boardwalk leading to the put-in on Brown Tract Inlet. This divide marks the highest point on the entire NFCT.

An informal alternative put-in (or take-out from the previous section) is to carry halfway to Brown Tract where the trail comes within sight of NY 28. The sandy pull-off on the side of the road here is about 0.6 mile north of Eighth Lake and is marked by a utility pole in its center. Although you can't leave a car here for any length of time, it provides another option as a start or end to a paddle trip.

Part of the adventure of paddling quiet Brown Tract Inlet is navigating through or over beaver dams on your way to Raquette Lake. Pass under a bridge as you emerge from the stream and enter Raquette Lake. The town of Raquette Lake is on your left. Here you can find the Raquette Lake Supply Co. General Store. Raquette Lake Hotel and Tap Room offers both lodging and refreshment. Overnight parking is available in the town of Raquette Lake.

Raquette Lake is the fourth-largest lake in the Adirondacks, with three basins. The lake is deceptively small in appearance, but its many bays and peninsulas provide almost 100 miles of shoreline. The lake is home to many of the Adirondack Great Camps (see "Adirondack Style and the Great Camps" sidebar earlier in the chapter). Several free lean-tos and primitive campsites are dispersed along the shores and on islands on public land. Tioga Point state campground and most sites associated with Forked Lake state campground are water-accessed-only and fee-based. Reservations are necessary to ensure a site is available upon your arrival. The Golden Beach state campground requires a day-use fee for each day of overnight parking.

Plan to paddle Raquette Lake in the morning, as afternoon winds can create rolling waves. As you head up the lake, there is little wind shadow from northwest winds until you round Bluff Point, so choose your route accordingly if you do encounter wind. You will paddle in and out of coves and around peninsulas and islands on your way north to Outlet Bay, the final cove. Several lean-tos are located along the northern shoreline of this cove between Boucher Point and the take-out.

Outlet Bay narrows just before the signed take-out on the north (left) shore. The 0.5-mile Forked Lake Carry follows a road over a 20-foot rise to the south shore of Forked Lake. **Note:** The first stretch of the Raquette River, which flows between Outlet Bay and Forked Lake, is not paddleable.

From the Forked Lake Carry dock and put-in on the south shore, you will paddle 3.5 miles into the eastern arm of Forked Lake toward the state campground at the outlet. Most of the northern shoreline is privately owned, but there are free primitive campsites near the put-in and one NYSDEC lean-to on the south shore outside of the state park boundary. Much of the west arm is also state-owned land and available for primitive camping.

Take out at Forked Lake state campground, where toilets and drinking water are available. A day-use permit is required if you park a vehicle here.

SECTION 3

Raquette River: Forked Lake to Long Lake

Classic Adirondack river and lake scenery characterize this segment, with a remote feel and mountain views. The 116-foot drop in 5 miles of the Raquette River between Forked Lake and Long Lake creates rapids and falls that are scenic but challenging from a paddling perspective. Portages are present to assist paddlers around technical whitewater and Class V Buttermilk Falls. Flatwater paddling on Long Lake brings you to the town of Long Lake.

TRIP DISTANCE: 9 miles
TRIP DURATION: Allow 1 day
FLOW/SEASON: Flatwater sections are navigable in all seasons from April ice-out to November freeze-up. Whitewater sections are navigable from April ice-out through mid-July and after a hard rain during the remainder of the paddling season.

DIRECTION OF CURRENT:
Raquette River, southwest to
northeast

**PUT-IN(S): Forked Lake state
campground boat launch,** 381
Forked Lake Campsite Rd., Long
Lake. Day-use fee. GPS: 43.90483°,
–74.527997°; **Forked Lake Campground Carry:** Portage trail
terminus on the Raquette River
to avoid rapids at boat launch.
Informal parking. GPS: 43.906747°,
–74.502415°

TAKE-OUT: Long Lake boat launch,
88 Dock Rd., Long Lake. Overnight
parking (use auxiliary lot). GPS:
43.978813°, –74.416154°

MAP: NFCT Map 1, Adirondack
North Country (West)

**PORTAGES (2–3): Forked Lake
Campground Carry,** 1.4 miles
(wheelable; only necessary if continuing a trip from the previous
section or avoiding the first section
of rapids); **Buttermilk Falls Carry,**
0.1 mile (not wheelable); **Deerland
Carry,** 0.4 mile (not wheelable)

HAZARDS: Raquette River's 5-mile
stretch between Forked Lake and
Long Lake contains Class II–III
rapids plus the mandatory portage
around Class V Buttermilk Falls.

OTHER ACCESS: North Point Rd.:
Informal parking at the Deerland
lean-tos and campsite access trail.
GPS: 43.924690°, –74.475268°; But-
termilk Falls offers day-use parking.
GPS: 43.914254°, –74.483011°; **Long
Lake town beach:** 1258 Main St.,
Long Lake. Overnight street park-
ing. GPS: 43.974244°, –74.423943°

CONTACT: Town of Long Lake
Parks & Recreation; New York State
Department of Environmental
Conservation (NYSDEC) Region 5;
NFCT Trip Planner

SERVICES: Food and lodging
available in the town of Long Lake

CAMPING: Free first-come, first-
served NYSDEC primitive campsites and lean-tos along the river;
Forked Lake state campground
charges a fee, reservations
recommended.

*Beautiful campsites and picturesque lean-tos like this one, can be found
throughout the Adirondacks in Maps 1 and 2. (Photo by NFCT)*

Alternative Trip: Marion River and Eckford Chain to Blue Mountain Lake Village

This historic paddle parallels the steamship-and-railroad route that Gilded Age tourists took from Raquette Lake to Blue Mountain Lake. After leaving Brown Tract, pass Raquette Lake dock and the north shore of Big Island. Paddle around the tip of Long Point and east into the mouth of the slow, winding Marion River. There, you'll observe second-growth forest, meadows, marsh with lily pads, and beaver dams. Where the water becomes very shallow, steamboats had to stop, and you do too. Carry 0.5 mile over private land on the old railroad bed to the dam at the foot of Utowana Lake. The shortest standard-gauge railroad line in the country ran 1300 feet here and operated from 1900 to 1929.

At the dam, tourists would embark on another steamship, and here you can get back in your boat. Paddle 7 miles through narrow Utowana and Eagle Lake, past a few cottages, to the mountain-ringed Blue Mountain Lake. These three lakes make up the Eckford Chain. Follow the right shore of Blue Mountain Lake for the best wind shadow, which will be especially important in the afternoon. On the west shore of the lake, a hiking trail leads 1.5 miles from the end of Maple Lodge Road to stunning views from Castle Rock. Blue Mountain Lake village is on the east side of the lake. The steam engine and passenger and baggage cars that traveled on the railroad bed you just carried are on display at the Adirondack Experience, The Museum on Blue Mountain Lake. This sprawling, multifaceted, award-winning museum is not to be missed!

This section technically begins with 1.4 miles of Class II–III "rock garden" rapids. Look for the US Geological Survey (USGS) gauge in Piercefield to be between 4.5 and 10 feet. However, nearly all canoeists and even most kayakers traveling with gear will choose to avoid these rapids by either following the Forked Lake Road Carry or beginning this section at the carry put-in. From the take-out on Forked Lake, portage east 1.25 miles on Forked Lake Road. At a sharp bend, bear left to follow a trail 0.15 mile to a put-in near a lean-to.

Paddle 1.5 miles of moving flatwater to the mandatory take-out, river-right, just above Class V Buttermilk Falls. This is a good place to stop and enjoy the scenery. Follow unwheelable paths over boulders and past a picnic area to put in below the falls.

Another 0.5 mile of flatwater paddling follows Buttermilk Falls. Then you can either portage around, or scout and run, the 0.5 mile of Class II rapids that follow. Below these rapids paddle about a half mile through pickerelweed and pond lilies, passing the Deerland lean-tos to the head of Long Lake.

The east shore and parts of the west shore of Long Lake are lined with boarding camps, cottages, and motels. Opposite Deerland, Owls Head Mountain rises 2780 feet, and its summit provides scenic views of the Fishing Brook Range and the High Peaks. Find the trailhead for this sometimes challenging 3.2-mile trail up Owls Head along Endion Lane, off New York Route 30 in the town of Long Lake. Primitive camping is limited on state-owned land on the north shore of the lake opposite Deerland in the bay north of Moose Island.

Heading north toward the town of Long Lake, you can relax and enjoy the panoramic views of the Seward Range in the northeast. Also, Blueberry and Kempshall Mountains are often in view in the east, and Buck Mountain in the west. At the town of Long Lake, paddle under the NY 30 bridge. The Adirondack Hotel, motels, stores, and restaurants are mostly on the eastern shore. Lake Eaton state campground is a short drive west on NY 30.

Stop at the town beach, where an NFCT kiosk perches alongside the road to access the village and its services, or paddle another 0.7 mile northeast to take out at the NYSDEC boat launch.

Paddling through the Adirondacks is characterized by broad lakes connected by remote, winding rivers. (Photo by Joe Geronimo)

NFCT MAP 2: ADIRONDACK NORTH COUNTRY (CENTRAL)

Long Lake to Saranac River

Located in the Adirondack Park, Long Lake, the remote Raquette River, and the Saranac Chain of Lakes offer beautiful stretches of predominantly flatwater paddling, breathtaking scenery, first-rate swimming, and opportunities to see ducks, mergansers, great blue herons, ospreys, and white-tailed deer, among other wildlife. Paddling is generally not challenging unless it's windy. Campsites and lean-tos abound along this section, and even staying overnight at an inn is possible. There are hiking and paddling side trips along the way, adding numerous options to extend the three to four days it normally takes to paddle between the communities of Long Lake and Saranac Lake.

You'll start this section by heading north on Long Lake, away from town and into the most remote area of the NFCT in New York. Long Lake is a slender, 13-mile finger of water, actually a widening of the Raquette River, about 1.5 miles across on average. The Northville–Placid hiking trail parallels your path on the lake, and hikers and paddlers share campsites along the eastern shore. The hiking trail connects the picturesque southern Adirondack foothills with the scenic northern High Peaks region.

The best smallmouth fishing is near the islands at the north end of the lake. The shallow weedy areas at Big Brook Bay, 1.5 miles north of the village of Long Lake on the west shore, and the lake's outlet in the northeast corner are the best for pike fishing.

From the end of Long Lake, paddlers glide onto the meandering Raquette River and float through a deep, silver maple forest. The river originates in the Eckford Chain of Blue Mountain, Eagle, and Utowana Lakes and acquires additional volume from Raquette, Forked, and Long Lakes. Its 170-mile course to the St. Lawrence River makes the Raquette the longest river in the northwestern Adirondacks and the second longest in the state of New York. The Raquette River's mouth is said to resemble the shape of a snowshoe, *raquette* in French.

As you paddle downstream from Long Lake, the river's tranquil nature is broken only by the scenic tumble of Raquette Falls, which you bypass on a

Century-old locks, operated by seasonal lock tenders or paddlers, continue to maintain water levels in the Saranac Lakes of New York. (Photo courtesy of Northstar Canoes)

rocky 1-mile carry trail. One Raquette Falls legend describes two young New Yorkers who decided to explore the Raquette in 1843. They started at Long Lake in a heavy yawl, which they wrecked in the rapids above Raquette Falls. Shortly thereafter, a birchbark canoe with five Native American adults and a baby came upon them. One of the adults, named Mitchell (possibly Mitchell Sabattis, a renowned guide and boatbuilder), proceeded to manufacture a second canoe. The two canoes continued 75 miles downriver to Matildaville (currently called Colton), where the two New Yorkers were told that they were the first white men to travel down the Raquette River.

Smallmouth bass, pike, and walleyes are found in the long pools and near rocks and trees along the shore below Raquette Falls. Fishing is best in the early morning during midsummer to avoid recreational traffic.

After the falls, you resume a leisurely pace downstream. At the mouth of Stony Creek, you must decide whether to head upstream to Stony Creek Ponds and over the carry to the Saranac Lakes, or continue winding your way downstream to Axton Landing or beyond to Tupper Lake (see "Extending Your Trip: Axton Landing to the Town of Tupper Lake" at the end of Section 1).

"Axetown" was once a lumber camp, and before roads existed in the Central Adirondacks, Axton Landing was the hub for travelers switching between the

HIKING IN THE ADIRONDACKS

The Adirondacks region offers not only premier paddling but also excellent hiking options for all abilities. Along the NFCT, easy and moderate hikes lead to panoramic views. Not far from the Trail, the forty-six High Peaks of the Adirondacks lure the adventurous to attempt steeper, longer, and more exposed hikes, including a 15-mile roundtrip hike to the windswept summit of Mount Marcy, the highest in New York at 5344 feet. For maps and advice, contact the Adirondack Mountain Club (see Resources).

Raquette and Saranac water trail systems. Indian Carry is the name for the low divide of glacial drift that separates the two drainage systems. The age of this carry is indicated by the large collection of arrowheads and Indian pottery collected by Jesse Corey, who operated Rustic Lodge at the north end of Indian Carry. At the turn of the twentieth century, Axton Landing was bought by Cornell University for its School of Forestry. Today, only stands of red, white and Scotch pine; Douglas-fir; and Norway spruce are left bearing witness.

The Saranac Chain of Lakes provide a diverse paddling experience. You'll cross broad lakes with views of distant peaks and shoreline camps; other times you'll wind along a narrow channel through marsh grass. Originating out of Upper Saranac Lake, the NFCT follows the Saranac River through the village of Saranac Lake to its mouth on Lake Champlain. A couple of century-old, hand-operated locks ease your transition on the river between Saranac lake levels.

Besides chop during the afternoon "westerlies," Middle Saranac offers Ship Island, with its evergreen sails set and a grand view of towering Ampersand Mountain. From the southeast corner of Middle Saranac, the Ampersand Mountain Trail climbs 1530 rugged feet from lake to granite summit in only 3.2 miles. South Creek joins Middle Saranac along its south shore where paddlers can access the lake from New York Route 3. To the northwest, Hungry Bay leads to Weller Pond and a 1-mile portage back to Upper Saranac Lake.

An ideal overnight trip begins at Indian Carry Landing on Upper Saranac Lake ending in the village of Saranac Lake. Dozens of numbered water-access-only campsites encircle these lakes. However, reserving a campsite on Middle Saranac or Lower Saranac through the Saranac Lake Islands state campground is a must. Book early in the season, as camping here is popular. Paddlers must check in with campground headquarters on Second Pond at the NY 3 bridge before occupying a campsite, so plan that into your paddling itinerary. For day two of the overnighter, the distance from the campground headquarters boat launch to the village of Saranac Lake is less than 7 miles, providing an excellent sampler of river, lake, and mountains. A shuttle is necessary for this one-way trip.

Another overnight or day-trip option is to launch at the north end of Lower Saranac Lake, at the public landing on Ampersand Bay, paddle down the lake to Bluff Island, and then follow the NFCT east and north to the village landing. By water it is 11 miles, but the shuttle is less than 1.5 miles, short enough to bike or walk. This trip follows the same route used by race participants in the annual 'Round the Mountain Canoe & Kayak Race. The May event hosted by the NFCT kicks off an unofficial start to the Adirondack paddling season.

Bumping right up against Scarface and the Sawtooth Range, Oseetah is one of the prettier lakes on the Saranac River. It was created when Lake Flower Dam flooded Miller Pond, Ray's Pond, and the marsh between. Kiwassa Lake, with several campsites, is a good side trip if time permits, but a better one is remote Pine Pond. To reach the carry trailhead, paddle east on Oseetah, then south, through a weedy bay to its southwest corner. Walk about a half mile (either fork of the trail is okay) and follow a path downhill to water visible through the trees. Though you will probably not have the wilderness pond to yourself, on a sunny day the sandy bottom invites a swim.

This section ends by paddling into the heart of Saranac Lake, New York, a larger town where many services are available. See NFCT Map 2 and the NFCT website for additional trip planning and navigational details.

SECTION 1

Raquette River: Long Lake to Axton Landing

Boarding camps, cottages, and motels dot the shores of the middle of Long Lake; the north end becomes more remote. A winding river through a remote forest, with scenic Class V Raquette Falls, follows flatwater lake paddling. Campsites and lean-tos are plentiful.

TRIP DISTANCE: 21.7 miles (add another 0.5 mile if launching from the town beach)

TRIP DURATION: Allow 2–3 days

FLOW/SEASON: Maintains a navigable water level from April ice-out to November freeze-up, but in dry years the upper Raquette River can challenge river-reading skills.

DIRECTION OF CURRENT: Raquette River, south to north to Stony Creek then east to west to Axton Landing; Stony Creek, north to south

PUT-IN: **Long Lake boat launch**, 88 Dock Rd., Long Lake. Overnight parking (use auxiliary lot). GPS: 43.978813°, –74.416154°; or **Long Lake town beach**, 1258 Main St., Long Lake. Overnight street parking. GPS: 43.974244°, –74.423943°

TAKE-OUT: **Axton Landing**. Gravel ramp at end of dirt road. Overnight parking. GPS: 44.20354°, –74.326626°

MAP: NFCT Map 2, Adirondack North Country (Central)

PORTAGES (1): Raquette Falls Carry, 1 mile (not easily wheeled; expect to carry in places)
HAZARDS: Late-morning and afternoon wind on Long Lake; Class V Raquette Falls (signed portage)
OTHER ACCESS: Stony Creek Ponds: Hand carry access on Coreys Rd. GPS: 44.222323°, −74.313336°

CONTACT: Town of Long Lake Parks & Recreation; New York State Department of Environmental Conservation (NYSDEC) Region 5; NFCT Trip Planner
SERVICES: Food and lodging available in the town of Long Lake
CAMPING: Free first-come, first-served primitive NYSDEC campsites and lean-tos.

From the NYSDEC boat launch on Long Lake, head north along the lake, past camps and boathouses. After about 1.5 miles, Big Marsh opens on the left shoreline and Catlin Bay on the right. Between two promontories, you will see the tall evergreens of Round Island as the most prominent feature another mile ahead of you.

The last several miles of the north end of Long Lake are less populated than the south end, particularly the forest preserve on the east shore, which is the western edge of the High Peaks Wilderness Area. Section D of the 133-mile Northville–Placid Trail parallels the east shore. As you continue paddling north, slivers of sandy beaches backed by dense forest provide good campsites. A dozen lean-tos line the shore between Catlin Bay and the foot of the lake, some of which are shared with hikers.

If you land on the narrow beach at the north end of the lake, you'll be standing on a natural dam that was pushed into the Raquette River by a glacier, forming Long Lake. Step into the trees that line the beach and see how narrow the top of this dam is. Just beyond the trees, the land drops away dramatically. The foot of Long Lake spreads across this natural dam in many shallow channels, and finding the main channel of the Raquette River can be tricky. Stay on the left side of a long narrow island, which is situated in the middle right of this maze of channels. To the extreme right, boulders on the shore indicate a channel that is impassable in low water. On the left is what appears to be another channel that goes nowhere.

As you paddle into the forest, the first of many side channels you'll drift past is Lost Channel on your right. A big oval boulder marks the beginning of an island that you will pass by just before you spot the Deep Hole lean-to on river-left, across from the mouth of Cold River. Cold River is classified as a wild river from its headwaters 14 miles upstream. However, few paddlers have attempted to paddle the 10 miles up to the camp area, once inhabited by Adirondack hermit Noah John Rondeau (the "Mayor of Cold River City— Population 1"). Most take the hiking trail on the left bank to Shattuck Clearing, where they pick up the Northville–Placid Trail to visit the site.

The carry around Raquette Falls provides scenic views of the river, picnic spots, and a refreshing swimming hole near the put-in. (Photo by NFCT)

From the Cold River confluence, you float on a slowly winding river through thick forests. The right bank of the river continues to border the High Peaks Wilderness Area almost all the way to Axton Landing. On river-left, Moose Creek flows through a large swamp before its confluence with the Raquette River, and you can turn upstream there and explore a couple miles of that area.

You'll hear the dull roar of rapids long before you see the big signs alerting you to the Raquette Falls Carry. Take out on river-right for the challenging 1-mile carry following a well-worn but rocky and rugged trail. Put in below the falls where a lean-to, a small clearing, and the caretaker's cabin are located. The small clearing once held Mother Johnson's boardinghouse, which produced the best wilderness flapjacks over a century ago. Today, a seasonal NYS-DEC ranger lives on-site to provide information and assistance to boaters and maintain the trail and area lean-tos. A side trail provides access to view the falls that drop 80 feet over a rocky bed with two 15-foot cascades. The second cascade, Lower Falls, plunges through a deep gorge. Heavy rapids create a torrent above, between, and below the two falls. Dispersed camping is available near the falls and lean-to. A pool at the put-in invites swimming, and riverside rocks provide a good place to eat lunch.

From the put-in, it's another 6 miles to Axton Landing. About a half mile before reaching the landing, Stony Creek flows in on the right marked with a sign at its mouth. Remain on the Raquette River, paddling past Stony Creek to Axton Landing. A small clearing provides a good tent campsite and overnight parking. The sandy beach of the landing is separated from the main current by a marshy stream and backwater.

From the mouth of Stony Creek, the NFCT follows the creek upstream to Stony Creek Ponds and across Indian Carry to the Saranac Lakes. An alternative trip finish could end at the hand carry access on Coreys Road in the westernmost arm of Stony Creek Ponds, but parking is limited. Another option is to knock off the historic Indian Carry portage ending on Upper Saranac Lake, where overnight parking is permitted. The northernmost Stony Creek Pond boasts several free first-come, first-served NYSDEC primitive campsites near the Indian Carry takeout. (See Section 2 below for navigational details.)

EXTENDING YOUR TRIP: AXTON LANDING TO THE TOWN OF TUPPER LAKE

From Axton Landing follow the Raquette River 15 miles through single and double oxbows with flanking lagoons and lost-channel crescents, floating among banks of silver and red maples, spruce, balsam, cedar, and pines to Tupper Lake. To give you an idea of the meanders of the river, from Axton Landing to the campsites at Trombley Landing is about 3 miles as the crow flies, but it is an 8-mile paddle.

Upon reaching Tupper Lake, you can turn left and take out at a public boat launch at the hamlet of Moody on the southeastern shore, or you can turn right and paddle 1 mile north into Raquette Pond to take out at the town of Tupper Lake. There are many additional paddling adventures to be found around Tupper Lake and dry-land excursions as well. You'd be remiss not to visit the WILD Center, a state-of-the-art, 31-acre natural history museum. Approaching the town of Tupper Lake from the south on NY 30, turn right at the traffic light onto Hosley Avenue, and find the museum entrance 500 yards on the left.

SECTION 2

Stony Creek to Saranac Lake Village

This is one of the great canoe areas of America. It is both stunningly beautiful and arguably the birthplace of recreational wilderness canoe tripping in the United States. When combined with the St. Regis Canoe Wilderness, the number of possible canoe trips through the headwater lakes is staggering.

To the south, rank on rank of mountains stand up, finally cresting in mile-high Mount Marcy.

TRIP DISTANCE: 21 miles

TRIP DURATION: Allow 2 days

FLOW/SEASON: Normally good from April ice-out to November freeze-up, though Stony Creek can become shallow in a dry summer.

DIRECTION OF CURRENT: Stony Creek, north to south; Saranac River from Middle Saranac Lake to Lower Saranac Lake, south to northeast and from Lower Saranac Lake to Oseetah Lake, west to east

PUT-IN: Axton Landing. Gravel ramp at end of dirt road. Overnight parking. GPS: 44.20354°, −74.326626°

TAKE-OUT: Village of Saranac Lake/ Lake Flower Kiwassa Rd. at NFCT kiosk. Hand carry access. Overnight parking in the lot off Dorsey St. or behind the police station at 3 Main St. GPS: 44.323832°, −74.131104°

MAP: NFCT Map 2, Adirondack North Country (Central)

PORTAGES (2): Indian Carry, 1.2 miles (not easily wheeled on the trail/wheelable on road); **Bartlett Carry,** 0.5 mile (mostly wheelable)

HAZARDS: Afternoon wind and waves, especially on Middle Saranac Lake

OTHER ACCESS: Stony Creek Ponds: Hand carry access on Coreys Rd. GPS: 44.222323°, −74.313330°, **Upper Saranac Lake:** South Shore Landing (Indian Carry), Old Dock Rd. off New York Route 3. Overnight parking. GPS: 44.238954°, −74.314928°; **Middle**

Saranac Lake: South Creek canoe access on NY 3. Hand carry launch with overnight parking. GPS: 44.244114°, −74.268805°; **Second Pond:** New York State Department of Environmental Conservation (NYSDEC) boat launch at Saranac Lake Islands state campground headquarters, 4468 NY 3, Saranac Lake. Overnight parking. GPS: 44.287367°, −74.184779°; **Lower Saranac Lake:** Ampersand Bay boat access on Bayside Dr. GPS: 44.325826°, −74.154389°; **Town of Saranac Lake:** Lake Flower boat launch, GPS: 44.323315°, −74.126059°; Baldwin Park hand carry access, GPS: 44.315584°, −74.120856°

CONTACT: New York State Adirondack Park Agency; NYSDEC Region 5; NFCT Trip Planner

SERVICES: Along River St. and Main St., the village of Saranac Lake offers restaurants and lodging to fit all tastes and budgets; outfitters and a wide variety of services available.

CAMPING: Free first-come, first-served NYSDEC campsites are available on Stony Creek Ponds, upstream of the Saranac River Lower Locks, and on Kiwassa Lake. Camping between Upper Saranac Lake and Cold Brook (just above the Lower Locks) is fee-based and by reservation only through Saranac Lake Islands state campground.

Paddling through Saranac Lake Village is a unique experience. (Photo by Chris Gill)

To pick up where the NFCT left off in Section 1, you will paddle a short distance upstream from Axton Landing and Stony Creek through the Stony Creek Ponds, then carry across NY 3 to Upper Saranac Lake. If you aren't up for this little challenge, put in at South Shore Landing on Upper Saranac Lake at the end of the Indian Carry.

From Axton Landing, paddle out into the main current of the Raquette River. Turn upstream (left) and paddle 0.5 mile to the mouth of Stony Creek. Turn left into the creek (which is not stony at all) and paddle up the slow stream. Pass under a bridge and follow the swampy creek as it winds to the first of two Stony Creek Ponds. In high water, Stony Creek can become more of a flooded wetland. A second bridge separates the lower pond from the upper. The start of Indian Carry is marked by a sign on the left shore of the uppermost pond where several free campsites are also located.

The 1.2-mile Indian Carry begins as an attractive—but mostly unwheelable—forest path, followed by a steep climb, then a gradual descent to NY 3. The second half is wheelable along Old Dock Road (gravel), which ends at a boat launch and dock on Upper Saranac Lake.

Eight-mile-long Upper Saranac Lake is barely sampled by the NFCT. The small Chapel Island, 0.75 mile from Indian Carry Landing, is a crossroads of the Adirondacks. Multiday canoe routes on the Saranac, St. Regis, and Osgood headwaters all join the NFCT here. Heading north off the NFCT route, the many fingers and coves of Upper Saranac Lake have progressively fewer camps and lead eventually into the St. Regis Canoe Area.

To continue following the NFCT, pass two free NYSDEC primitive shoreline campsites before turning right (east) just beyond Chapel Island. Enter Huckleberry Bay, where another campsite is located on the right shore. Take the left fork in 0.5 mile. The sandy take-out is located behind a small island. The wheelable carry follows a steep road to a trail leading to the put-in within a short, wide channel that connects to 3-mile-long Middle Saranac Lake.

The Saranac River subtly exits from the northeast reed-filled corner of Middle Saranac and twists through a wide, slack, marshy channel to the Upper Locks. In the summer, the keeper will lock you through to avoid a 3-foot drop. Not many wilderness canoe trails have such a convenience. In the spring or fall, you work the locks yourself, following directions on a signboard. To the right of the locks, a Class II rapid sluices down a ledge of anorthosite. If you choose the rapids, slide left to miss a rock at the end.

The river bends right, continuing through a marshy channel toward the blunt tower of Pulpit Rock. Lower Saranac Lake opens gradually over the next 1.5 miles. The mouths of two wide, woods-lined bays slide by on the right with occasional cabins poking out of the trees. The cliffs of Bluff Island provide a good landmark for the exit from Lower Saranac, but the red and green channel markers are better.

Turn right into the Saranac River, pass through First Pond, and go under NY 3 to the state campground boat launch on the right on Second Pond. This is the parking area for the Saranac Lake Islands state campground and the place to report for your reserved campsite. If you plan to leave a car overnight, let the ranger know.

Second Pond soon narrows to a slack river winding through deep woods. Powerboats can break the quiet on a typical summer day, but some of the wooden craft cruising by are beautifully maintained boats from the 1920s and '30s. About 1.5 miles downstream of the NY 3 bridge, you will pass a free first-come, first-served NYSDEC lean-to on the left (not part of the Saranac Lake Islands state campground). There is a campsite on the left shore 1200 feet beyond the lean-to and the marshy Cold Brook on the right. The deep brook snakes 0.7 mile south into the forest preserve. Just under a mile later, the Lower Locks simplify a 10-foot descent. A short, steep portage on the right is available for the impatient.

To cross island-studded Oseetah Lake, aim northwest, but avoid the first set of channel markers leading left to Kiwassa Lake. Follow channel markers out of the north end of Oseetah Lake, with cottages perched all about.

The river widens and then narrows again over the next mile as you paddle past many more cottages, and then widens into Lake Flower. The village landing (Lake Flower boat launch) is on the right shore, 2 miles down the winding lake. The NFCT kiosk in the town of Saranac Lake is just 0.3 mile farther, to the left of Lake Flower Dam, which marks the end of NFCT Map 2.

NFCT MAP 3: ADIRONDACK NORTH COUNTRY (EAST)

Saranac River to Lake Champlain

As it drops 1400 feet from the Adirondack Plateau to Lake Champlain, the Saranac River section of the Northern Forest Canoe Trail (NFCT) offers serene flatwater interspersed with some of the most challenging whitewater found along the route. This 61-mile stretch lends itself to day trips, as most paddlers will want to avoid the sections with rapids, which have drops ranging from Class II to V, and lengthy portages around rapids and dams.

More placid than wild from the town of Saranac Lake to Union Falls, the Saranac River opens vistas of mountains big and small. The forested shoreline gives way to a rural landscape from the whitewater stretch below Silver Lake Road to Plattsburgh.

From Union Falls to High Falls Gorge the river has fine intermediate-to-expert-level whitewater in a rather wild setting. For the whitewater enthusiast, this can be one of the most exciting segments of the route, especially in early spring when water levels are high. The upper stretches maintain the Adirondack Park feel, with wooded shorelines and frequent campsites. Separator Rapids provides an additional opportunity for skilled paddlers using appropriate whitewater boats.

At High Falls the Saranac drops 260 feet in a slot canyon, where a mandatory portage is present. After that, a 7-mile gentle coast through rural hills from Picketts Corners to Cadyville makes this segment a good choice for beginner paddlers. The final section from Cadyville to Lake Champlain is a giant staircase, with many portages past falls and dams and some fun whitewater in between.

Paddling the Saranac River is a more remote experience than one would guess, given the river's industrial past. Traces of the nineteenth-century iron industry that existed here are not visible, but remnants from logging days are. A series of about a dozen little mounded islands appear, angling downriver from left to right. They are "The Separator," where logs were once sorted into pens by the owner's brand and the namesake of the set of challenging Class

Adventure or tranquility? Both are to be found on the NFCT.
(Photo by Will Jeffries)

III rapids that appear just downstream. Set high on the hill to the left of Ore Bed Road Bridge near Separator Rapids is the site of the former Redford Glass Works, famous for its green bull's-eye windowpanes, with their unique swirl in the center. The story is that when the factory closed, the remaining glassware was dumped into the river here, and paddlers have found some fragments. The villages of Moffittsville and Saranac (The Hollow) were also once a thriving manufacturing complex, home to the Saranac Iron Works and a Catalan forge, where armor plate was fashioned during the Civil War.

This section of the Trail is further steeped in early American history. On September 7, 1814, approximately 500 British troops forced a crossing on the Saranac River at what is now the village of Morrisonville. There they met stiff resistance from local militia. Alexander Macomb, the American general, had been given the unenviable task of holding against the British army with a ragtag batch of soldiers. He built forts from river to lake, disguised roads, and broke bridges. The British army, ready to attack, retreated instead. Then, on September 11, 1814, under the command of United States Navy lieutenant Thomas Macdonough, the British lost the naval battle in Cumberland Bay on Lake Champlain, effectively ending the War of 1812.

In Plattsburgh, you paddle through the NFCT's largest city, seeing it from a perspective that few experience. Though in the heart of a city, this is a surprisingly pleasant section—an excellent finish to a trip down the Saranac. This is also a fine half-day whitewater run for novices looking to improve their skills.

Free primitive campsites and one private campground are dispersed throughout the route in this section. Services are limited or absent until reaching Plattsburgh. See NFCT Map 3 and the NFCT website for additional trip planning and navigational details.

SECTION 1

Saranac River: Saranac Lake Village to Union Falls Dam

This serene segment of the Saranac River is a combination of flowing flatwater and lake travel, cascading brooks, and remote campsites. Mountain views are spectacular at various points along this route.

TRIP DISTANCE: 22 miles

TRIP DURATION: Allow 2 days

FLOW/SEASON: Normally adequate water levels from April ice-out to November freeze-up

DIRECTION OF CURRENT: Southwest to northeast

PUT-IN: River Walk kayak launch. Hand carry access below Lake Flower Dam along the walkway to Beaver Park. Overnight parking available at Dorsey St. parking lot or behind the police station at 3 Main St. GPS: 44.325624°, −74.133135°

TAKE-OUT: Union Falls Dam. Hand carry access above dam from Union Falls Rd. Overnight parking and camping. GPS: 44.506812°, −73.915343°

MAP: NFCT Map 3, Adirondack North Country (East)

PORTAGES (2–3): Saranac Lake Carry, 0.2 mile (wheelable; only necessary if continuing a trip from the previous section); **Permanent Rapids Carry,** 1 or 1.2 miles

(wheelable); **Franklin Falls Dam Carry,** 0.4 mile (wheelable)

HAZARDS: Short Class III gorge within Permanent Rapids; possible strong winds on the lakes

OTHER ACCESS: Saranac Lake: St. Regis Canoe Outfitters (with permission), 73 Dorsey St., Saranac Lake. GPS: 44.327634°, −74.132332°; **Saranac River:** Multiple locations along New York Route 3 and River Rd.; **Franklin Falls Pond:** New York State Department of Environmental Conservation (NYSDEC) boat launch with overnight parking. GPS: 44.416011°, −74.002273°

CONTACT: New York State Adirondack Park Agency, NYSDEC Region 5; NFCT Trip Planner

SERVICES: The town of Saranac Lake provides lodging, restaurants, groceries, and outfitters.

CAMPING: Many free first-come, first-served primitive NYSDEC campsites

The Saranac Lake Carry from Lake Flower crosses Main Street and passes through a parking lot where it joins river access trails. Proceed under the NY

The Saranac River below Saranac Lake Village is mostly calm, with views of Whiteface and other northern Adirondack peaks. (Photo by Mike Lynch)

3 bridge, river-left, to put in downstream within a pool below a set of artificial rapids.

The start of this Saranac River trip conducts you between the buildings of downtown, with windows of local businesses overlooking the river, and canoes stacked on the St. Regis Canoe Outfitters' rack above the current. As you exit town, at the last bridge you pass under (Pine Street), Class I rapids flow by a small park on the left.

Except for a riffle or two, the river is flowing flatwater for the next 10 miles from the outskirts of the town of Saranac Lake to Permanent Rapids. The shores vary from rural fields to open marshland.

At 3.5 miles, Moose Creek joins on the right, with a public primitive campsite topping the bluff at the mouth of the creek. If you paddle the 1.2-mile side trip up the marshy creek, it feels like you are paddling into the arms of towering Little McKenzie Mountain, a scenic highlight of this segment.

Two miles beyond the creek are the trailhead and parking area for Moose Pond Trail. Hop out and stretch your legs on this easy, 1.5-mile walk to Moose Pond. Rows of peaks line the distant shoreline of the pond, and a rocky bluff provides a good picnic spot. Privately owned Five Fauls Lean-to appears less than a mile below the Moose Pond Trail. The landowner asks paddlers planning to stay at the lean-to to inquire prior to arrival. See NFCT Map 3 or visit the NFCT Trip Planner for more details and contact information.

At high water, plan to carry (river-left) around McCasland Bridge (privately owned) just downstream of the lean-to. In another mile on the left, Sumner

Brook comes sliding in from Bloomingdale. Not quite 2 miles farther, Moose Pond Road Bridge crosses the river. This would be a good place to end a day trip from the town of Saranac Lake.

As you approach Permanent Rapids, be aware there are two take-outs available. Adding only 0.2 mile to your carry, the first take-out option is much safer to use in high water. Just beyond the high-water take-out, there is a primitive campsite on the left shore where the river bends. It is easy to miss, but is also accessible from River Road, the wheelable carry used as the portage route. And 500 feet beyond the campsite is the low-water take-out for the 1-mile portage avoiding the rapids. This second take-out option is within eyesight of the start of Permanent Rapids.

Class II–III Permanent Rapids is normally runnable all summer, hence "permanent," though the name is suspiciously similar to its nineteenth-century name, Permit Rapids. *(Caution: Permanent Rapids should only be attempted by intermediate or better whitewater paddlers with durable boat layups.* Once away from the road, a portage is not easy.) For the first 1000 feet, from where the river leaves the road, the rapids are Class I. Then the difficulty bumps up to Class II. Where cliffs pinch the river, known to locals as "The Narrows," there are several holes to avoid, followed by two ledges. The gut is Class II–III at most levels, and with water levels above 2000 CFS, you'll experience an exhilarating wave train. The little gorge opens, and the rapids finish with a curving Class II rock garden. With River Road nearby for a shuttle, multiple runs are easy for whitewater enthusiasts.

The Permanent Rapids Carry ends at the Ledges, a large primitive campsite under the pines. From the put-in, the river opens up into Franklin Falls Pond. A state fishing access and boat launch is located 0.7 mile beyond the Ledges campsite, on the left.

Franklin Falls Pond is about 2 miles long and quite pretty, with only a few private cabins along the shore. There are campsites on the first half of the pond, including one on the southern end of a small island. Take out at the far end of the pond to the left of the bridge and boom. Timber steps lead up to River Road.

Franklin Falls Dam Carry is a short walk past the dam and dry falls. Follow River Road/Franklin Falls Road for 0.4 mile to an obvious trail leading to the river and the head of 6-mile-long Union Falls Pond, a lesser-known gem of the Adirondacks. The pond offers glimpses of the barren summit of Whiteface soaring over 3400 feet above. In a storm, the view fades into the mist and bone-white waves illuminated by silvery light stand out against black clouds.

After 1.5 miles, Woodruff Bay opens to the right behind Seberts Point. Follow the sound of falling water to cascading Frenchs Brook, another highlight of the trip. As the lake opens to its full width, look back to see another view of Whiteface Mountain. Above the dam, take out on the right where a signpost announces the start of Union Falls Carry. Please sign the register. For day-trippers, this landing is a good launch point for exploring the pond.

Union Falls Pond offers several free primitive campsites along its eastern shores, including some developed by NFCT staff and volunteers. The first is located about halfway between Watsons Point and Seberts Point. Bear Point, 3 miles past the first campsite, hosts two more sites. There are also several NYS-DEC sites (also shared with car campers) located near the take-out.

SECTION 2

Saranac River: Union Falls Dam to Clayburg

Scenic falls and continuous technical whitewater in a remote setting characterize this segment of the Saranac River, which is reserved *for experienced paddlers only*. Portaging is not easy around the Class II–III and III–IV whitewater, and only a primitive trail skirts Class IV-V Tefft Pond Falls. The rapids are a delight for paddlers confident in Class III+ water but a danger for the less experienced. Capsizing here can be more consequential than other stretches where roads can be more easily accessed. Thru-Paddlers with lesser whitewater skills should steel themselves for a long road portage.

TRIP DISTANCE: 9 miles

TRIP DURATION: Allow a half to full day

FLOW/SEASON: Usually runnable from ice-out in April to mid-June; 600–800 CFS recommended for paddling whitewater stretch from Silver Lake Rd. to Clayburg

DIRECTION OF CURRENT: Southwest to northeast

PUT-IN: Union Falls. Park in the small lot near the Union Falls generation station off Casey Rd. at the north end of Union Falls Pond. Carry 500 feet following the marked path along the buried penstock to the put-in below the powerhouse. GPS: 44.510947°, –73.912875°

TAKE-OUT: Clayburg, at the confluence of the Saranac and its North Branch. Hand carry access. Parking is available on the left side of Silver Lake Rd., prior to the New York Route 1 bridge. GPS: 44.595655°, –73.838600°. Do not take out at the posted Silver Lake Rd. Bridge abutting private property.

MAP: NFCT Map 3, Adirondack North Country (East)

PORTAGES (1–2): Union Falls Dam Carry, 0.3 mile (mostly wheelable; only necessary if continuing a trip from the previous section); **Casey Rd./Silver Lake Rd.,** 4.6 miles (only if completely avoiding the hazards below Trail Rapids, wheelable); or unsigned, unmaintained **Tefft Pond Falls Carry,** 500 feet (carry) if remaining on the river

HAZARDS: Class V Tefft Pond Falls; Class III–IV staircase ledges; Class III–IV Stord Brook Ledge. High water increases the difficulty of all.

OTHER ACCESS: Casey Rd. access trail, which is difficult to find from the road. GPS: 44.542798°, −73.876193° (from river)

CONTACT: New York State Department of Environmental Conservation (NYSDEC) Region 5; NFCT Trip Planner

SERVICES: None

CAMPING: Free primitive campsite on NYSDEC land at Trail Rapids/ Casey Rd. access; downstream from Casey Rd. access there is no camping.

Paddlers should approach the area with caution. For the first 2 miles the Saranac is deceptively flat as it flows through forest. Then, around a left turn is a Class II rapid, followed by a pool. Half a mile later is Trail Rapids, also Class II. During times of higher flow, many features of this section are washed out, becoming swiftwater and rolling waves. In lower water, large rocks lying just below the water's surface turn the river into a technical boulder garden.

Near the end of Trail Rapids, on the left, is the namesake trail to Casey Road. The Casey Road Carry take-out appears immediately below a small cove and large boulder outcrop, and just above a rapid. Swiftwater is present both upstream and downstream of the take-out. Although marked as clearly as possible, this portage is still easy to miss if you are not paying attention. This is

The Saranac River drops off the Adirondack Plateau, creating challenging rapids in Sections 2 and 3. Some sections are suitable only for the most experienced whitewater paddlers. (Photo by John Klopfer)

the last piece of state land along the river and the only place where camping is permitted.

Caution: Only experts possessing whitewater reading and rescue skills should attempt to paddle beyond the Casey Road access. If you had any problems at all in the rapids up to this point, take out here to portage along Casey and Silver Lake Roads to Clayburg. The river only gets harder. The NFCT recommends bypassing this area by using the Casey Road Carry to Clayburg.

The next rapid after passing the access trail is a short Class II rock garden followed by a Class II rapid tumbling through a scenic rock cleft another 1000 feet later. Minor rapids for the next 0.4 mile end in a short pool before Silver Lake Road. There is unfortunately no access at the bridge. All four corners are posted by private property owners. A long, rocky Class II stretch begins under the bridge and ends in the stillwater of Tefft Pond, the narrow 1.3-mile-long swampy remnant of a past pond.

When the stillwater ends, land on the rock pile on river-right. Riverbanks on either side of the falls are privately owned and posted, so scouting is challenging. Neither marked nor maintained, Tefft Pond Falls Carry (not an official part of the NFCT) is a short but rough scramble over the rocks to a pool below the falls. Cascading into the pool is Tefft Pond Falls, beside the spiky remains of a log sluice. An old anglers' access trail on the left shore is blocked by storm damage and an ownership dispute. Please respect the landowners, pass through unobtrusively, and leave no trace of your visit.

Just below Tefft Pond Falls is a Class II rapid. Be prepared to eddy out immediately below it. The Ledges, a challenging Class III–IV staircase, comes up fast. The first ledge appears as a horizontal line until you're just about on top of it. The route is complex and more challenging during high water. Several large holes lie immediately after the drop, especially at levels above 6 feet. Open canoes have swamped and been pinned in this area. Remain vigilant. Scout first, and, if you don't feel up to running the rapids, line from shore, although log jams can complicate this maneuver. There is no easy portage.

From the Ledges to Stord Brook, continuous Class II and III boulder gardens tumble for 1.8 miles. Tall hills hide the road and fields above, so the river feels very remote in its ravine. On the sharp right turn following Stord Brook is a Class III–IV ledge to run or line. The narrow chute on the right is a little more straightforward than the double ledge on the left. Either side may be holding washed down trees. On the left shore, a public anglers' access trail drops 0.2 mile steeply down to the river from Silver Lake Road.

Below the Stord Brook Ledge, the river continues to drop through Class II rock gardens for another 0.7 mile but then eases off to Class I–II in the final stretch. The section ends in Clayburg at an access area with parking located along Silver Lake Road, river-left, before the bridge under which the North Branch enters.

SECTION 3

Saranac River: Clayburg to Cadyville Dam

At High Falls the Saranac leaps from the North Woods into a pastoral valley. The river is mostly moving flatwater and riffles, with the exception of Separator Rapids and High Falls, both of which are portaged. The entire section makes a good two-day paddle. The NFCT Forest to Field campsite or Bakers Acres Campground provide midpoint camping options. This trip can be extended by starting 4 miles west of Clayburg on the North Branch of the Saranac River.

TRIP DISTANCE: 16 miles (or more)
TRIP DURATION: Allow 1–2 days
FLOW/SEASON: From early April to mid-June, or after a rain. Turns bony below 930 CFS; below Picketts Corners is runnable much of summer.
DIRECTION OF CURRENT: Southwest to northeast
PUT-IN: Clayburg, at the confluence of the Saranac and its North Branch. Hand carry access. Parking is available on the left side of Silver Lake Rd., above the bridge. GPS: 44.595655°, –73.838600°
TAKE-OUT: Trail above Cadyville Dam to Park Row Rd., river-left. Roadside parking. GPS: 44.697503°, –73.628741°
MAP: NFCT Map 3, Adirondack North Country (East)
PORTAGES (2): Separator Rapids Carry, 0.4 mile (carry on trail, wheelable on road); **High Falls Gorge Carry**, 1 or 1.4 miles (wheelable)

HAZARDS: Separator Rapids, High Falls Dam and Gorge
OTHER ACCESS: Moffitsville: New York State Electric and Gas (NYSEG) anglers' access with a parking area below High Falls hydro off Soper Rd. GPS: 44.639954°, –73.747008°;
Picketts Corners: Hand carry access by Bowen Rd. Bridge along New York Route 3. GPS: 44.659322°, –73.732519°; **Cadyville Beach:** 2199 NY 3. Boat launch and parking lot. GPS: 44.696218°, –73.635973°
CONTACT: New York State Adirondack Park Agency; New York State Department of Environmental Conservation (NYSDEC); NYSEG; NFCT Trip Planner
SERVICES: Gas station, country store, and restaurant in Picketts Corners
CAMPING: Free NFCT primitive campsite (Forest to Field); private Bakers Acres Campground (fee)

At Clayburg, the Saranac River turns east and spreads wide across shallow Class I gravel bars. For the next 2 miles, careful rock-picking will help you slither through.

HIGH FALLS GORGE

In High Falls Gorge the Saranac goes downhill fast, 260 feet in about half a mile. The river foams down the face of the dam and spills onto ledges to each side. The water then plunges into a seemingly bottomless slot canyon. It was first scouted and partly run October 17, 2003, by an American Whitewater study group of expert paddlers. At 250 CFS, most drops were found to be challenging Class V, with the exception of the last falls, a 50-foot corkscrew plunge that was clearly unrunnable. Vantage points on either rim all require bushwhacking (well worth it). No boardwalks thread this canyon.

Separator Rapids consists of two challenging Class III rapids with a short pool between. *Caution: Only experienced whitewater paddlers should attempt running them.* The upper rapid has a series of ledges to thread through, with a hole on the lower left to munch the careless. Downstream 500 feet is the second Class III rapid that starts as a rock garden but funnels into a powerful drop, with a cleaver rock to avoid, right under the bridge. It flushes into a big pool, where the portage also ends. The portage trail is useful for scouting.

Watch the right shore for a portage sign marking the start of the Separator Rapids Carry. The carry begins as a well-traveled fishing access trail before reaching Ore Bed Road. The rocky point by the scenic pool that lies between the upper ledges and the lower rapid churning downstream provides a good spot to scout a route. A little farther down the portage trail, slumbering in the trees to the right are the stone foundations of Lanes Shingle Mill, one of many mills that once enclosed the rapids. Continue following the portage along Ore Bed Road to put in below the bridge, river-left.

Another 0.7 mile below Ore Bed Road Bridge, the river passes under Pup Hill Road Bridge, then chatters between wooded hills sprinkled with cabins. About 1 mile from the High Falls Dam, the river slows to slackwater. Approaching the dam, you see ahead only blue sky and distant Dannemora Mountain.

Land on shore between the booms (shielding the dam and the overflow powerhouse), marked by an NFCT medallion. Get out the portage wheels if you have them. The High Falls Carry follows the NYSEG access road from the dam around the shoulder of Russia Mountain and down into the valley. Follow the portage directions on the NFCT map or the FarOut NFCT app to access one of the two put-in options, or continue following Soper Road for 0.5 mile to reach the NFCT Forest to Field campsite.

The river holds minor Class I–II rapids for the next 1.5 miles. At the Bowen Road Bridge in Picketts Corners, there is an excellent canoe access on the left, with parking and a paved path to the river. A sign and path leading to private Bakers Acres Campground appears another 0.7 mile below the Bowen Road Bridge.

In spring, summer, or fall, many parts of the Trail are enjoyed by kayakers and canoeists alike. (Photo by John Klopfer)

The 7-mile segment between the Bowen Road Bridge access and Cadyville Beach makes for a fine novice day trip—a pastoral coast. In full view are the broad back of Burnt Hill to the south, Johnson and Dannemora Mountains to the north.

The Duquette Road Bridge signals the approach of the Blue Line, the invisible boundary of the Adirondack Park. About 0.7 mile below the bridge, watch for a spot on the left shore to pull over and enjoy an icy drink from Gougeville Spring. It is just one more mile to Cadyville Beach, river-left, an alternative trip-ending take-out option located less than 0.5 mile before Cadyville Dam.

At the next bridge, the rocky shores pinch close together in "The Rocks," the site of a waterfall drowned by Cadyville Dam. After crossing a round pond, look for an NFCT medallion on a tree on the left shore, above a boom warning of the Cadyville Dam and gorge. This is the take-out point ending this section or beginning the 2.1-mile carry circumventing Kent Falls. A short trail leads to Park Row Road.

SECTION 4

Saranac River: Cadyville Dam to Lake Champlain

The Saranac River passes through cliffs and canyons, then descends past industrial ruins, and finishes as whitewater in the suburbs of Plattsburgh. *Caution: This is a somewhat challenging segment, with long Class II rapids between long portages around several dams.* Day-trippers should cherry-pick short segments.

TRIP DISTANCE: 12.5 miles

TRIP DURATION: Allow 1 day

FLOW/SEASON: The rapids are often too shallow by midsummer, but dam releases can bring the river level up. A gauge reading of 1850 CFS is suggested to run whitewater from Treadwell Mills Dam to Imperial Mills Dam. *Caution: This can be a dangerous whitewater run.* Imperial Mills Dam to Lake Champlain is runnable below 929 CFS but is recommended at 1850 CFS or above.

DIRECTION OF CURRENT: West to east

PUT-IN: New York State Electric and Gas (NYSEG) public access area and overnight parking lot below Kent Falls Hydro facility. Hand carry. GPS: 44.705062°, –73.594936°

TAKE-OUT(S): Saranac River mouth, Green St. Landing (on river). GPS: 44.699364°, –73.44859°; or **New York State Department of Environmental Conservation (NYSDEC) Plattsburgh boat launch**, 2 Dock St., Plattsburgh, New York (on Lake Champlain). GPS: 44.697954°, –73.444684°

MAP: NFCT Map 3, Adirondack North Country (East)

PORTAGES (2–3): Cadyville Dam/ Kent Falls Carry, 2.1 miles (wheelable; only necessary if continuing a trip from the previous section); **Treadwell Mills Dam–Fredenburgh**

Falls Carry, 0.8 mile (wheelable; option to wheel another 0.5 mile to put in below Indian Rapids and the location of the former dam); **Imperial Mills Dam Carry**, 0.2 mile (not wheelable)

HAZARDS: Kent Falls Dam, Treadwell Mills Dam, and Imperial Mills Dam; turbulent water at the put-in below the Treadwell Mills Dam–Fredenburgh Falls Carry, Class II+ Indian Rapids, and a continuous run of Class I–II rapids and ledges between Imperial Mills Dam and the Broad St. Bridge when water levels are high

OTHER ACCESS: Treadwell Mills Impoundment: Military Turnpike Rd., hand carry access with small parking area. GPS: 44.668988°, –73.507915°; **Imperial Mills Dam:** Public fishing access area at the end of Adirondack Lane. Hand carry access with a small parking lot. GPS: 44.681732°, –73.472283°

CONTACT: New York State Adirondack Park Agency; NYSEG; NFCT Trip Planner

SERVICES: Within a short walk of the Bridge St. bridge are restaurants and a food co-op in Plattsburgh's historic downtown.

CAMPING: Free first-come, first-served NFCT primitive campsites (LaPierre Lane and Treadwell Mills); Cumberland Bay State Park, 2 miles northeast from takeout (fee)

If you are continuing a trip that began prior to Kent Falls, refer to NFCT Map 3 or the FarOut NFCT app for portage information. Otherwise, you avoid the 2.1-mile carry (with its short, but mandatory river crossing) by beginning this section below Kent Falls at the public fishing access. The 7-mile run from here to Treadwell Mills Dam delivers a fun half-day trip suitable for beginner

WATERFALLS AND CHASMS

Below Cadyville, the Saranac River once plunged over waterfalls in a series of deep slots carved through flat-bedded sandstone. They are close cousins of touristy Ausable Chasm, cut through the same rock by the same geological processes. Cadyville Dam plugs the first gorge, a box canyon running 0.5 mile to Goddeau Road. Just upstream of Cadyville Hydro Power Station is a waterfall with a V-shaped crest pointing downstream. Parking for a public fishing access area is located on the upstream south end of the Goddeau Road Bridge where a kiosk provides information about the area and its hydro facilities.

Near Oxbow Lane (once Kent Falls Road), shelving ledges on the west shore are a popular swimming hole. The low ledges are actually the tops of cliffs now beneath the pond. Paddlers who are using the Cadyville Dam–Kent Falls Carry can paddle upstream to explore the flooded gorge and view sandstone walls. From the put-in at the dead end of Oxbow Lane (and the location of the former Kent Falls Road Bridge), paddle the oxbow 0.7 mile up to the base of Mill C Dam, before returning to the take-out on the riverbank opposite the put-in. Do not paddle downstream of the carry access points where Kent Falls Dam is located.

Below Kent Falls Dam a series of four waterfalls still foam through a sheer-walled chasm not visible from the road. This area is only accessible by permission of the landowners or by paddling and tracking upstream from the put-in at the public fishing access area below the Kent Falls Hydro Power Station.

whitewater paddlers. There are 6 miles of fast, continuous Class I and II rapids, which are often too dry to run after midsummer. Though the gradient is from 20 to 40 feet per mile, there are no hard drops.

The first mile winds below high, forested bluffs. Soon cabins start to appear on the right shore. After 2.2 miles there is access from the river to the Mill Historic Marker and wayside on New York Route 22B. Commemorating logging days, it is a stack of three huge millstones. Downstream 0.5 mile is the NY 22B bridge in Morrisonville, where access is not good—the banks are steep, and traffic is dangerous. A better option is to take a break 0.3 mile downstream of the bridge at the LaPierre Lane Riverway, river-left. The park is one of the first completed sections of the Saranac River Trail Greenway, managed by Friends of Saranac River Trail, and home to a unique playground and an NFCT primitive campsite.

For the next 2.5 miles, rapids are continuous Class I to I–II and the shores are mostly wooded and undeveloped. The left shore is part of the closed Clinton County Airport, replaced by Plattsburgh International, itself a former air force base. After the river curves left, the current fades into 1 mile of slackwater, the Treadwell Mills Dam impoundment. From here Lake Champlain is only 7 miles away, but you will first encounter whitewater and dams requiring mandatory portages.

The Treadwell Mills Dam Carry overlaps with the Saranac River Trail Greenway (SRTG). From the take-out at the NY 190/Military Turnpike Bridge, cross the road and pass through the chain-link gate, following the multi-use trail along the canal. A primitive NFCT campsite is located in the woods to the left of the canal across a marshy area.

Put in upstream of the I-87 bridge in sometimes sporty water. Upriver of the put-in are the sloping ledges of Fredenburgh Falls, where Zephaniah Platt built his first mill. In partnership with the US Fish and Wildlife Service, Trout Unlimited, and NYSEG, the industrial ruins and breached remains of Fredenburgh Falls Dam and Indian Rapids Dam were removed in 2023, and the river once again flows freely to Imperial Mills Dam. Downriver of the put-in are 0.5 mile of Class I rapids followed by Indian Rapids, a whitewater area that has been closely restored to its historic pre-dam condition.

As the Saranac River enters the Champlain Valley, the landscape changes from heavily forested to more agrarian. Watching the sun set over the valley from the NFCT Forest to Field campsite is a lovely way to end a full day of paddling and portaging. (Photo by Katina Daanen)

Northern Forest waterways entice paddlers who want to explore new horizons. (Photo by Joe Geronimo)

An alternative option to launching from the carry put-in is to continue another 0.5 mile of the SRTG by foot, following the wheelable Treadwell Mills Connector Trail, reentering the river below Indian Rapids. A 0.2-mile footpath leads from a parking area off of NY 22, back to the Saranac River, where paddlers can put in below the rapids and the former site of Indian Rapids Dam.

Class I riffles run for only 1000 feet before the current dies in the pool of Imperial Mills Dam. Paddle for 1 mile around the curve of the forested pond. Land on the left, in a marshy area beside the berm, well away from the unbarricaded dam. Carry over the berm and follow a gravel road to put in downstream of the dam at the park located at the end of Adirondack Lane.

The last 3 miles of the river consists of continuous Class I–II rapids and ledges, passing by the State University of New York at Plattsburgh campus and onward right through the center of Plattsburgh.

About 0.6 mile from the put-in below Imperial Dam, pass under a pedestrian bridge at the head of a 0.3-mile-long island. Though not especially big, the island is the longest on the entire river below Saranac Lake. Below the next bridge (Catherine Street) is a Class II ledge and more whitewater action. A hand-carry boat launch with access to Pine Street parking and the Saranac River Trail Greenway appears just above the next (pedestrian) bridge, river-left. In high water, the spirited ride continues through the city where a good surfing wave appears below the Broad Street Bridge. Riverwalk Park, river-left, is

SARANAC RIVER TRAIL

The Saranac River Trail Greenway (SRTG) vision is to become a braided network of trails connecting downtown Plattsburgh to the foothills of the Adirondack Mountains. Development of this 27-mile Clinton County corridor is occurring in stages, and it may someday connect riverside communities as far west of Plattsburgh as Redford. Currently the NFCT shares a section of the Treadwell Mills Dam Carry with the SRTG.

where the pillar of the Macdonough Monument, commemorating the Battle of Plattsburgh, rises between the NY 9 bridge and two final sets of bridges—a railroad and a green pedestrian suspension bridge.

As the mouth of the Saranac River opens up to Lake Champlain, the Green Street Landing appears on the right. There is an NFCT kiosk in the parking area. The Plattsburgh boat launch on Lake Champlain is only another 0.3 mile beyond the Green Street Landing. Most will take out here, 61 miles from the town of Saranac Lake and its River Walk. Ahead for Thru-Paddlers is Lake Champlain. The statue of its namesake looks out from the Samuel de Champlain memorial on the bluff above the meeting of lake and river.

Next page: *The Nulhegan River starts out as a narrow, slow-moving, beaver dam–strewn stream before its frothy descent through gorges, boulder fields, and boreal forests in the Silvio O. Conte National Fish & Wildlife Refuge.* (Photo by Chris Gill)

Vermont

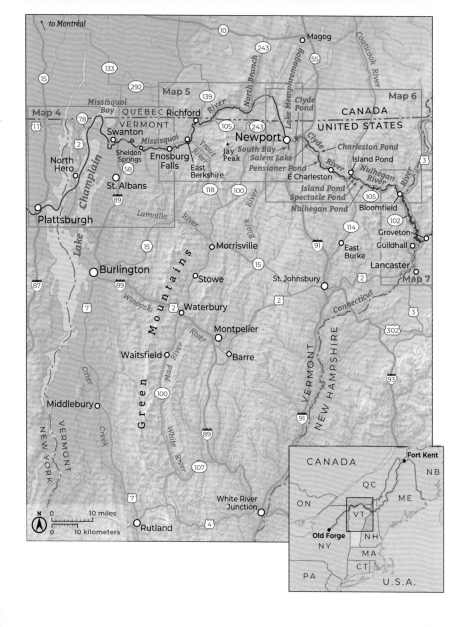

Vermont has been called the most rural state in the nation, and because of its broad valleys and sweet soils, it is the most-farmed state in New England.

However, as you traverse the Northern Forest Canoe Trail's (NFCT's) more than 133 miles across northern Vermont, you will experience many different types of water and scenery. Vermont offers many attractive NFCT campsites located along the route, making Thru-Paddling and multiday trips feasible. In addition to quiet rivers that wander through broad, farmed valleys, there are brisk stretches of challenging whitewater, intimate winding streams bound by marshland, and the placid meanders of the Missisquoi River, historically one of the region's major passageways for the Abenaki, who knew the river as *Mazipskoisibo*, meaning the "crooked river." In addition, you'll be thrilled to paddle spectacularly beautiful expanses of open water on two of New England's largest lakes—Lakes Champlain (*Bitawbakw*, meaning "waters that lie between") and Memphremagog (*Mamlowbaugog*, meaning "great pond place").

Vermont's waterways have long been tied to its dynamic social and political history. The first European to visit the region was the French explorer Samuel de Champlain, who in 1609 came south from French Canada into a long, beautiful lake surrounded by mountains and was so impressed that he immediately named it for himself: Lac Champlain. The lake is more than 110 miles long and has been a major factor in Vermont's history and economy for four centuries.

The Champlain Valley was a major battleground in the Revolutionary War and later an important trade and lumber transport route. Vermont's early years as an independent republic lasted from 1777 to 1791 and, some say, stamped Vermont forever as a place where independence, ingenuity, and self-reliance would be especially important character traits. Even today, fringe groups of Vermonters dissatisfied with the policies of the United States government spark debates on secession. The exploits of Ethan Allen, his brothers, and the Green Mountain Boys gave Vermonters a heroic past to take pride in.

The Abenaki had lived in the area for thousands of years before Champlain "discovered" the big lake and the British settled the regions nearby. From Lake Champlain to the Connecticut River, Indigenous people traveled across northern Vermont by dugout and bark canoe. They founded a large settlement near the mouth of the Missisquoi River, at present-day Swanton, which is still home to many Abenaki.

Logging played a historical role in northern Vermont, as it did in the rest of the region. Every major river in Vermont was used for transporting logs in the

CONNECTING INTERNATIONALLY SHARED WATERS

While some of the NFCT section descriptions listed below begin or end at the international border, waterways, of course, do not. Both the Missisquoi River and Lake Memphremagog flow through Vermont and Québec. This chapter covers the Vermont trail sections of the Missisquoi River and Lake Memphremagog south of the international border. For the Québec segment of the Missisquoi River and Lake Memphremagog north of the international border, refer to the Québec chapter.

Paddlers who wish to follow the navigable sections of the Trail through both countries will need to use the CBP ROAM app and carry a valid passport for entry. For more information about border crossings and government restrictions, refer to the Planning a Trip section.

nineteenth century, and Burlington, on Lake Champlain, was a major timber transport center in the mid-1800s.

Generally speaking, the section in Vermont is more open and less forested than the other states through which the NFCT flows. But even that generalization has its exceptions. From a subtle height of land just east of the village of Island Pond (named for its adjacent pond), both the Clyde River (*Onkawbegok*, meaning "at the chain of connected lakes") and Missisquoi River flow west, while the Nulhegan River (*Galahigen*, meaning "the place of log traps") flows east some 16 miles to join the Connecticut River. That high point, which is located in Vermont's rugged and rural Northeast Kingdom, provides a subtle boundary between the open pastoral valleys through which the Clyde and Missisquoi Rivers wander and the heavily forested, often swampy section of far-northeastern Vermont traversed by the Nulhegan.

In addition to being more open, most of Vermont's Northern Forest is more settled than it is in the other three states. Five significant communities and several smaller hamlets are located along the NFCT in Vermont. From west to east, they are: Swanton, near the shores of Lake Champlain; Enosburg Falls, midway along the Missisquoi; Richford, on the upper Missisquoi; Newport, on Lake Memphremagog; and Island Pond, on the northeastern pond of the same name.

None of these settlements is large. Newport, the most substantial community and the only one incorporated as a city, has roughly 4400 inhabitants. Yet what they lack in size, they more than make up for in accessibility. One of the pleasures of paddling through northern Vermont is stopping for a bank-side sandwich or a conversation at one of the small communities along the way.

Lake Champlain is undeniably huge and stunningly spectacular; paddlers must use caution on its waters. However, even in the midst of this great lake,

VERMONT'S NATIONAL WILD AND SCENIC RIVERS AND COVERED BRIDGES

Sections of the Missisquoi River, including the NFCT segment from the Canadian border north of Richford to Samsonville, and the Trout River, from the confluence of the Jay and Wade Brooks in Montgomery to its confluence with the Missisquoi River in East Berkshire, are designated National Wild and Scenic Rivers. The National Wild and Scenic Rivers System was created by Congress in 1968 to preserve certain rivers with outstanding natural, cultural, and recreational values in a free-flowing condition for the enjoyment of present and future generations. Both of these Vermont bedrock rivers provide exceptional recreational opportunities and are renowned for their numerous deep swimming holes.

The Trout is also spanned by the greatest concentration of covered bridges of any area in the United States, most of which are still in use today. Built by the Jewett brothers in the 1800s, they are now listed on the National Register of Historic Places. The bridges are popular destinations for sightseers and add to the unique local character of the region.

which can seem very large and overpowering, the spiffy little island town of North Hero, with its paddle-friendly marina and well-appointed general store, brings the paddler back to human scale and the pleasures of a small freshwater "port."

Likewise, Lake Memphremagog, a 31-mile-long glacial lake ringed with mountains, is blessed with breathtaking scenery. Memphremagog's South Bay Wildlife Management Area, protected by the State of Vermont, is one of the premier birding spots in Vermont. In the spring, migratory songbirds can be seen here by the hundreds.

Both Lake Champlain and Lake Memphremagog straddle the international border flowing north to the St. Lawrence River. They were important waterways for the Abenaki and later became vacation and recreational areas because of their natural beauty and pristine northern location.

It's easy to tailor a paddling trip to your own desires and skill level in Vermont. If you are looking for an extreme whitewater challenge, the steep, bony, Class III–IV rapids of the lower Nulhegan River will keep you busy as you descend through a protected boreal forest to the Connecticut River. The Clyde River below West Charleston also has some brisk whitewater segments, generally less demanding than the Nulhegan, but enjoyable and scenic Class II and III rips.

On the other hand, if your ideal trip is a quiet day on the river, drifting and paddling on placid waters, perhaps getting in some fishing along the way, the middle stretches of the Missisquoi offer a pleasant interlude. One of the most delightful sections of the Missisquoi starts at the US-Canada border and continues to Enosburg Falls. The river is modest in size here, and in spring, its clear waters flow briskly through open farmland. There is a challenging Class III–IV set of rapids for the skilled paddler as the river courses right through downtown Richford, but this section can be easily portaged. And on the west end of town, you'll find pretty little Davis Park next to the river. There are benches and a bandstand that make this spot just right for a lunch break!

It is the blend of new and old that typifies much of today's Vermont and makes it so enjoyable. The traditional farm-and-village economy that prevailed here until the 1960s was joined in more recent years by a wave of incoming immigrants who liked the state's laid-back, rural lifestyle and generally fit in well as they adopted upcountry ways, found jobs, started new businesses, and began to meet their neighbors.

Today, country stores and farm stands have been joined by natural-food outlets, coffee shops, and supermarkets. Busy recreation and tourism economies have augmented more traditional manufacturing and agriculture jobs. But despite the changes, informality and a cautious friendliness still characterize Vermont's people. And from on high, the Green Mountains still watch over Vermont's rivers and lakes, which provide an ideal and enjoyable paddling environment for all.

The Abenaki people founded a large settlement near the mouth of the Missisquoi River, at present-day Swanton, that is still home to many of the Abenaki nation. The waterway is a favorite destination for family paddling trips and riverbank picnics. (Photo by NFCT)

NFCT MAP 4: ISLANDS AND FARMS REGION

Lake Champlain and Missisquoi River

This section of the Northern Forest Canoe Trail (NFCT) encompasses a wide variety of paddleable water: the spectacularly scenic expanses of Lake Champlain; the 34 miles of the lower Missisquoi River that contain some interesting rapids and long stretches of serene flatwater; and the bayou-like passages of the Missisquoi Delta. Whether on river or lake, throughout this section paddlers will enjoy attractive small villages where supplies, a meal, or lodging can be obtained. NFCT primitive campsites are available at regular intervals along most of the route.

See NFCT Map 4 and the NFCT website for additional trip planning and navigational details. For information about the Missisquoi River upstream of Enosburg Falls, refer to the Map 5 chapter, Vermont: Sections 1 and 2, and Québec: Section 1.

LAKE CHAMPLAIN

Although Lake Champlain enjoyed a short-lived eighteen-day designation as the sixth Great Lake, it is actually the tenth-largest naturally occurring freshwater lake by area in the United States. An amendment classifying Lake Champlain as a Great Lake in 1998 was slipped into a routine federal funding bill creating eligibility for sea-grant program participation. But as news spread of the limnological change, Lake Champlain was soon redefined as a cousin to the Great Lakes, a resolution that still secured the source of important funding. Even without a Great Lakes title, at 490 square miles, Lake Champlain retains its status as a top paddler's adventure, offering grand vistas of water, mountains, and sky, and an array of interesting routes to follow and places to visit.

The lake lies between Vermont and New York and is banked on both the east and west by rugged mountain ranges. It has been described as the most historic body of water in North America because of its association with the exploration of Samuel de Champlain and others, and because it became a strategic thoroughfare during the French and Indian Wars and, later, the American

RAILS-TO-TRAILS

Vermont is home to a growing Rails-to-Trails network including two that intersect with the NFCT: the Missisquoi Valley Rail Trail (MVRT) and the Lamoille Valley Rail Trail (LVRT).

The MVRT mostly parallels the Missisquoi River for more than 17 miles from Richford to Sheldon. The presence of the Missisquoi Valley Rail Trail makes it possible to consider using a bike for shuttling after several hours spent paddling the river. In fact, this concept is brought to life each summer when the NFCT hosts the Missisquoi Paddle-Pedal. The family-friendly event combines 6.5 miles of paddling down the Missisquoi River with 5 miles of cycling back to Richford on the MVRT.

The LVRT runs inland between the villages of Sheldon Junction and Swanton, and passes near East Highgate and Highgate Center. The LVRT crosses the MVRT in Sheldon Junction. Both trails offer visitors to north-central Vermont options combining biking with paddling. Detailed maps and additional information for these trails can be found from the Rails-to-Trails Conservancy.

Revolution. You will travel south along the shores of Lake Champlain's two largest islands, North Hero and South Hero. Ira Allen, one of the founders of Vermont, named these islands following the Revolutionary War. Today the lake is an important environmental resource, a major flyway for migratory birds, and a source of recreational pleasure for those who visit and live along its shores.

Though beautiful and exciting, Lake Champlain can be dangerous. Weather can change very quickly, making paddling unsafe, even in closed boats. For this reason, only experienced paddlers should consider crossing the open water of the lake. Planning shorter trips that follow shorelines is generally a safer and more enjoyable way to experience the paddling and scenery of this unique lake.

Century-old Hero's Welcome General Store and other services are available in the village of North Hero, located midway on North Hero Island's east shore. Marinas, motels, inns, B&Bs, and many public and private camping opportunities are present throughout the Lake Champlain region.

ENOSBURG FALLS

Enosburg Falls is a busy trading center in serious dairy farming country. Some street signs have little cow silhouettes, and the biggest event of the year is the Vermont Dairy Festival, traditionally held the first weekend of June.

On Depot Street, near the center of town, stands the historic Enosburg Opera House, a reminder of the days when Dr. B. J. Kendall, a local pharmacist, made himself and the village prosperous with his invention and marketing of "Kendall's Spavin Cure," a popular horse liniment. This handsome wood-frame building with its tower was built in 1892. It has been restored and is used today for public meetings and concerts.

There are many very striking Victorian houses in Enosburg Falls, several of which have been beautifully restored. Just west of Enosburg Falls Dam is the Bridge of Flowers and Light, a single-arch, concrete footbridge with cast-iron lampposts, flower planters, and an NFCT kiosk.

With the exception of Class I–II ledges just downstream of Enosburg Falls Dam, this section of the Missisquoi River is moving flatwater. Primitive camping, lodging, dining, an outfitter, and many other services are available in Enosburg Falls.

SHELDON JUNCTION

In 1864, near the end of the Civil War, a covered bridge located just below Abbey Rapids was used as a getaway route by a band of Confederate soldiers who had robbed the banks in Albans, about 10 miles to the south, by far the most northerly engagement of the Civil War. After shooting up the town, the raiders headed for Canada with their plunder. They thundered across the old bridge on horseback and unsuccessfully attempted to burn it to thwart their pursuers. Though the robbers made it into Canada, their raid did little to help the failing Confederacy. While the old covered railroad bridge is now gone, today a trestle approximates its location transporting bicyclists and other outdoor recreational users as part of the Lamoille Valley Rail Trail.

The Missisquoi Valley Rail Trail parallels the river between the North Sheldon Bridge (Kane Road) and Sheldon Junction and can be used as a means of avoiding Class II–III Abbey Rapids or as a bicycling shuttle option for day trippers. Both the Lamoille Valley Rail Trail and the Missisquoi Valley Rail Trail intersect near Vermont Route 105 in Sheldon Junction. The NFCT maintains a primitive campsite near the end of Abbey Rapids.

SHELDON SPRINGS AND EAST HIGHGATE

Prior to industrialization, the Missisquoi River freely flowed over ledges and cascaded through gorges. Today, only a few areas of whitewater are present in an otherwise tamed waterway. In addition to Abbey Rapids, two other notable areas exist within this section to either paddle or avoid: Sheldon Springs Rapids and the East Highgate ledges.

Unless you are an experienced whitewater paddler specifically seeking the big volume Class IV–V rapids below Sheldon Springs Dam, most NFCT visitors easily dodge this area either by starting their section paddle below the dam and rapids or by portaging around them. The short run is only suitable for those possessing the appropriate skill set during high-water releases using whitewater boats.

Many sections of the Missisquoi River are suitable for novice paddlers, and the adjacent Missisquoi River Valley Trail makes bike shuttling a nice option for day trips. (Photo by NFCT)

East Highgate was once home to Rixford Manufacturing, makers of scythes and axes. At one point, the company sold 3500 axes a year. The dam used to power the factory remained a fixture in the river until 1927, when most of it was demolished in a flood. The flood was one of the most destructive in Vermont's history, razing 1285 bridges and killing 84 people.

In 2017, the dangerous remains of the breached East Highgate Dam were removed in an effort led by the NFCT, with support from the US Fish and Wildlife Service, the village of Swanton, the town of Highgate, and other partners. Today, paddlers can choose to run or line the Class I–II ledges or avoid them by portaging along Vermont Route 78.

There are no services in the former mill town of East Highgate, but convenience stores can be found in Sheldon Springs. The nearest campsite is located downstream at Highgate Falls.

HIGHGATE FALLS

The villages of Highgate Center and Highgate Falls lie on opposite banks of the river, with the dam roughly between them, where the great falls of the Missisquoi once dropped 75 feet. Dammed at an early date, the falls provided power for a sawmill, a gristmill, and later a foundry and machine shops. Today it generates electricity for the towns of Highgate and Swanton. The dam uses an unusual 240-foot-long inflatable rubberized spillway, one of the largest pneumatic crest control "gates" in North America.

Also remarkable is the 1887 Douglas & Jarvis Patent Parabolic Truss Iron Bridge located below Highgate Falls Dam. This unique lenticular truss bridge

Abenaki guides and their clients, known as "sports," camped on a Missisquoi River island. (Photo courtesy of Fred Wiseman)

is a Historic Civil Engineering Landmark and listed on the National Register of Historic Places.

Both Highgate Center and Highgate Falls are interesting little villages that sit amid a wide array of farms and fields but offer only a few visitor amenities. The Highgate Falls green (south side of the Missisquoi) is long and rectangular, with Highgate Manor (a.k.a. Baxter House)—an ornate mansard-roofed mansion that, at times, has operated as an inn—near one end and the brick 1831 St. John's Episcopal Church near the other. Highgate Center's green is smaller but is watched over by a Civil War statue and has picnic tables and a collection of nineteenth-century buildings around it.

Spring Rapids, Sheldon Springs, and Highgate Springs were all named in the nineteenth century for various mineral springs whose waters were promoted as healing. "Taking the cure" at mineral springs and spas was a nineteenth-century medical craze, and healing springs were fortuitously discovered all over the Northeast.

This section of the river is moving flatwater. The NFCT maintains a free primitive campsite below the dam, along the Highgate Falls portage.

SWANTON

Swanton has been an Abenaki dwelling place since prehistoric times, one of many such villages established by Native Americans along the river. The

Missisquoi was their primary means of travel into the heartland of northern Vermont. Today Swanton is a center for Abenaki history and culture and a thriving contemporary village with a large, attractive green surrounded by restaurants, shops, and other commercial establishments. A motel is located less than a mile away from Marble Mill Park.

The Railroad Depot Museum, on the west side of the river near Swanton Dam, is operated by the Swanton Historical Society and has exhibits detailing the town's railroading past and other aspects of its history. You can climb up a short path from the river to the museum where the old railroad bridge abutment stands in the current.

Below Swanton, the Missisquoi becomes deeper and the current slows as it flows northwest through the wildlife refuge to Lake Champlain.

MISSISQUOI NATIONAL WILDLIFE REFUGE

One of the best sections of Vermont's NFCT for viewing waterfowl, herons, beavers, and other wild creatures is the Missisquoi National Wildlife Refuge, a rich river-mouth delta where the Missisquoi River enters Lake Champlain. This large, federally protected area is home to many species of wild birds and animals, all in a protected complex of river channels, islands, and wetlands that is unique in Vermont.

As you paddle southwest across Long Marsh Bay, remember that Missisquoi Bay is an international waterway and the Canadian border is just north of the NFCT route. The border patrol regularly travels the bay, interviewing boaters. Be sure to carry proper ID while in this section of the lake.

The refuge headquarters is located in an attractive building on Tabor Road, which branches south from VT 78 about 5 miles west of Swanton. There are displays and audiovisual presentations about the refuge's marshes and delta, maps and pamphlets, a bookshop, and informed staff who are ready to answer questions. The building is located on Hog Island, so named because nineteenth-century farmers used to row their pigs across the inlet to the island each spring and let them roam and fatten, then bring them back to the mainland for slaughter in the fall.

If you want to stretch your legs after a day of paddling, there are several nature trails within the refuge. Near the headquarters building is the Discovery Trail. A controlled-access road (open only during hunting season in the fall) leads north from Louie's Landing to Mac's Bend, where it becomes a more primitive jeep trail that continues farther into the delta. It is open to walkers in all seasons. On the south (left) side of VT 78, a couple of miles north of Swanton, an information kiosk marks the beginning of the Black Creek/Maquam Creek nature trails, which skirt the edges of Maquam Bog.

Camping is not permitted in the refuge, but private campgrounds are located on either end of Hog Island.

SECTION 1

Lake Champlain

The suggested route proceeds south from Missisquoi Bay, following the island shoreline of North and South Hero, Vermont, eventually reaching Plattsburgh, New York. Although beautiful, the lake is often dangerous, due to its size and changeable weather. The lake is best explored with touring kayaks.

TRIP DISTANCE: 27 miles

TRIP DURATION: Allow 2 days

FLOW/SEASON: May to October; busiest in July and August

DIRECTION OF CURRENT: n/a

PUT-IN: Sandy Point boat launch (on the east side of the Vermont Route 78 bridge spanning the entrance to Missisquoi Bay). 72-hour parking. GPS: 44.970612°, −73.210439°

TAKE-OUT: New York State Department of Environmental Conservation (NYSDEC) Platts-burgh boat launch, 5 Dock St. Large parking lot and marina. GPS: 44.697954°, −73.444684°

MAP: NFCT Map 4, Islands and Farms Region

PORTAGES (0–1): Carry Bay (optional), 100 yards (carry)

HAZARDS: Waves, wind, and quickly changing weather; powerboat traffic, particularly on the open-water crossings in midsummer.

OTHER ACCESS: North Hero Island: North Hero State Park day-use area. Hand carry access. No overnight parking. GPS: 44.920782°, −73.241965°; North Hero Marina, GPS: 44.836351°, −73.300664°;

City Bay, GPS: 44.816257°, −73.290044°; Knight Point State Park boat launch, GPS: 44.769823°, −73.293048°; **Isle La Motte:** Stoney Point boat launch on West Shore Rd., GPS: 44.871507°, −73.358879°; **Plattsburgh:** Cumberland Bay State Park, 152 Cumberland Head Rd. Beach/hand carry access. Day-use fees for parking. GPS: 44.723103°, −73.422261°; Green St. boat launch with small parking area and location of the NFCT kiosk. GPS: 44.699364°, −73.44859°

CONTACT: Vermont Agency of Natural Resources; Lake Champlain Committee; NYSDEC; US Coast Guard; NFCT Trip Planner

SERVICES: North Hero/City Bay (mid-lake) has a full range of services, food, and lodging. Marinas and a variety of shoreline lodging options are also present throughout the region; Grand Isle Ferry.

CAMPING: Vermont and New York State Parks (reservation recommended, fee charged); Lake Champlain Paddlers' Trail primitive campsites (with membership); North Hero Island paddler-only free primitive campsite (no facilities); private campgrounds on Hog Island (fee)

LAKE CHAMPLAIN: BIRD THOROUGHFARE

Because of its immense size, its north–south configuration, and the many islands, bays, and wetlands that are intermingled throughout its more than 110-mile length, Lake Champlain is a natural home and major flyway for all sorts of migratory birds. It is also one of the best places in Vermont for those who like to watch birds.

In spring and fall, especially, the lake is a magnet for many kinds of waterfowl. Most of these birds are very shy and commonly swim far offshore. So be sure to pack the binoculars—and a spotting scope if you have one. A variety of shorebirds, including herons, hawks, and songbirds, are plentiful on and around the lake.

Best places to look for birds along or near the NFCT suggested route include Cumberland Bay on the New York side, and in Vermont the Grand Isle ferry landing (Gordon Landing); the Gut, between North and South Hero Islands; the Missisquoi Bay Bridge (a.k.a. the Alburg–Swanton Bridge); and the Missisquoi National Wildlife Refuge (see also Section 4 below). Walking trails within the refuge are often very productive birding routes.

Because of the changeable nature of Lake Champlain weather, the NFCT route may need to be modified as plans and weather conditions dictate.

From the boat launch, you will paddle south passing under the VT 78 bridge, leaving Missisquoi Bay and entering Lake Champlain proper. Keep a careful lookout while passing the bridge, and you may see spiny softshell turtles, a threatened species in Vermont, basking nearby.

Follow the western shore of Hog Island south to Hog Island Point, where in calm weather you may cross the broad lake to Stephenson Point and North Hero State Park. A day-use area with a public beach is located at the northernmost end of North Hero Island. A paddler-only primitive campsite can be found between Bull Rush and Stony Points on the island's west shore. Marked by a Lake Champlain Paddlers' Trail sign, a path from the lake leads through the woods to a site on one of the state park's old campground loops.

From Stephenson Point, the NFCT now bifurcates. The suggested route follows the east shore of North Hero Island to the town of North Hero. If the weather is threatening, you may wish to follow the more sheltered western shore of the island south from the state park, through Alburg Passage and Carry Bay.

North of the village of North Hero is a narrow isthmus known as the Carrying Place. This historic spot provided the native Abenaki people with a handy portage between eastern and western sections of the lake. It provides you with another choice of routes when you head south from the state park. Use it to gain quick access to either side of the island by crossing the narrow strip of land (or paddling through the culvert beneath).

Lake Champlain, the Lake Between, separates New York and Vermont and provides island camping and open water conditions for paddlers. (Photo by John Klopfer)

Pleasant lakeside North Hero village has the feel of a maritime community, though the water here is fresh, not salty. At the center of town, close to the boat landing, is Hero's Welcome General Store, where you will find sandwiches, groceries, fresh-baked bread, marine equipment, books, maps, and a variety of other wares. Nearby is the North Hero House, an outstanding inn with a fine restaurant. The village also has a boat landing with rentals, a post office, and an NFCT kiosk.

Continue south along the eastern shore of North Hero until you come to the US Highway 2 bridge that joins North and South Hero Islands. Knight Point State Park is located here, on the southern tip of North Hero Island. Paddlers may camp here in emergencies but must inform park authorities.

After leaving Knight Point, cross the Gut, a sheltered bay between North and South Hero, then paddle southward along the west shore of South Hero Island toward Wilcox Point and Gordon Landing. Make your crossing, staying well clear of the Grand Isle Ferry route. Ferries run year-round between Cumberland Head and Gordon Landing. Paddle along the north shore of Cumberland Bay (passing Cumberland State Park) to Plattsburgh, New York.

The Plattsburgh boat launch on Dock Street is located on Lake Champlain by Peace Point Park, just south of the mouth of the Saranac River. Alternatively, you can take out at the Green Street Landing located within the mouth of the Saranac River, river-right. An NFCT kiosk is found here.

SECTION 2

Missisquoi River: Enosburg Falls to Sheldon Springs

Below Enosburg Falls, the Missisquoi is a sizable west-running river flowing through a broad pastoral valley to Lake Champlain. Most of the river here is serene flatwater. Class I–II ledges below the Island View Park put-in in Enosburg Falls and Abbey Rapids provide the only whitewater action within this section. Abbey Rapids range from Class II to III thrills in high water to a boney, bumpy ride in low water. For information on the Missisquoi River above Enosburg Falls refer to the Map 5 chapter, Vermont.

TRIP DISTANCE: 11 miles

TRIP DURATION: Allow a half to full day

FLOW/SEASON: Spring, summer, fall. Spring runoff (not flood stage) is the most enjoyable time, as some riffles must be lined or walked at summer water levels. A flow of 650–3000 CFS is recommended.

DIRECTION OF CURRENT: East to west

PUT-IN(S): To run the up-to-Class-II ledges in **high water**, put in at Island View Park, 0.2 mile from Lawyer's Landing on Duffy Hill Rd. Hand carry access. Overnight parking. GPS: 44.900468°, –72.808105°; **alternative low-water put-in,** 0.5 mile from Lawyer's Landing off St. Albans St. near Pearl St. Hand carry access. GPS: 44.905562°, –72.814945°

TAKE-OUT: Signed canoe route hand carry access upstream of Shawville Rd. Bridge. A trail leads from the river to a roadside pullover area. GPS: 44.909999°, –72.967404°. *Note: Taking out at the bridge above Sheldon Springs Dam is not recommended.*

MAP: NFCT Map 4, Islands and Farms Region

PORTAGES (0–2): Enosburg Falls Carry, 0.2 mile or 0.5 mile (wheelable; only necessary if continuing downstream from Enosburg Falls, Map 5 chapter, Section 2); **Sheldon Springs Dam Carry,** 1.3 miles (wheelable; only necessary if continuing downstream to next section)

HAZARDS: Class II–III Abbey Rapids in high water; presence of dams— do not approach at high water.

OTHER ACCESS: North Sheldon Bridge, Vermont Route 120 (Kane Rd.). Informal access by trail. Roadside parking. GPS: 44.908013°, –72.90413°

CONTACT: Vermont Agency of Natural Resources; Missisquoi Valley Rail Trail (MVRT); NFCT Trip Planner

SERVICES: Enosburg Falls offers lodging, restaurants, and other services.

CAMPING: Free first-come, first-served NFCT site (Lussier) below Abbey Rapids

Paddlers enjoy areas of whitewater on the Missisquoi River downstream of Enosburg Falls, Vermont. (Photo by Chris Gill)

Just above Enosburg Falls Dam, on the south bank of an embayment created by the dam, is Lawyer's Landing, a grassy spot with a parking lot. This is the take-out for the upper end of the Enosburg Falls Carry around the Enosburg Falls Dam and a put-in for those wishing to paddle the impounded waters above it. The access road is gated, but paddlers are welcome to drive in to reach the launch. See Lawyer's Landing in the NFCT Trip Planner for the gate access code.

There are two put-in options below Enosburg Falls Dam. If the Class I–II ledges immediately below Island View Park are runnable, you can start here, river-left from the Duffy Hill Road access. If the water level is too low, use the St. Albans Street alternative put-in, river-right, in moving flatwater. Unimproved riverside access from St. Albans Street is beyond a gated fire lane and small substation.

For the next 6 miles the river flows smoothly through a broad, farmed valley. Meadows line the left shore and the Tyler Branch enters from the south. The North Sheldon Bridge, a green iron truss that carries VT 120 (Kane Road) across the river, provides another unimproved access point and an indication that the character of the Missisquoi is about to change.

Just below the bridge, Abbey Rapids begins a mile-long stretch of ledges and rock gardens. Class II under normal conditions, it approaches Class III at spring runoff and other high-water times. The long series of ledges and rocks offer ample opportunity to practice ferrying, eddy turns, and other maneuvers. You should scout this rapid carefully before entering it. Near the bottom of the left side of the rapids is the attractive NFCT-built Lussier campsite in the pines atop the bank. A register, fire ring, and picnic table are located there. Look across the adjacent meadow for a sign to the composting toilet. The Lussier family of Sheldon owns the land, and you may find evidence of their farming activities around the campsite.

The former Black Creek Railroad Bridge, now part of the Lamoille Valley Rail Trail (LVRT), is 0.5 mile below the end of Abbey Rapids. Below the trestle, Black Creek enters, river-left, shortly after which two other bridges cross the river. One is a three-span iron truss that carries the Missisquoi Valley Rail Trail (MVRT), another abandoned railroad bed turned into a multi-use recreational path. The MVRT parallels the river between Kane Road and Sheldon Junction and can be used as an alternative portage option circumventing Abbey Rapids. The other bridge carries VT 105, heading south to St. Albans.

Water impounded by Sheldon Dam backs up below here, creating a calm, pondlike backwater. The river pulls away from the road, and the dam's quiet impoundment is a secluded area where you are likely to see wildlife, including waterfowl and ospreys. As you approach Sheldon Springs Dam, you'll see a warning sign, DAM AHEAD, on the right, near where the river divides. Take out at the signed Canoe Route that follows a trail to the road and parking area to end your trip. Or continue following the portage around Sheldon Springs Dam if connecting to the next section.

SECTION 3

Missisquoi River: Sheldon Springs to Swanton

The Missisquoi assumes its full size, in places reaching more than 100 yards across, and is a large, smooth-flowing river, with a few small rapids between long sections of quiet flatwater. Class II–II+ ledges below the Machia Road Bridge in East Highgate, where an old dam has been removed, provide a beautiful run.

TRIP DISTANCE: 14.5 miles

TRIP DURATION: Allow 1 day

FLOW/SEASON: Spring, summer, fall. At low summer levels, some shallow sections may have to be walked.

DIRECTION OF CURRENT: East to west

PUT-IN: Low-water put-in below Sheldon Springs Dam, river-right. Follow the hydro access road from Shawville Rd. to powerhouse. Hand carry access. Day-use parking only. GPS: 44.909733°, –72.982374°; **Alternate high-water** put-in, river-left off Mill St. Hand carry access. Roadside parking only. GPS: 44.906515°, –72.980794°

TAKE-OUT: Above Swanton Dam by Vermont Route 78. Hand carry access. Overnight parking permitted across the street at Marble Mill Park. GPS: 44.92001°, –73.127563°

MAP: NFCT Map 4, Islands and Farms Region

PORTAGES (1): Highgate Falls Carry, 0.5 mile (mostly wheelable)

HAZARDS: The series of Class II rapids below Sheldon Springs can be challenging at high water. Up to

Class III East Highgate ledges.
OTHER ACCESS: Highgate Falls:
Highgate Falls Dam paddler parking lot on VT 207. GPS: 44.933625°, −73.05393°; **Swanton:** Vermont Fish and Wildlife Department Babbie access area, at US Highway 7 bridge, river-left. Hand carry access with parking area. GPS: 44.9103°, −73.106089°

CONTACT: Vermont Agency of Natural Resources; NFCT Trip Planner
SERVICES: Swanton is the largest village, with restaurants, lodging, and other services. Highgate Center has a small market and convenience store.
CAMPING: Free first-come, first-served (small) NFCT site along the Highgate Falls Carry

Paddlers who are continuing their trip by river from upstream of Sheldon Springs will first need to portage 1.3 miles from the take-out above Sheldon Springs Dam to reenter the river below it. Paddlers beginning here have two put-in options accessing the river from either bank via Shawville Road. To enter on the right (north) bank, enter the paved hydroelectric access road marked with a CANOE ROUTE sign and follow it through a field of solar collectors to its end. Day-use parking is available at a small riverside gravel lot. During high water releases, the rocky put-in downstream of the rapids and above the overflow channel/powerhouse may be turbulent. To enter the river from the left (south) bank, use Mill Street following the gravel driveway of an electric substation. The driveway entrance is found 0.2-mile west of the Mill Street and Shawville Road intersection. River access is several hundred yards down a rough trail, on the right.

A quarter mile below the put-in, the river consists of a short series of riffles, ledges, and a boulder garden that can be up to Class II at high water levels or scratchy and bumpy at low. Beyond that, the river opens up into a broad, gentle flow that continues for about 5 miles to a green iron bridge (Machia Road). A quarter-mile stretch of rapids and Class II ledges begins just above the bridge. Below the bridge—and the site of the former dam—are several more ledges capable of swamping boats that are rated Class II or III in higher water but are shallow and scratchy in low water. Consider scouting from the bridge or lining individual ledges. If necessary, use Vermont Route 78 downstream of Machia Road Bridge to portage, but be mindful of traffic at all times.

The East Highgate ledges are the last significant rapids on the lower Missisquoi. The 4-plus miles between the ledges and Highgate Falls Dam are mostly a flat backwater paddle, swinging away from VT 78 and proceeding quietly to Highgate Falls Dam. Spring Rapids, a former series of challenging ledges in this stretch of river, drowned in 1994 when the dam was raised.

To portage Highgate Falls Dam, take out river-right of the dam's barriers and follow the signed trail 0.5 mile, crossing Mill Hill Road and VT 207 before descending into the gorge below the dam. The second half of the carry is shared with ATV riders. Shortly before reaching the river, there's a small NFCT

Lake Champlain is a natural home and major flyway for all sorts of migratory birds. (Photo by Rob Center)

campsite tucked into the softwoods on the left side of the trail. The campsite has a tent pad, sign-in box, and moldering privy. Fires are prohibited.

From Highgate Falls Dam to Swanton Dam, the river is deep, slow-moving flatwater. Watch for wildlife and birds—ospreys, waterfowl, and herons—among the islands as the river widens. About 4 miles below Highgate Falls Dam, you will pass under Interstate 89, with the US 7 bridge just beyond. Near US 7, a fishing access area makes a good put-in/take-out point if you want to end here. It is another 3 miles downriver from here to the village of Swanton and Swanton Dam.

Use caution as you approach Swanton Dam, especially in high water, as it does not have a line of warning buoys. Take out on river-right and portage 150 yards to Marble Mill Park, where you can leave a vehicle or reenter the river.

From here, the Missisquoi drifts through the wildlife refuge (Section 4) to its outlet on Lake Champlain (Section 1).

SECTION 4

Missisquoi National Wildlife Refuge and Missisquoi Bay

The Missisquoi River flows slowly through a large, swampy delta that is alive with songbirds, waterfowl, muskrats, otters, and a wide array of reptiles and fish. The bayou-like passages open onto the broad, shallow, slightly eutrophic waters of Missisquoi Bay, the northeastern arm of Lake Champlain. As you exit the refuge, be mindful that this section is close to the international border and the waters are patrolled.

TRIP DISTANCE: 11.5 miles

TRIP DURATION: Allow 1 day

FLOW/SEASON: Spring, summer, fall

DIRECTION OF CURRENT: Southeast to northwest

PUT-IN: Marble Mill Park, below Swanton Dam, river-right. Hand carry access. Overnight parking. GPS: 44.921147°, –73.124975°

TAKE-OUT: Sandy Point boat launch (on the east side of the Vermont Route 78 bridge spanning the entrance to Missisquoi Bay). 72-hour parking. GPS: 44.970612°, –73.210439°

MAP: NFCT Map 4, Islands and Farms Region

PORTAGES (0–1): Swanton Dam Carry, 0.2 mile (wheelable; only necessary if connecting sections)

HAZARDS: Winds and quickly changing weather conditions on Missisquoi Bay

OTHER ACCESS: Louie's Landing in the Missisquoi National Wildlife Refuge on Vermont Route 78. Overnight parking. GPS: 44.958513°, –73.166566°

CONTACT: US Fish and Wildlife Service (for the refuge); Vermont Agency of Natural Resources; Lake Champlain Committee; US Coast Guard (for lake); NFCT Trip Planner

SERVICES: Food, lodging, and other services are available in Swanton. Some lodging is available along Missisquoi Bay.

CAMPING: Not allowed in the refuge; private campgrounds on Missisquoi Bay and south end of Hog Island (fee)

Below the dam and Marble Mill Park, paddle away from Swanton with VT 78 on your left. About 2.5 miles below Swanton Dam, just before Dead Creek intersects with the Missisquoi, river-right, a low stone monument and totem pole marks the site of a historic Abenaki settlement. The site is hidden beyond shoreline trees and not easily seen from the water.

Beyond Dead Creek, on both sides of the river, lies the Missisquoi National Wildlife Refuge, a 6729-acre complex of wetlands and river channels that encompasses the entire delta of the Missisquoi River and teems with life. The refuge, established by the federal government in 1943, is managed for the benefit of the wide variety of birds. More than two hundred species of waterfowl, shorebirds, herons, warblers, and other species migrate through the Champlain Valley each spring and fall, including more than twenty thousand ducks. Beds of wild rice, arrowhead, bulrush, and wild celery, attract large flocks of ringnecked ducks, black ducks, mallards, wood ducks, and green- and blue-winged teal.

Alternative Trips within Missisquoi National Wildlife Refuge

For a day trip within the refuge, put in at Louie's Landing on Vermont Route 78. There are two day-trip options, both of which follow the main channel of the Missisquoi north to Metcalfe Island, then bear right to reach Shad Island and the blue heron rookery. Bear right again to continue past Shad Island to the open waters of Missisquoi Bay.

One popular option once you reach the bay is to bear left, paddle completely around Shad Island, back into the Missisquoi's main channel, and return the way you came (upstream this time, which isn't too difficult on the delta's slow current), back to Louie's Landing.

An alternate 10-mile loop, if the wind is calm and the waters of Missisquoi Bay are not too unruly, is to bear right as you leave Shad Island behind and enter the bay. Continue to your right and paddle roughly southward, staying close to the shore. Traverse Gander Bay, Martindale Point, and Goose Bay, and enter the mouth of Dead Creek. Dead Creek is not an actual creek but a canal-like passageway opened by the great Flood of 1927. Follow Dead Creek back to the main stem of the Missisquoi, and bear right again, completing the loop back to Louie's Landing. This is a full day's paddle, and if weather conditions are favorable, a very satisfying trip.

The delta is a classic bird-foot shape, so named for the way the river channels flow through it, and is the only such one in Vermont. There are few roads within the refuge and none within the delta itself. The best way to explore the refuge is by boat. Canoes and kayaks are perfect for getting to know this fecund delta, which in places feels more like a Louisiana bayou than a part of the Northern Forest. There are some areas where boats— even paddle craft—are forbidden to go, to protect and foster bird life. Please heed signs barring boats and people from entering restricted areas. The refuge provides nesting habitat for many uncommon and rare wild birds and is an important breeding ground for the rare black tern. The largest great blue heron rookery in Vermont is located here on Shad Island.

Flowing past Louie's Landing, a popular paddler access for day trips in the refuge, the main channel of the Missisquoi will lead you roughly northward the length of this extensive delta. The channels and bays here can be confusing, so carry a map. The river's main channel is wide, deep, and calm. Spiny softshell turtles can be spotted sunning on logs or swimming alongside your boat.

Many areas along the Trail, like the Missisquoi National Wildlife Refuge with its large great blue heron rookery, provide prime wildlife viewing opportunities. (Photo by Katina Daanen)

If you are headed for the Missisquoi Bay Bridge, bear left at Metcalfe Island. From the mouth of the Missisquoi River, you will enter Missisquoi Bay, a broad, shallow arm of Lake Champlain that extends into Canada. Paddlers should remain aware that weather on the open lake can deteriorate rapidly, turning the bay's waters dangerous. Be prepared to alter your plans and seek shore and shelter if necessary. Paddle west past Donaldson Point on Hog Island, then farther southwest to the Missisquoi Bay Bridge and VT 78, where there is a boat access ramp and small parking area.

Take VT 78 for a quick and direct shuttle route between this segment's put-in and take-out, but be aware this is an extremely busy highway. It is not recommended to be used as a return option by bicycle or by foot.

NFCT MAP 5: UPPER MISSISQUOI VALLEY

Missisquoi River to Lake Memphremagog

As in its lower stretches, the Missisquoi expresses itself as a placid river meandering through a broad, farmed valley. Here the river is a mostly calm journey through a pastoral landscape dotted with farms and small villages.

From the US-Canada border to Richford, the Missisquoi resembles a sprightly mountain stream more than the placid, substantial river it will later become as it progresses toward Lake Champlain. Several decades ago, the Missisquoi, feeling frisky, jumped its banks and ran through a farmer's fields, trading its older single-channel course along the south side of the valley for a braided course along the north side. Rivers are organic, evolving ecosystems, and this lovely section of river is of recent origin.

There are several short sections of whitewater, including one significant, but avoidable, Class III–IV rapid where the Missisquoi charges through Richford. Historically a logging and manufacturing town, Richford was devastated by the Flood of 1927, which wiped out Main Street Bridge and much of River Street. Furniture, hockey sticks, plywood, and Scrabble tiles were made here, but as the local timberlands were exhausted, the town's economy dwindled. About 1600 people live in Richford now.

Richford's many Victorian homes and the impressive St. Ann's Episcopal Church still testify to its prosperity at the turn of the century. Across the street from Davis Park is Grey Gables Mansion, an ornate, three-story, Queen Anne-style house built in 1890 as the home of local lumber baron Sheldon Boright. The mansion is a strikingly elaborate building, both inside and out. Its design and much of its detailing are from a nineteenth-century architectural pattern book entitled *Palliser's American Cottage Homes* (although Grey Gables does not resemble a cottage at all). The building is on the National Register of Historic Places and has at times operated as a bed-and-breakfast inn.

Below Richford, the Missisquoi glides gently through its broad farmed and forested valley. This section between Richford and Samsonville is among the most scenic of the NFCT and notable in its designation as a National Wild and

Scenic River. This is rural Vermont at its prettiest, and this stretch makes for a lovely, mostly quiet paddle. Wary brown trout lurk in some of the deeper holes, and in season you'll see anglers fishing for them.

About a half mile upstream of the confluence of Trout River, also designated in Vermont's National Wild and Scenic River System, you'll spot a tall clay bluff, sparsely vegetated, rising above the river's left bank. Look closely, and you'll see that the sandy top layers are different from the clay layers farther down. The various layers were laid down at different times in the valley's geologic past. The lower portion of the bank reveals varved clay, annual sediment layers laid down by a glacial lake that covered the valley roughly 20,000 years ago. The lighter and darker layers here were caused by variations in the lake's rate of sedimentation. The sandy layers near the top are more recent and were laid down by the ancestral Missisquoi River after the lake receded. Then the river carved out the valley and eroded its way into its present course. This bluff is home to the NFCT Doe campsite.

There are good opportunities for wildlife viewing along the stretches of the river that wander away from Vermont Route 105. As you get closer to Enosburg Falls Dam, you'll see some structures, river-right, made from steel pipe and concrete. These are ice deflectors, designed to protect several thousand trees from the ice backed up from Enosburg Falls Dam each spring. The trees are part of a project to restore the native floodplain forest on 30 acres of former farmland. Such forests preserve native plants, shade the river to provide

Community paddles and events are a great way to share the Trail with others. (Photo by NFCT)

Alternative Trip: Upper Missisquoi River from Raboin Farm Access

The Missisquoi River is unique in that it originates in Vermont, flows north into Canada where it joins the Northern Forest Canoe Trail (NFCT) route in Highwater, then flows back into Vermont, and out to Lake Champlain. Land along the Missisquoi is privately held or owned by local communities. The upper Missisquoi River received designation in 2014 as part of the National Wild and Scenic Rivers System. Designated by local communities, Wild and Scenic rivers are federally protected and funded to ensure their special historic, environmental, and recreational features are maintained. The Upper Missisquoi and Trout Rivers (UMATR) Wild and Scenic Committee oversees the management of the waterway.

Lovely half- or full-day paddles allow you to sample the upper stretches of the river, which travel through beautiful mixed forests, lush open fields, and interesting rock formations. Put in at Raboin Farm access just south of the Lowell-Westfield town line off Vermont Route 100 and paddle 8.1 miles to Lane Road, 11.9 miles to River Road, or 16 miles to the River Road Covered Bridge. This section offers some excellent views of the northern Green Mountains while providing an adventure through some easy quick water. For more information and to download a map of this section, visit the NFCT website.

habitat for some fish, and protect against flooding and soil erosion. The NFCT Brownway campsite is located on this property. Land on river-right by a ledge outcrop and follow steps to the campsite.

Some of Vermont's largest dairy farms, with 350 or more cows, are located along this stretch of the Missisquoi, which makes for a beautiful countryside, but manure runoff from some of the farms does not do much for the water quality of the river. Dairy farmers use their cows' manure to fertilize their fields, and during spring runoff and rainy periods, manure can wash off the fields and into the river. It is unlikely you'll roll your boat in these placid stretches. But if you do take a swim—voluntary or involuntary—keep your mouth closed. It's also a good idea to carry your own drinking water.

Richford and Enosburg Falls offer many services including supplies, restaurants, and lodging. See NFCT Map 5 and the NFCT website for additional trip planning and navigational details. **Note:** For the Québec segment of the Missisquoi River and Lake Memphremagog north of the international border, refer to the Québec chapter. For Lake Memphremagog trip planning information in the United States, refer to Section 3 in the Map 6 chapter, Vermont, and NFCT Map 6.

SECTION 1

Missisquoi River: International Border to Richford

From the US-Canada border to the town of Richford, the Missisquoi River is an attractive stream of moderate size that flows, for the most part, through open farmland. Above Richford, it flows briskly along over various shallow riffles and Class II rapids. There are more trees and meandering channels above Richford than below. An avoidable stretch of Class III–IV rapids passes through Richford. Below the village, the river assumes a generally more placid character.

TRIP DISTANCE: 5.7 miles

TRIP DURATION: Allow a half day

FLOW/SEASON: Best run in spring or other high-water time; shallow rapids may need to be walked at low water.

DIRECTION OF CURRENT: East to west

PUT-IN: US Customs and Border Protection station, 1683 Glen Sutton Rd., East Richford. Hand carry access. No overnight parking. GPS: 45.011145°, –72.588076°

TAKE-OUT: Leatherneck Landing boat access and campsite, river-left, above Richford. Hand carry access. Overnight parking on Main St. GPS: 44.994166°, –72.672093°

MAP: NFCT Map 5, Upper Missisquoi Valley

PORTAGES (0–1): Richford Carry, 0.5 mile (mostly wheelable; only necessary if continuing downstream beyond Richford)

HAZARDS: Three Class II rapids; challenging Class III–IV ledges if you miss the portage take-out in Richford

OTHER ACCESS: Downstream of the border: Glen Sutton Rd. south of East Richford, Vermont. Hand carry access. Small parking area for day-trippers. GPS: 44.997414°, –72.611042°; **Upstream of the border:** Canoe & Co., 1120 Chemin Burnett, Sutton, Québec, Canada (with a fee). Overnight parking. GPS: 45.041559°, –72.502106°

CONTACT: Vermont Agency of Natural Resources; NFCT Trip Planner

SERVICES: Food and lodging are available in Richford.

CAMPING: Free first-come, first-served NFCT primitive campsites (Coons, Leatherneck Landing); Davis Park in Richford

The route detailed for this short, but very pretty, stretch of the river begins right at the US-Canada border Vermont Route 105A in East Richford (the village itself is hidden behind a railroad embankment) and is best suited for a day trip. Overnight parking is not available near the border station.

The Missisquoi River flows primarily through farmland, with distant mountains visible on some stretches. (Photo by NFCT)

The red brick US Customs and Border Protection building is on your left as you approach the iron truss bridge from VT 105A leading into the province of Québec. A US Customs stop is not required unless you are proceeding into Canada, but even so, it's not a bad idea to pull in and let the Border Protection people know your plans. Follow a well-worn path behind the Customs building directly down the river. After putting in, you'll immediately enter (at high water) an easy Class I+ rapid. At low water, this and other gravel runs above Richford may need to be walked.

The water here is clear, and it moves right along, paralleling VT 105A for about 1.5 miles, until it reaches the Stevens Mills Rapids. This is a Class II wave train that becomes Class II+ at high water. Two brisk mountain brooks, Mountain and Stanhope, come tumbling off Jay Peak, entering on river-left. In flood time, the brooks carry rocks and gravel that they dump here, changing the rapid's configuration from time to time. It's a good idea to scout the rapid before running it, though it should not present a serious problem at most water levels.

A hand carry access and parking area on Glen Sutton Road is located about 0.2 mile above Mountain and Stanhope Brooks and the Stevens Mills rapids, river-left. Below the rapid, watch for rebar in the water, and note, also on the left, the remains of an old mill building and dam—the "mill" of Stevens Mills. The NFCT Coons paddler-access-only campsite is located just below the rapid and the remains of the old mill. The Missisquoi now breaks into four channels, threading its way through small, woodsy islands. Take whichever channel has the most flow, and keep an eye out in these passages for "sweepers" or "strainers"—stationary fallen trees that can be dangerous.

THE TROUT RIVER: DESIGNATED NATIONAL WILD AND SCENIC RIVER

The Trout River flows into the Missisquoi just upstream of East Berkshire. In 2014, the Trout River joined the prestigious network of the National Wild and Scenic Rivers System when a congressional action designated 46.1 miles of the upper Missisquoi and Trout Rivers as wild and scenic. The Upper Missisquoi and Trout Rivers (UMATR) Wild and Scenic Committee oversees the management of the waterway. For more information and to view an interactive map of the rivers, visit the UMATR website (see Resources).

As the river reforms into a single channel, it becomes larger, slower, and more powerful. One mile upstream of the take-out in Richford, you will pass under a railroad bridge and go through a sweeping right-hand turn.

In Richford, buildings and sheer retaining walls contain the river as it drops over a series of ledges that can be Class IV. The serious rapids may be run by skilled paddlers but must be scouted first before deciding whether to run the rapids or not. There is no exit once you enter them, especially at high water.

To portage or scout, stay left as you approach the village and paddle into shallow water on the left side of a small island. Take-out at an improved landing where camping is allowed. Leatherneck Landing is a parcel of land protected through the work of the NFCT, the Vermont River Conservancy, and local partners.

From the take-out, follow the trail and gravel road to a gas station parking lot connecting to Main Street. The portage continues across the bridge where you can scout the rapids if considering a run. After crossing the bridge, turn left onto River Street and carry 0.2 mile to Davis Park, where you can reenter the river below the ledges.

Davis Park is a nice spot for lunch, with benches along the sides and a bandstand in the center. Sandwiches, drinks, and snacks are available in downtown Richford. The town of Richford also permits paddlers and bicyclists to camp in Davis Park. The NFCT Believe It or Not primitive campsite is a short paddle downstream of Davis Park, tucked into an overflow channel.

EXTENDING YOUR TRIP: COMBINE SECTIONS FOR AN INTERNATIONAL OVERNIGHT TRIP

Add 16.9 miles to this short segment by beginning north of the border at Mansonville, Québec, where overnight parking is permitted. Carry the appropriate documentation and use the CBP ROAM app for entry at the US Customs and Border Protection station, located river-left, downstream of the iron bridge at East Richford, Vermont. See the trip description for Québec, Section 1: North Branch Missisquoi River to International Border.

SECTION 2

Missisquoi River: Richford to Enosburg Falls

For the most part, this segment of the Missisquoi River flows smoothly through a wide, farmed and forested valley paralleling Vermont Route 105. Some riffles, the Magoon ledges (up to Class II), and the Samsonville ledges (up to Class III) and rapids near the site of the old breached dam below East Berkshire, break up an otherwise placid waterway.

TRIP DISTANCE: 13 miles

TRIP DURATION: Allow 1–2 days

FLOW/SEASON: Spring through fall; 650–3000 CFS is recommended

DIRECTION OF CURRENT: Northeast to southwest

PUT-IN: Davis Park, below the rapids on River St. in Richford, Vermont. Hand carry access. Overnight parking. GPS: 44.997901°, –72.676214°

TAKE-OUT: Lawyer's Landing above Enosburg Dam on VT 108. Hand carry access on gated private property. See Lawyer's Landing in Trip Planner for gate access code. Overnight parking and camping permitted. GPS: 44.902543°, –72.805605°

MAP: NFCT Map 5, Upper Missisquoi Valley

PORTAGES (0–1): Richford Carry, 0.5 mile (mostly wheelable; only necessary if continuing downstream from previous section)

HAZARDS: Magoon ledges may reach Class II in high water; two sets of Samsonville ledges (Class II–III) and rapids in the area of the old dam

OTHER ACCESS: East Berkshire: Upstream VT 118 bridge, river-right. Informal hand carry access. Parking across the bridge. GPS: 44.934734°, –72.709281°; **Enosburg Falls:** Brownway access off Missisquoi St. Hand carry access. Overnight parking. GPS: 44.908134°, –72.796632°; river is also accessible at various points along VT 105 between Richford and Enosburg Falls

CONTACT: Vermont Agency of Natural Resources; Missisquoi River Basin Association; Missisquoi Valley Rail Trail (MVRT); NFCT Trip Planner

SERVICES: East Berkshire has a convenience store; Richford and Enosburg Falls have various services, including restaurants and lodging

CAMPING: Davis Park in Richford; free first-come, first-served NFCT primitive campsites (Leatherneck Landing, Believe It or Not, Doe, Brownway, Lawyer's Landing)

Paddling away from Davis Park, you'll pass under a bridge, circling around a large island and past an overflow channel (river-left) where the NFCT Believe It or Not campsite is located. The first hint of whitewater or rocks signaling Magoon Ledge appear about 1 mile from the put-in. At some water levels, the Magoon Ledge forms a Class II rapid. Paddlers should stay right or carry over exposed ledges.

West-to-east traveling NFCT Thru-Paddlers paddle the Missisquoi River upstream. When water levels are low, tracking is necessary! (Photo by Andrew Aderman)

About 4.5 miles below Richford, the twin bridges of VT 105 and the Missisquoi Valley Rail Trail cross the river. Another mile below the bridges and atop a geologically significant bluff is the very pleasant NFCT Doe campsite, named after the local family that has allowed its use. Access is at a signed take-out just downriver from and on the same side (river-left) as the high bluff. A trail leads uphill through the trees to a clearing amid blackberry brambles. There is a fire ring, a picnic table, a register, and a composting toilet. The campsite is breezy and therefore relatively bug-free, with a nice view of the river.

A half mile below the high bank and the Doe campsite, the Trout River enters on the left. Just below, the VT 118 bridge crosses the Missisquoi, leading to the little town of East Berkshire. Take out river-right, upstream of the bridge and up a short, steep bank. Parking is on the other side of the bridge, on the wide dirt shoulder of VT 118.

For about 2.2 miles below East Berkshire, the water is placid. A large island in the center of the river marks the approach to the former site of the Samsonville Dam. You will encounter several ledges here. Scout, line, or portage (100 yards) river-left. The ledges are soon followed by a short series of Class II–III rapids. The whitewater ends in flatwater backed up 4.3 miles from the Enosburg Falls Dam.

Two NFCT primitive campsites are available in the Enosburg Falls area. The more private Brownway site is located river-right, less than half a mile above the dam. Approaching the VT 108 bridge that crosses the river just above the dam, look for Lawyer's Landing, river-left, above the bridge, a privately owned access built specifically for use by paddlers. Camping is also permitted in this open, exposed area near town, but there are no facilities. Enosburg Falls offers many other services including lodging and dining.

Lawyer's Landing is the official terminus of this section and is a good take-out or put-in point for those who wish to paddle the calm section of the Missisquoi upriver from the dam.

NFCT MAP 6: NORTHEAST KINGDOM

Lake Memphremagog to Connecticut River

The Trail's two principal Vermont waterways covered on NFCT Map 6, the Clyde and Nulhegan Rivers, are strikingly different in character. Both rivers rise at Island Pond and, with an appropriate skill set, both offer the opportunity to be paddled in their entirety from source to mouth. From their headwaters, each river begins calmly, providing miles of quiet paddling suitable for novices, but includes a descent through spirited whitewater and boulder fields that should be attempted only by expert paddlers. The Clyde flows westward, through wetlands and a farmed valley, to Newport and Lake Memphremagog. The Nulhegan flows east, through deep forest, bogs, and alder swamps, to the Connecticut River.

Lake Memphremagog, a vast glacial lake, is situated between Newport, Vermont, and Magog, Québec. The lake is a source of recreation and provides drinking water for 200,000 people. Map 6 covers the section that falls within the United States. For the Canadian segment of Lake Memphremagog above the international border, refer to Section 2 in the Map 5 chapter, Québec.

Many services are available in the larger villages of Island Pond and Newport, and public and private campgrounds, as well as NFCT primitive campsites, are evenly spaced out, making multiple-day trips feasible. See NFCT Map 6 and the NFCT website for additional trip planning and navigational details.

CLYDE RIVER

Island Pond, a small waterbody with an island near its center, is the source of the Clyde River. The village of Island Pond, which has a rugged, northern frontier-like feel to it, clusters at the pond's north end and has restaurants, lodging, and a grocery store. A private campground and access to Brighton State Park on Spectacle Pond are located on the pond's southeast end.

The Clyde River leaves Island Pond between a motel and information center and then passes directly under a historic hotel. The hotel was built in 1866, when Island Pond was a rough-and-tumble logging town and an important rail

SPECTACLE POND

Spectacle Pond was added as a waterbody to the NFCT several years after the Trail's inception. Thru-Paddlers use this short but scenic segment connecting Island Pond to the headwaters of the Nulhegan River. Visitors can enjoy paddling right up to Brighton State Park shoreline campsites (reservations highly recommended). If you are journeying east from Island Pond, portage 0.3 mile through Lakeside Camping and launch from the Vermont Fish & Wildlife Department access point off of Fishing Village Road, where parking is also available. Access is also available from the Brighton State Park boat launch on Spectacle Pond (day-use fee). After crossing Spectacle Pond, paddlers who wish to connect sections as part of a larger trip will then need to portage 1.9 miles following wheelable trails and Vermont Route 105 to the put-in on Nulhegan Pond.

center for the Northeast Kingdom. The river begins here as a narrow stream, meandering through tall marsh grasses, alder thickets, and lowland cedar forests while also passing over numerous beaver dams.

Below Five Mile Square Road, the Clyde enters a large flatwater-wetland complex that leads through a black ash–silver maple floodplain forest and a wide wetland dominated by bog sedge. This is known as an intermediate fen—a very rare type of wetland. Some paddlers have experienced wayfinding difficulty when paddling upstream through Bucks Flat because the flow is very slow and there are several channels, some of which are dead ends.

Nevertheless, this wild wetland will reward the extra effort. Bucks Flat is a fecund area that provides potential nesting sites for two large raptors, the osprey and the bald eagle; sightings of both birds are not uncommon here. Other more common marsh birds, such as red-winged blackbirds and great blue herons, are likely to be seen. Mink, muskrats, and river otters may also show themselves. The mountain that rises off to the northeast is 1800-foot Dolif Mountain.

From Ten Mile Square Road, the Clyde passes through forests of silver maple and cedar, and a farmed valley with occasional views of the rolling, open countryside that surrounds the river. While the paddling through this section is not exciting, and blowdowns can be a problem, this is a scenic section of the river. Its winding, tree-shaded course offers an air of mystery as you proceed. You never know just what you'll see around the next bend.

Twin Bridges Road (Cross Road) provides an informal access point near the bridge. A short walk will bring you to the hamlet of East Charleston with its white-steepled church. Seymour and Echo Lakes enter through the large backwater northeast of the village and are known to locals as good trout-fishing sites. Below Twin Bridges Road, the Clyde passes through a classic floodplain forest also dominated by silver maple, white cedar, and other lowland trees.

From Pensioner Pond, the Clyde links a series of small ponds interspersed with rapids as it descends to Lake Memphremagog. Challenging ledges and Class II–III rapids are best suited to whitewater enthusiasts, while public boat launches allow easy access for exploring each of the quieter ponds.

Little Salem Lake (known for its good pickerel fishing) connects to Salem Lake, where an NFCT campsite and residences line the shores. You can paddle between the two ponds or take out at the northeast end of Little Salem Lake, where there's a parking area and access point off Hayward Road. Just uphill, overlooking the lake is the private Char-Bo Campground, offering campsites, a camp store, and other amenities.

The Clyde River leaves Salem Lake at its northwest corner and quickly changes character again. It plunges into a narrow, cedar-forested valley and picks up speed as it descends toward Derby Center and Clyde Pond. The river is mostly pushy Class II rapids in this section and should be attempted by experienced paddlers only. The same holds true for the river spilling below the Great Bay Hydro powerhouse on Clyde Street after Clyde Pond. This is the put-in for experts possessing whitewater skills and boats who purposely want to paddle Class II–III rapids. Most paddlers will follow the wheelable street portage downhill to the Clyde Street Bridge where the Clyde placidly flows into Lake Memphremagog at Newport. Newport is a large town offering many services.

Many of the Trail's rivers and streams are "maintained" by resident beaver populations. (Photo courtesy of Northstar Canoes)

LAKE MEMPHREMAGOG

Although three-fourths of this impressive freshwater lake extends into Canada, the section of the lake that lies within the United States provides two quite distinctively different paddling experiences that are separated by the city of Newport.

South Bay is narrower, river-like, and surrounded by cattail marshes and other boggy areas that make ideal wildlife habitat. It is home to the South Bay Wildlife Management Area, an 1800-acre preserve protecting some of the finest wetlands in the state. Here, you are likely to see herons, turtles, and beavers, especially during early morning paddles. Wood ducks and other waterfowl are common.

The lake north of Newport is wide open, broadly scenic, and windswept. Paddlers wishing to explore the lake should first consult a local weather forecast. There are few public access points and north winds can kick up big waves. The NFCT Eagle Point campsite is located near the border within a sandy cove on the lake's east shore.

Newport was a railroad and logging center in the nineteenth century. It developed as a vacation center during the height of the railroad era but by the middle of the twentieth century had entered a period of decline. Today, Newport is enjoying a bit of a renaissance, with an attractive waterfront boardwalk and marina right downtown as well as restaurants, a good natural foods store, a sporting goods store, excellent coffee, and a tasting room for locally made cider, beer, and spirits. Camping is available at municipally owned Prouty Beach.

The Memphremagog Historical Society of Newport, located in the Emory Hebard State Office Building, has murals and displays related to the history of the region, including Native American history. An NFCT kiosk on the lawn next to the Emory Hebard building provides more local information. St. Mary Star of the Sea (the large Catholic cathedral on top of the hill) is an impressive church with a nice view of the lake from its front steps.

If you intend to enter Canada, you must carry a valid passport or passport card and stop at the Leadville Pier, Québec, Customs Office on the west shore to report entry. The border is marked with buoys and delineated on land with clear-cutting. For more information about border crossings and government restrictions refer to the Planning a Trip section.

NULHEGAN RIVER

The ring of mountains that contains the Nulhegan basin is believed by geologists to be the remnants of an ancient volcanic ring dike, formed and eroded eons ago. The underlying granitic bedrock is much more acidic than the bedrock to the west of Island Pond and is therefore less conducive to farming. Also, the Nulhegan basin tends to hold cold air and so is chillier than other nearby regions. This deeply forested basin remains one of Vermont's wildest and most

LOGGING AND THE NULHEGAN BASIN

Since the area was first settled by Europeans, much of the Nulhegan's deep forests and swamps were logged. Over time, industrial timberlands were acquired by large timber companies. Before World War II, rugged camps of loggers cut timber all winter and stacked logs beside the Nulhegan and other streams. Spring logging drives sent rafts of logs down the Nulhegan to the Connecticut. The log drives ended in the 1940s and '50s as trucks, railways, and better roads became the primary means of transporting lumber to the mills downcountry.

In the 1990s, ownership patterns in this area began to change. The big timber companies began to sell off their holdings, and it was feared that the area might become developed. However, land purchases by the state and federal governments, the Nature Conservancy, the Vermont Land Trust, and the Vermont Housing & Conservation Board conserved much of the area. The Silvio O. Conte National Fish and Wildlife Refuge was established along the Connecticut River watershed, and federal and state authorities quickly decided that the Nulhegan basin would be a high priority for conservation, with its rare species of plants and animals and the unusual wetland habitat throughout the basin.

Today, as you paddle on the Nulhegan and upper Connecticut Rivers you'll be within a few miles of more than 300,000 acres of conserved land in Vermont and New Hampshire. Not all of it is designated wilderness; the majority of the conserved acreage is designated working forest, where timber harvesting and other human activities are encouraged. But this unique, wild corner of Vermont has been protected from widespread development forever.

undeveloped regions with a completely different feel than the farmed valley of the Clyde River, just a few miles to the west.

Moose Bog, located near Wenlock Crossing, drains into the upper Nulhegan and is known to birders throughout the region as the home of several rare boreal bird species, the black-backed woodpecker, boreal chickadee, and spruce grouse among them. In fact, the basin contains the only spruce grouse nesting area known in Vermont. Many other species are seen here in spring and summer. The Nulhegan basin has been designated an official Important Bird Area, Vermont's largest.

The Nulhegan should be approached with the idea that this river is of two minds. In its upper reaches, the Nulhegan River is small, slow, and tea-colored. It usually holds enough water that it can be paddled throughout the season. Paddlers who choose to explore this wild section of river should be prepared to cross multiple beaver dams and other obstacles and should not be in a hurry.

As it winds back and forth, the river drains a huge wild basin of boreal forests, swamps, and streams inhabited mostly by deer, moose, bear, and blackflies. Novice paddlers should plan to take out at Wenlock Crossing where Vermont Route 105 again crosses the river, a 6-mile paddle from the headwaters put-in.

Wenlock Crossing was once a thriving logging camp, where a rough-and-ready backwoods community revolved around the Beattie sawmill. It remained an active log yard until the 1980s, and you'll see large boom derricks and other heavy industrial equipment nearby. The rail line also crosses here. Today, though it has been heavily logged, the area is remote, rugged, and wild.

Only expert boaters should consider paddling beyond Wenlock Crossing, which is only runnable with enough water. In spring, the lower Nulhegan contains sections of serious whitewater. It rushes over Class II–IV boulder fields and rapids, and churns through a narrow gorge surrounded by Vermont Wildlife Management Areas and the Silvio O. Conte National Fish and Wildlife Refuge. During low water, canoes must be walked or lined through much of this part of the river.

At the confluence of the East Branch Nulhegan, the river continues another few miles through Class I and II boulder fields, which are runnable in high water, but make for a bumpy, scratchy, or impassable ride in low. The river spreads out over gravel bars at its outlet on the Connecticut River.

SECTION 1

Clyde River: Island Pond to Pensioner Pond

The Clyde River begins at Island Pond, then meanders lazily, except for one short Class II rapid, for the next 17 miles, entering Pensioner Pond through a small wetland at its east end. Though quiet, it traverses some pleasantly wild wetlands where paddlers may encounter beaver dams and other obstacles.

TRIP DISTANCE: 18.7 miles
TRIP DURATION: Allow 2 days
FLOW/SEASON: This segment of the Clyde is navigable, with some portages, throughout the paddling season. Very high or low water may make parts of the first 10 miles more difficult. A flow of 600 CFS is recommended for a clean run of the short Class II rapid; 150–200 CFS is considered normal flow.

DIRECTION OF CURRENT: Southeast to northwest
PUT-IN(S): Island Pond boat launch: 16 Ripple Cove, Island Pond. 72-hour parking. GPS: 44.7926710°, –71.8663790°; or **Lakeslde Park** in the village of Island Pond, 32 Mill St., public dock and hand carry access. Overnight parking. GPS: 44.813713°, –71.879906°
TAKE-OUT: Pensioner Pond,

Vermont Department of Fish and Wildlife public access boat ramp off Vermont Route 105. 72-hour parking. GPS: 44.877367°, −72.052235°
MAP: NFCT Map 6, Northeast Kingdom
PORTAGES (0–1+): Blowdowns and beaver dams may necessitate short portages at various points along this section. Use an informal, unmaintained trail (150 feet) to avoid a Class II rapid (about 2 miles west of Island Pond), if not running
HAZARDS: One Class II rapid, occasional beaver dams, or down trees blocking the narrow channel
OTHER ACCESS: **Island Pond south shore beach**, 381 Lakeshore Dr. Hand carry access away from the beach. Inform the staff if parking overnight. Day-use fees apply during the operating season. GPS: 44.792265°, −71.862486°; **Five Mile Square Rd.:** A.k.a. "The Tubes"

on VT 105. Hand carry access. 72-hour parking. GPS: 44.801612°, −71.914849°; **Ten Mile Square Rd.:** Adjacent to VT 105 bridge. Gravel boat ramp with 72-hour parking. GPS: 44.827662°, −71.973852°; **Center School Rd.:** Informal hand carry access at bridge. GPS: 44.840891°, −72.021956°
CONTACT: Vermont Agency of Natural Resources; NorthWoods Stewardship Center; NFCT Trip Planner
SERVICES: Island Pond has several lodging and restaurant options. A boat livery located below Pensioner Pond rents kayaks and offers shuttle services (by prior arrangement) for much of this section.
CAMPING: Free first-come, first-served NFCT primitive campsite (NorthWoods Landing); Island Pond, private Lakeside Camping (fee); Spectacle Pond, Brighton State Park (fee)

Island Pond has many services, including food and lodging. If time permits, hike the 3.5-mile roundtrip Bluff Mountain Trail just north of town. Stunning views of the pond and the Nulhegan basin are seen from the summit.

There are two ways to begin your paddle on the Clyde. The mileage for this section derives from the public boat access located at the south shore of Island Pond, on Lakeshore Drive. Explore the attractive pond with its large namesake island and beaches, or paddle roughly 1.7 miles to the northwest, near the center of the village of Island Pond where the Clyde leaves the pond. If you choose not to paddle the length of the pond, you can put in at the town beach and paddle the channel that passes under the historic hotel, or use the handcarry access behind the hotel.

The river's passage underneath the historic hotel can be run at normal water levels but should be scouted first. Use the alternative put-in behind the hotel during high water. The river flows beside local backyards, over beaver dams, and under a low-clearance bridge crossing. The Pherrins River joins the Clyde from the right soon after passing the low-clearance bridge. About 1 mile beyond the confluence of the Pherrins River, you'll encounter a short Class II rapid that can be tricky at higher water levels. This rapid ends in a plunge pool that was once a millpond. Scout, line, or portage on an informal trail river-right.

Once past this rapid, the river flows quietly along, roughly paralleling VT 114 and VT 105. It passes the mouth of Oswegatchie Brook before reaching a double-culvert bridge and a parking area with an easy access point at Five Mile Square Road. These two large, paddleable culverts are unmistakable and are known locally as "The Tubes."

After passing Five Mile Square Road, paddlers should be prepared for more beaver dams that may block the river as the Clyde leads westward through the fen's maze of wetlands and larger areas of open backwaters. The river begins to widen and picks up more volume where Webster Brook enters from the right.

About 3.5 miles after "The Tubes," look for NFCT's NorthWoods Landing campsite tucked along the right shoreline. The primitive campsite is the halfway stopping point on an overnight trip. The site is a short walk up from a dock used by the NorthWoods Stewardship Center. Footpaths lead to the center's campus.

The Clyde will again narrow at the bridge carrying VT 105 across the river at Ten Mile Square Road. A Vermont Fish & Wildlife access point here makes an excellent put-in/take-out point dividing this section into two day trips. Just across the street from the Fish & Wildlife river access parking is a farm stand. Here you will find an NFCT interpretive panel and, depending on the time of

The top of the Clyde River flows beneath a hotel in Island Pond, making an easy transition from bed to boat. (Photo by NFCT)

KINGDOM TRAILS

Not far south of the Northeast Kingdom section of the NFCT is a unique and popular trail destination: Kingdom Trails in East Burke. Known mostly as a mountain bike trail system, Kingdom Trails are actually multi-use and open to nonmotorized recreation year-round. The mile after mile of winding single track, old cart roads, broad fire roads, and scenic country roads can be explored on foot, bicycle, skis, or snowshoes. The variety of trail types means that there's a section for any ability of biker, skier, or hiker, and the knowledgeable staff will set you up with a map and advice about the routes. This diverse trail system uses both privately and state-owned land and is a unique example of successful public/private partnership. The small fee collected from day passes helps trail crews maintain the routes and manage use in environmentally appropriate ways. Local shops provide gear rentals and guiding services, and lodging establishments provide accommodations with trail packages. For more information, contact Kingdom Trail Association.

year, fresh vegetables, baked goods, and homemade ice-cream sandwiches available for purchase.

The current picks up a little below the bridge, and the river's main channel carries paddlers through a silver maple forest. The river proceeds through farmlands and becomes more sinuous, with numerous oxbows as it meanders on its way to the east end of Pensioner Pond.

Twin Bridges Road is less than 2 miles from Ten Mile Square Road with informal access to East Charleston (no services). Center School Road crosses the river about 2.5 miles below East Charleston, providing a better paddler take-out or put-in. However, care must be taken not to obstruct the fire hydrant located at this crossing.

You'll reach the open waters of Pensioner Pond in another 5 miles or so beyond the Center School Road bridge. Pensioner Pond is a small, attractive lake surrounded by farmlands and camps. Cross to its east (right) shore, and take out at the Vermont Fish & Wildlife access and parking area on the far north end.

SECTION 2

Clyde River: Pensioner Pond to Lake Memphremagog

Shortly after Pensioner Pond, the Clyde begins its descent to Lake Memphremagog's South Bay. The route is primarily a series of small ponds interspersed with rapids, some runnable and some unrunnable. *Challenging ledges and Class III rapids make the lower section best suited to whitewater enthusiasts.*

TRIP DISTANCE: 13.6 miles

TRIP DURATION: Allow 1 day

FLOW/SEASON: The rapids are best paddled in the spring during high water. Low water may make passage difficult or impossible. Ponds may be paddled spring to fall.

DIRECTION OF CURRENT: Southeast to northwest

PUT-IN: Northeast end of Pensioner Pond, Vermont Fish & Wildlife Department public access boat ramp off Vermont Route 105. 72-hour parking. GPS: 44.877367°, −72.052235°

TAKE-OUT: Newport City Dock/ Gateway Center, 84 Fyfe Dr. Improved launch. Overnight parking. GPS: 44.936842°, −72.212062°

MAP: NFCT Map 6, Northeast Kingdom

PORTAGES (3–4): Great Falls Carry, 0.4 mile (wheelable); **West Charleston Pond Dam Carry**, 0.5 mile (wheelable); **Yale Dale Carry** (optional), 1.2 miles (mostly wheelable); **Clyde St. Bridge Carry**, 0.4 or 1 mile (wheelable)

HAZARDS: West Charleston ledges and Class II boulder field, 3 miles of continuous Class II–III rapids below Salem Lake; 0.5 mile of Class II–III rapids below powerhouse put-in after Clyde Pond. Paddlers should carefully scout all rapids before running. Caution: The rapids at Great Falls and at the village of West Charleston are dangerous and must be portaged.

OTHER ACCESS: Charleston Pond: South end via Great Falls Rd. below Barton Hydro facility. Hand carry access. Small parking area. GPS: 44.887536°, −72.055295°; North end via dirt road from Gratton Hill Rd. above West Charleston Dam. Hand carry access. Small parking area. GPS: 44.895188°, −72.054335°; **Little Salem Lake:** Public access area from Hayward Rd. Hand carry with limited parking. GPS: 44.9188310°, −72.1000210°; **Salem Lake:** David H. Wood public access, improved boat launch with parking area also off Hayward Rd. GPS: 44.920743°, −72.098566°; **Derby Center:** A long section of Class II–III rapids below Salem Lake is best accessed through the lake's outlet or at the riverside park adjacent to the VT 105 bridge in Derby Center. Overnight parking. GPS: 44.945289°, −72.13626721°; **Clyde Pond:** North end boat launch. GPS: 44.940037°, −72.17185°; South end. Hand carry access only. GPS: 44.935029°, −72.175217°; both access areas are located off Crawford Rd. and allow overnight parking; **Lake Memphremagog South Bay:** Vermont Fish & Wildlife Department South Bay access area, 619 Coventry St., Newport. 72-hour parking. GPS: 44.929059°, −72.213021°; **Lake Memphremagog:** Prouty Beach and Campground, 386 Prouty Beach Rd. Municipal park. Hand carry access. GPS: 44.946828°, −72.207465°

CONTACT: Vermont Agency of Natural Resources; NorthWoods Stewardship Center; NFCT Trip Planner **SERVICES:** West Charleston has a general store. Derby Center and Newport offer lodging, food, and supplies.

CAMPING: Free first-come, first-served NFCT primitive campsites (Great Falls, Coutts, Yale Dale, Pond View, Hidden Leaf); Char-Bo private campground by Salem Lake (fee); Prouty Beach municipal park on Lake Memphremagog (fee)

After putting in at the Vermont Fish & Wildlife boat launch on Pensioner Pond, paddle due north, reentering the Clyde River from the pond's northern outlet. After 0.6 mile, take out on the left above the VT 105 bridge. Great Falls gorge and the dam is located below the bridge within the next half mile. All boaters must exit here. The portage route crosses the river on the VT 105 bridge and turns left onto Great Falls Road. Follow this road down to a parking lot at its end. The little brick powerhouse (marked with a brick-inlay date of 1930) still generates power for the town of Barton, and you may hear its turbines running as you near the end of your portage. Heed the signs warning paddlers to stay well clear of the raceway and its sometimes dangerous outflow currents.

From the small parking lot at the end of Great Falls Road, the trail heads down the right-hand side of the outlet and powerhouse raceway through the NFCT Great Falls primitive campsite to a public-access put-in on the south shore of Charleston Pond.

Charleston Pond is an enjoyable paddle with undeveloped shorelines, but it's short, since the West Charleston Pond Dam and falls on the pond's north end must be portaged. Take out river-right before the bridge and trail that leads to a parking area, then follow the NFCT arrows to portage west on VT 105 through the village of West Charleston. Put in below the Fontaine Road Bridge and ledges in quickwater. Alternatively, expert paddlers may choose to follow Citizens Road, put in by the powerhouse substation, and run a section of Class II+ ledges in high water that should first be scouted. Fontaine Road Bridge is a low-profile bridge spanning the last ledge drop. Beyond the bridge, it's a calm 2.5-mile glide to reedy Little Salem Lake.

Paddle through Little Salem Lake, passing under Hayward Road Bridge through the narrow inlet connecting Salem Lake. Both lakes can be accessed from Vermont Department of Fish & Wildlife public access areas off Hayward Road (Little Salem Lake and David H. Wood on Salem Lake) where parking is available. Private Char-Bo Campground is also located uphill off Hayward Road. Campground information is listed on the NFCT website.

After leaving Salem Lake, the Clyde arrives in Derby Center in lively fashion, on a sharp zigzag turn at Derby Center and the bridge that carries VT 105 across the river. Here you will find a small riverside park turnout with parking and access to the Yale Dale Carry from Bridge Street. The Yale Dale Carry was established to help Thru-Paddlers avoid ascending more than a mile of

Wildlife-rich paddling is to be found on the upper stretch of the Clyde River and the fen. The course of the river becomes more apparent in autumn. (Photo courtesy of Northstar Canoes)

challenging rapids. The portage route passes by the home of a landowner who has generously provided a paddler campsite and lean-to on a height of land.

Below the Bridge Street turnout, the quick Class II+ rapids are almost continuous as the river flows under Interstate 91 for more than a mile and into little Clyde Pond, a 200-acre impoundment managed by Great Bay Hydro to feed its hydroelectric generating facilities downstream. There are two public access points on Clyde Pond, one on the pond's western shore at Pond View campsite, and the other, a little farther down that same shore, beside Newport Dam. Parking is permitted at both access areas. For birders and anglers, there is a nature trail that follows the pond's western shore southward from the dam, giving access to the bays along the south end of the pond. A second campsite, water-access-only Hidden Leaf, is located on the eastern shore under pines.

For most paddlers, Clyde Pond should be considered the end of downstream paddling. For paddlers interested in finishing in Newport, portage 1 mile downhill to the Clyde Street Bridge to rejoin the river in quickwater, or continue walking another 0.2 mile to a public access area adjacent to the Western Avenue Bridge. This gives access to the last mile of the Clyde River, which flows wide and deep from here into Lake Memphremagog's South Bay. Expert paddlers may want to shorten the portage by running the 0.5 mile of Class II–III rapids below the hydro powerhouse off Clyde Street.

Take out at the Newport City Dock, one of the several public access areas in South Bay, or boat launches on either side of Lake Memphremagog.

SECTION 3

Lake Memphremagog and South Bay

Newport is an attractive border city, advantageously sited on the spectacular northern Lake Memphremagog. South Bay and its marshy, fertile Wildlife Management Area, replete with plants and wildlife, are worthy of exploration. The NFCT route follows the west shore of Lake Memphremagog from City Dock and the Gateway Center north roughly 5.5 miles to the Canadian border at Leadville Pier, Québec. Touring kayaks are the most suitable craft for paddling on this big lake.

For the Québec segment of Lake Memphremagog, see the Québec chapter, NFCT Map 5, Section 2.

TRIP DISTANCE: 7 miles roundtrip south/12.5 miles roundtrip north

TRIP DURATION: Allow a half to full day

FLOW/SEASON: May through foliage season in October

DIRECTION OF CURRENT: n/a

PUT-IN/TAKE-OUT: Vermont Fish & Wildlife South Bay access area, 619 Coventry St., Newport. Improved boat launch. GPS: 44.929059°, –72.213021°

MAP: NFCT Map 6, Northeast Kingdom

PORTAGES (0): None

HAZARDS: Winds and rough weather on the open lake

OTHER ACCESS: South Bay: Glen Rd. Hand carry access. GPS: 44.902637°, –72.192167°; Gardner Memorial Park, 155 Gardner Park Rd. Hand carry access.

GPS: 44.940585°, –72.201917°; **Lake Memphremagog:** Newport City Dock/Gateway Center, 84 Fyfe Dr. Improved launch. Overnight parking. GPS: 44.936842°, –72.212062°; Vermont Fish & Wildlife Department Whipple Point access area, 155 Fishing Access Rd., Derby Line. Improved boat launch. 72-hour parking. GPS: 44.953861°, –72.234016°

CONTACT: Vermont Agency of Natural Resources, US Coast Guard; NFCT Trip Planner

SERVICES: Newport has a wide range of shops, services, lodging, and restaurant options.

CAMPING: Free first-come, first-served NFCT primitive campsite with three tent platforms (Eagle Point); Prouty Beach municipal park (fee)

The city of Newport, Vermont, lies at the south end of Lake Memphremagog.
(Photo by John DiSalvo)

From the Vermont Fish & Wildlife public access, turn south to paddle into the reedy bay or north to paddle toward and into the main lake. The northern end of the bay feels decidedly urban—and slightly noisy, with traffic making its way into Newport. However, as you paddle southward, the marshy character of the bay asserts itself and a narrow channel leads through areas of pickerelweed, water lily, and cattails. A hand carry boat launch located along Glen Road about 3 miles south of Newport provides another put-in option on the far south end of the South Bay Wildlife Management Area. Like the Clyde, other rivers terminate in South Bay, including the Black River. The lower Black River provides an additional paddling opportunity (see "Extending Your Trip: Lower Black River" below).

Paddling north from the Vermont Fish & Wildlife access, you will pass underneath the bridge and railroad trestle that separate South Bay from the main part of Lake Memphremagog. You are now close to downtown Newport and can sense why this small city has a decidedly maritime feel.

Consult a local weather forecast before exploring the open lake beyond Newport. The NFCT route follows the shoreline north to Québec. Paddle west of the Newport City Dock, past Whipple Point, across Holbrook Bay, and beyond Maxfield Point toward the border where the NFCT continues north to Perkins Landing. If you intend to enter Canada, you must stop at the Leadville Pier, Québec, Customs Office. For border crossing information, refer to the Québec chapter.

Eagle Point, just south of the international border on the east shore of the lake, is home to an NFCT paddler campsite within a cove. Camping here overnight would turn this section into a pleasant two-day excursion. If conditions allow, make the 2-mile crossing, keeping south of Province Island and the international border. Alternatively, you can reach Eagle Point by paddling north from Newport and following the eastern shoreline.

Camping and picnicking is also available at Prouty Beach, a lakeside municipal park less than a mile by water north of Newport's city center.

EXTENDING YOUR TRIP: LOWER BLACK RIVER

The lower Black River is an excellent 8-mile quiet water paddle that can be done as a one-way trip, taking about three hours, or an out-and-back day trip from Newport. A town park in Coventry and a state launch on Lake Memphremagog's South Bay make for easy access. The paddle is almost entirely flatwater, with only very small sections of quickwater. The majority of this paddle takes you through another section of the South Bay Wildlife Management Area. The trip ends (or starts if you are doing an out-and-back trip) in the South Bay of Lake Memphremagog, which has beautiful views all around.

SECTION 4

Nulhegan River

The Nulhegan, a small wilderness river, has two distinctly different sections. Its first 6 miles wind slowly through a series of highland bogs and alder swamps. *After Wenlock Crossing, the river plunges abruptly downhill, racing through a series of difficult Class II–IV rapids suitable for expert paddlers only.* Quickwater ends shortly before the Nulhegan joins the Connecticut River in Bloomfield.

TRIP DISTANCE: 16 or 16.9 miles

TRIP DURATION: Allow 1–2 days

FLOW/SEASON: At normal or low water levels, the lower section may have to be lined or walked.

DIRECTION OF CURRENT: West to east

PUT-IN(S): Both access options are located along Vermont Route 105. Hand carry access. Park along the highway shoulder. **Nulhegan Pond**, GPS: 44.786089°, –71.817054° or **Nulhegan River**, GPS: 44.785888°, –71.809201°

TAKE-OUT: Debanville Landing, at the confluence of the Nulhegan and Connecticut Rivers in Bloomfield. Take out by field. Hand carry access. Overnight parking by NFCT kiosk on VT 102. GPS: 44.751425°, –71.632742°

MAP: NFCT Map 6, Northeast Kingdom

PORTAGES (2–3): Silvio Carry (optional), 0.3 mile (not wheelable); **Nulhegan (Upper) Gorge Carry**, 0.2 mile (not wheelable); **Stone Dam Rapids Carry**, 1 mile (wheelable)

HAZARDS: The lower section of the river, starting at mile 9, below Wenlock Crossing, is dangerous and should be attempted by expert

whitewater paddlers only.
OTHER ACCESS: Wenlock Crossing: VT 105. Improved hand carry access. 72-hour parking. GPS: 44.771503°, –71.741672°; **Stone Dam:** VT 105. Improved hand carry access. Overnight parking. GPS: 44.779172°, –71.676881°
CONTACT: US Fish and Wildlife Service (for the refuge); Vermont

Agency of Natural Resources; NFCT Trip Planner
SERVICES: Groceries, supplies, and lodging are available in Island Pond. A general store with a deli is near the take-out in Bloomfield.
CAMPING: Free first-come, first-served NFCT primitive campsites (Walker, Nulhegan Confluence); state-managed campsite (Belknap)

East of Island Pond on VT 105, just past the John H. Boylan State Airport (named for a longtime local legislator), you'll see Nulhegan Pond—small, shallow, and boggy—on your left. This is the source of the Nulhegan River. Paddlers who are continuing their trip from Spectacle Pond will first need to portage 1.9 miles (see "Spectacle Pond" sidebar in the Map 6 chapter overview for portage details).

If the water's high enough, put in here and paddle just under a mile, looping around the pond's south side to the Nulhegan riverhead. A second access point is located another 0.4 mile east of the pond put-in on VT 105, where the river flows under the highway bridge. Beginning here eliminates the 0.9 mile pond paddle. Timbered steps provide hand carry access to the water, river-right, between VT 105 and the railroad bridge. Keep an eye out for traffic, especially the heavy lumber trucks that frequent this stretch of road. There's no parking area, but the road shoulder is wide enough for a single car.

The NFCT Walker primitive campsite is present on an elevated terrace under a stand of towering pine trees, river-left, within the first half mile. For the next several miles, the river winds its way through a complex and extensive wetland, passing through a series of bogs and alder swamps, groves of cedars, and banks of marsh grass, and over numerous beaver dams, as it makes its way eastward. In this wildlife-rich upper stretch, the river can feel more like a choked creek than a river. A couple of low bridges may necessitate portaging when water is high.

Most paddlers will end their Nulhegan River trip at Wenlock Crossing, where VT 105 crosses the river on a concrete bridge, 6 miles from its headwaters. A vehicle turnout a short distance east of the bridge provides parking off the two lane highway.

Do not attempt this section unless you are a highly skilled paddler. From Wenlock Crossing, the Nulhegan River continues its wandering course for a few more miles, picking up speed as it negotiates some boulder fields. The river abruptly becomes steep and rocky approaching the National Fish and Wildlife Refuge, and paddlers need to remain vigilant. The Silvio Carry is a nature trail associated with the Silvio O. Conte Nulhegan Basin Visitor Center. It can be

The boreal forests surrounding the Nulhegan River support habitat for many northern species including great horned owls. (Photo by Russ Ford)

used to scout the rapids or carry around them, but it does not provide a practical exit because the visitor center is perched high above the gorge.

Just beyond the nature trail, you will encounter an iron railroad bridge. This is immediately above the upper gorge, a steep section of whitewater. Take out river-left and portage 0.2 mile to avoid a Class IV drop beneath the railroad bridge. This is a must-make maneuver. Put back in below the gorge. From here, Class I–II rapids continue for a half mile before dissolving in the impounded waters behind the old Stone Dam.

Below Stone Dam, the river becomes steeper, passing through a narrow gorge with Class III–IV rapids that can be avoided by using the Stone Dam Rapids Carry. This run is unsuitable for loaded canoes. Take out at the VT 105 bridge and portage 1 mile along VT 105. The put-in is situated on conserved land home to the timber-framed Nulhegan Confluence Hut (advance reservation required through Vermont Huts Association). The NFCT Nulhegan primitive campsite is located downriver of the hut, at the confluence of the East Branch and the Nulhegan's main stem. Class I and II rapids continue through boulder fields on the river's main branch for 3 miles below this campsite. The rapids here are runnable, but the river will be shallow and scratchy during low water.

The Nulhegan washes out over gravel bars where it joins the Connecticut River at Debanville Landing in Bloomfield. State-owned Belknap primitive campsite is situated upstream of the VT 102 iron bridge on the left bank; Debanville's General Store & Cafe and an NFCT kiosk with a small parking area are also located nearby.

Next page: Silver maples are common along NFCT rivers and streams, creating floodplain forests, which moderate river speed. (Photo by Will Jeffries)

Québec

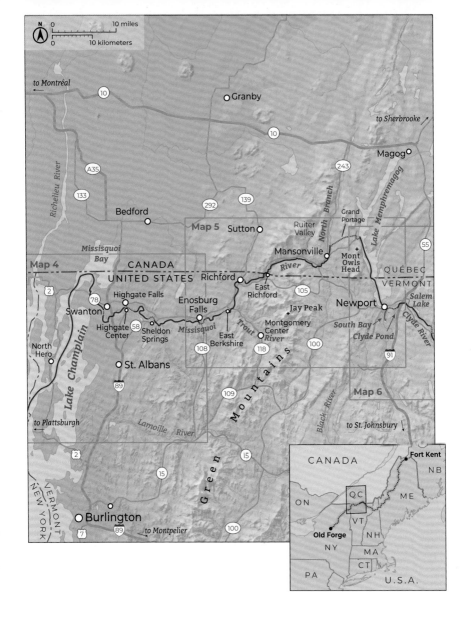

N

0 ___ 10 miles
0 ___ 10 kilometers

to Montréal ←

10

Granby

to Sherbrooke ↗

10

Magog

A35

243

133

292

139

North Branch

Lake Memphremagog

55

Bedford

Map 5

Sutton

Ruiter Valley

Grand Portage

Missisquoi Bay

Mansonville

Mont Owls Head

Map 4

CANADA

River

QUÉBEC

UNITED STATES

Richford

VERMONT

2

Highgate Falls

78

Swanton

Enosburg Falls

East Richford

105

Salem Lake

Jay Peak

Newport

Highgate Center

58

Sheldon Springs

Missisquoi

Trout River

Montgomery Center

South Bay

Clyde Pond

Clyde River

91

North Hero

St. Albans

East Berkshire

108

118

100

Map 6

89

109

Lake Champlain

to Plattsburgh ←

Lamoille River

Green Mountains

Black River

to St. Johnsbury ↓

2

15

CANADA

Fort Kent

NB

VERMONT

15

QC

ME

NEW YORK

ON

Burlington

89

to Montpelier →

100

Old Forge

VT

NH

7

NY

MA

CT

PA

U.S.A.

135

The Northern Forest Canoe Trail includes early Abenaki routes through this region of Québec.

The Abenaki people first inhabited this region and traveled regularly between Lakes Memphremagog and Champlain via the Grand Portage and the Missisquoi River. The Missisquoi River is much revered as a travel route given its few swifts (rapids) and gentle flow, making upriver travel easier than many rivers in the larger region.

The first Europeans to settle here were British Loyalists from the American Revolution conflicts in the early 1790s. They resided along the Missisquoi, while immigrants from the British Isles settled mainly in the northern region of the 96.5-square-mile Potton Township. Potton Township (Canton de Potton) was created in 1797 and included the hamlets of Dunkin, Mansonville, Knowlton Landing, and Vale Perkins.

Between 1840 and the 1850s a wave of French Canadian settlers swelled the population, and by the 1871 census, French Canadians dominated the region. Today, a multicultural festival celebrates the twenty nationalities represented in the township. Historic sites in the region include the wooden covered bridge at Province Hill, built in 1896, and the Round Barn in Mansonville, built in 1910.

The round barn in Mansonville is a fine example of an architectural style that used to be more common on regional farms. (Photo courtesy of North Vermont RC&D Council)

As occurring elsewhere throughout the region, logging found a foothold here shaping Québécois history as well as the landscape. The wide valley of the Missisquoi and the hillsides above it were logged heavily from the early 1800s to the mid-1900s. Today, the mountains are largely reforested with maple, ash, beech, and a few evergreens, while impressive willows, oaks, and maples line the Missisquoi River.

Québec contains the continuation of Vermont's Green Mountains. Rising above the Missisquoi River valley and the glacial Lake Memphremagog, Monts Owls Head, Pevee, Sugar Loaf, and Bear dominate the landscape. These peaks are part of the Appalachians, a continuous chain of ancient mountains extending for almost 2000 miles from Newfoundland and Labrador in Canada to central Alabama in the United States.

Potton is part of the Eastern Townships (Cantons de l'Est), so named for their proximity to the metropolitan region of Montréal, and is blessed with panoramic views of its patchwork landscape of farm fields, forests, villages, river valleys, and broad lakes. The townships are known for charming lakes and waterside towns. The rural scenery amid gentle mountainous terrain offers a wide array of fine dining, elegant bed-and-breakfast lodging, and outstanding recreational opportunities. In addition to paddling options, there are many downhill ski areas and golf courses, as well as trails for hiking, cross-country skiing, snowshoeing, and cycling on quiet paved and gravel roads. From Lakes Memphremagog and Champlain, which serve as hub lakes, it is easy to travel in many directions along early trails and waterways.

NFCT MAP 5: UPPER MISSISQUOI VALLEY

Missisquoi River to Lake Memphremagog

The Canadian portion of the NFCT is divided into two distinct segments: the first is the wide Missisquoi River, with its steady, gentle current winding its way through the valley, and a tributary, the North Branch Missiquoi River. And the second is impressive Lake Memphremagog. The US-Canada border transects both the Missisquoi River and Lake Memphremagog.

The 5.7-mile Grand Portage crosses the watershed divide on Chemin Peabody, connecting the two segments (see "The Grand Portage" sidebar in Section 2). Most paddlers will choose not to portage across this distance, but Thru-Paddlers traveling the whole Trail will need to follow this ancient route. The majority of the Grand Portage follows scenic Chemin Peabody, and the height of land provides views of the surrounding mountains and farmlands. Approaching Lake Memphremagog, the portage passes a general store and descends steeply to Perkins Landing, where paddlers need to wash their boats to prevent introducing new species to the lake ecosystem.

The NFCT Missisquoi paddle is the recreational gem of the area for outdoor enthusiasts. The North Branch of the Missisquoi flows through the village of Mansonville in Potton Township before joining the main branch of the river. A highlight of the area is taking a self-guided walking tour through Mansonville. Historical interpretive plaques pepper the town and portage route, and there are tourist-friendly picnic gazebos. If you add the upper section of the North Branch onto the NFCT route, the river is a fine two-day outing (see "Extending Your Trip: Headwaters of the North Branch Missisquoi" at the end of Section 1).

Potton and Sutton Townships offer a wealth of additional recreational activities. The cycling is superb due to a network of quiet, paved and dirt roads; 20- to 30-mile loops are easily found. There is also excellent hiking, mostly northwest of the village of Mansonville, in the conservation lands of the Ruiter Valley Land Trust. Here you will find a network of trails with grand vistas of the surrounding mountains in all directions, including an extensive forest on the southeast face of Sommet Rond. The lush greens of summer are surpassed

The Trail crosses the international border on Lake Memphremagog, within sight of the water access–only NFCT campsite at Eagle Point. (Photo by Katina Daanen)

only by the rich colors of autumn. This view, while possible to see from the Missisquoi River valley, is especially stunning from the pasture in the upper valley floor. To learn more about the area, contact the Ruiter Valley Land Trust (see Resources). The area has a good mix of restaurants and a few bed-and-breakfasts to suit a range of tastes and pocketbooks. If you are planning to stay in this region for a few days, visit the Tourism Eastern Townships website for current information (see Resources).

Early settler Hendrick Ruiter was among many British Loyalists who lost their land during the American Revolution and resettled north of the border. In the 1790s farming and communities developed along the Missisquoi and up the Ruiter Valley. Approaching Glen Sutton on the Missisquoi, you will pass some houses along Chemin Burnett on the south side of the river. The first house, built on stilts (presumably due to threats of high water), is now the base of Canoe & Co., which rents canoes and kayaks and offers guiding services along the river. Another good rest area is on river-left at Dufour Creek before the Glen Sutton Bridge, with fine views of the surrounding mountains. The river offers a remote, big-valley feel here.

With normal spring water levels, you should not be dragging your boat anywhere along the North Branch. Unless there has been a heavy rain and runoff, the river water is clear with a steady, easy flow. Bends are gentle, tree limbs overhang, and sweepers are generally not a factor, but you should remain watchful particularly with increased spring river flow. (Potton Township clears the river of excessive shoreline debris.) Silver maple and spruce trees line the shore, offering a full river canopy and glorious shade on hot days. Muskrats, beavers, otters, and deer may be seen from the river. This is an intimate river experience given the forest canopy shrouding the waterway. Paddle the entire Québec river section in one long day run or break it up into two easy sightseeing days.

Majestic Lake Memphremagog can be paddled in one day, although you should be aware of weather conditions before launching, as winds can kick up high waves quickly on this large, open body of water. There is limited public access along the eastern shoreline and banks are steep. Only a few small, sheltered beaches offer emergency take-out locations. Weather tends to come in from over the mountains from the west, so inclement weather can be easily missed. Always keep an eye out for black clouds rolling in—a sign it is time to get off the lake. The Canadian western shore of the lake is mostly straight but affords little break from strong winds. You should plan to be on the water early in the day for the lightest winds.

See NFCT Map 5 and the NFCT website for additional trip planning, camping, and navigational details.

SECTION 1

North Branch Missisquoi River to International Border

The North Branch of the Missisquoi is a well-shaded, narrow river flowing into the rapids and falls at Mansonville. Below the Mansonville portage and the hamlet of Highwater, where the North Branch joins the Missisquoi proper, the pastoral wide-river valley provides a grand view and the current slows but remains helpful and gentle to the international border. This river provides a critical east–west link between Lakes Memphremagog and Champlain, both of which were dominant hubs of early travel.

Note: A passport is required for crossing the international border. There is no other Canadian take-out above the international bridge at East Richford. US Customs and Border Protection is downstream of the bridge and accessed by a trail river-left, but the Canada Border Services Agency on Chemin de la Vallée-Missisquoi is not accessible from the water.

To continue on the US segments of the Missisquoi River south of the international border, see the Vermont chapter.

TRIP DISTANCE: 16.9 miles

TRIP DURATION: Allow 1–2 days

FLOW/SEASON: Best paddled in spring. Some river dragging and walking your boat down short shallow sections may be necessary in the summer on upper stretches. The Missisquoi proper tends to be reliable water through the summer.

DIRECTION OF CURRENT: North Branch, north to south; Missisquoi River, east to west

PUT-IN: The **Diorio access** (northwest corner of the bridge on Chemin Peabody) off of Québec Route 243. Hand carry access. See NFCT Map 5 or the NFCT Trip Planner for overnight parking instructions. GPS: 45.072969°, –72.387478°

TAKE-OUT: **US Customs and Border Protection station**, 1683 Glen Sutton Rd., East Richford, Vermont. Hand carry access. No overnight parking. GPS: 45.011145°, –72.588076°

MAP: NFCT Map 5, Upper Missisquoi Valley

PORTAGES (1): Mansonville Carry, 0.8 mile (wheelable); the route follows QC 243 through town between Secteur Nautique and the Mansonville public access below the falls

HAZARDS: Mansonville mill waterfall (avoidable)

OTHER ACCESS: Parc de la Rivière Missisquoi-Nord: Secteur André Gagnon access off QC 243. Hand carry access. Overnight parking. GPS: 45.057411°, –72.389718°; **Secteur Nautique:** Park entrance from QC 243. Hand carry access. Overnight parking. GPS: 45.054795°, –72.391885°; **Mansonville:** Riverside access below falls and town on QC 243. GPS: 45.045146°, –72.396605°; **Camping Nature Plein Air:** 2733 Chemin de la Vallée-Missisquoi, Mansonville. Overnight parking or day-use access fee. GPS: 45.032925°, –72.440796°; **Canoe & Co.:** 1120 Chemin Burnett, Glen Sutton. Overnight parking or day-use access fee. GPS: 45.041559°, –72.502106°; **Downstream of the border:** Glen Sutton Rd. hand carry access south of East Richford, Vermont. Small parking area for day trippers. GPS: 44.997414°, –72.611042°

CONTACT: Potton Township Tourism Office; Tourism Eastern Townships (Tourisme Cantons-de-l'Est); NFCT Trip Planner

SERVICES: Mansonville offers lodging, restaurants, outfitting, and other services.

CAMPING: Private campgrounds (fee)

The Diorio access to the North Branch of the Missisquoi is found where Chemin Peabody crosses the river not far from Rue Principale (QC 243), north of Mansonville. The river and road are quite close together along the North Branch of the river, but the road is surprisingly unobtrusive while paddling.

In 2.4 miles, you will see the NFCT medallion and dock of the Secteur Nautique access on river-right, at a significant bend to the east. The 0.8-mile portage around Mansonville Falls begins here and follows QC 243 through town to a put-in below the village. At Secteur Nautique, you will see the start of an interpretative foot trail along the riverbank.

The Missisquoi River flows through bucolic farmland and the forested Sutton Mountains of southern Québec. (Photo by Will Jeffries)

Walking south through the village, you will come to a park at the corner of QC 243 and Chemin de Vale Perkins. Here you will find historical plaques and a gazebo. Walk a block east on Chemin de Vale Perkins to view the old mill site and falls. Aided by the interpretative signage, you can get a sense of a bygone era. It is a fine location to experience the then-and-now quality of traveling this historic waterway. If you've gotten off to a midmorning start from the Chemin Peabody access, Boulangerie Owl's Bread, a gourmet French bakery, grocery, and restaurant, is a perfect place to eat or pick up a picnic lunch. Be sure to check days of operation to avoid disappointment.

Relaunch on the river at the signed access area off QC 243 below Mansonville. The river valley widens, and the vegetation along the bank lessens. As the valley opens up, the absence of shade trees allows picturesque views of the lush green mountains framing the river. The North Branch joins the main branch just beyond the QC 243 crossing and before the town of Highwater. From here, water levels are most reliable.

From Highwater to the border crossing at East Richford (10 miles), the river corridor is generally 100 feet wide with a mix of forest and pastures opening to mountain views. Along the way is the Camping Nature Plein Air, which offers tent sites along the shore, showers, and restrooms. You'll also pass the remains of an old bridge just past the mouth of Ruiter Brook.

The stilted house appearing river-left, two miles beyond Ruiter Brook, belongs to Canoe & Co., a family-owned business offering shuttle services and canoe, kayak, and paddleboard rentals. The location makes for a good alternative stopping point. There are no other access points between here and the US border. Overnight parking is available at Canoe & Co. for a small fee.

Glen Sutton is a small settlement with nice examples of period architecture but offers no services. Private property abuts the bridge with no public access from the river, so the town is best seen from the road.

The river flows steadily from the Glen Sutton Bridge to the international border at East Richford. Take out, river-left, immediately after paddling under the green truss bridge. The river take-out for US Customs and Border Protection is well signed. Announce yourself at the customs office; they are familiar with paddlers' entries. Let them know whether you are stopping here or continuing on into the United States. The Canada Border Services Agency station is located on Chemin de la Vallée-Missisquoi, away from the water.

It is a full six-hour paddling day from the Chemin Peabody access to Canoe & Co., including extra time to explore Mansonville as you are passing through. Allow another one to two hours to continue 4.5 miles on to the international border. Service information for this section is listed on the NFCT website.

EXTENDING YOUR TRIP: HEADWATERS OF THE NORTH BRANCH MISSISQUOI

You can also begin paddling farther upriver on the North Branch of the Missisquoi River. Access at Chemin Fontaine adds a lovely 6-mile paddle to the Chemin Peabody access. In the spring, the North Branch is paddleable from its headwaters at Lac d'Argent. A fine two-day paddle excursion would involve the North Branch of the Missisquoi from the Chemin Fontaine access to Mansonville on day one. On day two paddle from Mansonville to the border. For more information about the Missisquoi Nord contact the Potton Township Tourism Office (see Resources).

SECTION 2

Lake Memphremagog: Perkins Landing to International Border

Lake Memphremagog is majestic. It is not just big (31 miles long), but it has the feeling of a mountain lake, surrounded by steep, dramatic mountains—a special place indeed, but one that demands respect. Seventy-three percent of the lake's surface area is in Québec. However, three-quarters of its watershed, 489 square miles, is in Vermont. The lake's elevation is 682 feet, and twenty islands are scattered within it. The watersheds are a mix of agricultural and forest land. The name *Memphremagog* is derived from the Algonquian language, meaning "where there is a big expanse of water." Touring kayaks are the most suitable craft for paddling on this big lake.

For the Vermont segment of Lake Memphremagog, see the Vermont chapter, Map 6, Section 3.

TRIP DISTANCE: 13.2 miles (roundtrip)

TRIP DURATION: Allow 1 day

FLOW/SEASON: May through foliage season in October

DIRECTION OF CURRENT: n/a

PUT-IN/TAKE-OUT: Perkins Landing, 77 Chemin George-R.-Jewett. Improved launch. Mandatory boat wash station. Overnight parking. GPS: 45.092003°, –72.294141°

MAP: NFCT Map 5: Upper Missiquoi Valley

PORTAGES (0): None

HAZARDS: Wind, waves, and weather on the lake

OTHER ACCESS: None

CONTACT: Potton Township Tourism Office; Tourism Eastern Townships (Tourisme Cantons-de-l'Est); NFCT Trip Planner

SERVICES: Mansonville provides a good selection of food and lodging options. The general store in Vale Perkins has supplies and a fine deli.

CAMPING: Free first-come, first-served NFCT primitive campsite with three tent platforms (Eagle Point), on eastern shore near international border on US side

---

From the east side of the Grand Portage, paddle south on Lake Memphremagog from Perkins Landing. (**Note:** You must spray your boat to remove invasive species to get a clean-boat pass [fee]. Without a pass, you may be fined on the lake.) Notice the cottages that line the western shore, many of them perched high over the steep rocky banks. It is an interesting mix of old and new, rustic and fancy cottages. The forest along the shoreline is dominated by cedar, hemlock, and birch.

This section of the lake is home to some interesting history. One mile south of Perkins Landing is a privately owned marina, the site of a former children's camp. The old cabins built on the rocks were impressive buildings dating back to its heyday in the 1920s through 1940s. The camp was closed down in the 1960s, and the docks and beach are not open to the public.

A little over a mile later, at the foot of Mont Owls Head opposite Skinner Island, is the former site of Mountain House. This late-1800s five-star hotel was once a choice destination for well-heeled vacationers. The hotel burned down in 1899 and was not rebuilt. Full-time residents and cottages now occupy the land where the grand hotel once stood.

Skinner Island is notable for a significant cave that was fully exposed until the lake's water levels were raised in the 1870s. Only a portion of the cave can be seen today. The island is named for Skinner the rumrunner, who allegedly died in the cave with his contraband. A crossing of 1 mile is needed to reach

THE GRAND PORTAGE

The Grand Portage between the Missisquoi Valley and Lake Memphremagog is the longest official carry along the Northern Forest Canoe Trail (NFCT). While most day-paddlers and weekend-trippers will find ways to avoid this 5.7-mile portage across the watershed divide, it is an essential link that Thru-Paddlers must reckon with.

If paddlers have portage wheels, the quiet road and beautiful scenery make this a more pleasant portage than one might expect. Traveling west to east, from the take-out at the bridge crossing the North Branch Missisquoi River, you start with a long, gradual climb, gaining 540 feet to the height of land. From this hilltop plateau, you get a fine view of Mont Owls Head and a glimpse of Lake Memphremagog. A stop here to take in the view is a must. One can't help but see why Mont Owls Head has been revered as a sacred site in different times of human experience. Today there is a popular ski hill, a golf course, condos, and a lodge on the mountain. A summer climb up Mont Owls Head for the spectacular view would be a grand addition to your travels in the area.

From here, you descend 780 feet to Lake Memphremagog, passing by a place where large stones have been removed from the farm field and relocated beside the road. Locals call this spot Stonehenge and not so erroneously, because faint petroglyphs (human-carved lines) can be seen on some of the stones.

At the end of Chemin Peabody, go right (south) on Chemin du Lac for 400 yards to the Jewett's General Store, a must-stop. On Saturday morning, the arrival of fresh bread and amazing croissants is a local event. The store has been run by the Jewett family for decades—a family whose Vale Perkins roots date back six generations.

The final descent down Chemin George-R.-Jewett is a steep 0.5 mile to Perkins Landing. Although this portage may have been used by First Nations (the general name used for Native peoples of Canada), area historian Gérard Leduc suggests that a more common portage may have followed the longer but more gradual Chemin Vale Perkins into Mansonville. Today, this is a much busier road than Chemin Peabody, and not as scenic, so if you have to portage, the NFCT route is the better way to go.

the island, where it rests close to the eastern shore. Past Mont Owls Head and Skinner Island, the lake maintains its steep banks. Ahead, Ronde Island signals that the lake has widened to over 3 miles across. Mont Bear is visible if you are not close against the shore near the Canada-US border.

The international border is clearly delineated by a conspicuous timber cut on either side of the lake as well as a cut bisecting the southern tip of Île de

la Province (Province Island). Turn back at the border, returning to Perkins Landing.

If continuing into the United States from Canada, you can either use the CBP ROAM mobile app on a smart phone to check in remotely or present your passport in person to US Customs and Border Protection at the Memphremagog Gateway Center/Newport City boat dock another 5 miles south in Newport, Vermont. Cameras exist along the border. Following proper procedures is a must.

Note: This section is also shown on NFCT Map 6.

Opposite: *Mont Owls Head and ancient petroglyphs carved on some of the stones edging a farm field can be seen when traversing the Grand Portage via Chemin Peabody.* (Photo by Katina Daanen)

Next page: *The Upper Ammonoosuc River meanders through silver maple tunnels and past the twin points of Percy Peaks.* (Photo by Chris Gill)

New Hampshire

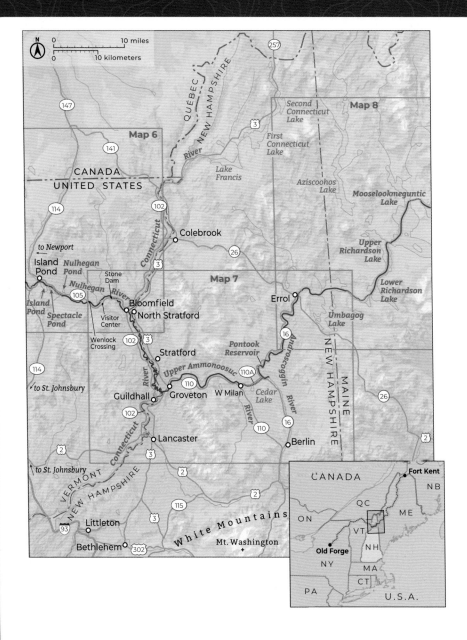

N

0 — 10 miles
0 — 10 kilometers

257

QUEBEC

NEW HAMPSHIRE

River

147

Map 6

141

Second
Connecticut
Lake

Map 8

3

First
Connecticut
Lake

CANADA

UNITED STATES

Lake
Francis

Aziscoohos
Lake

Mooselookmeguntic
Lake

114

102

Connecticut

Colebrook

26

Upper
Richardson
Lake

to Newport

Island
Pond

Nulhegan
Pond

Stone
Dam

3

Map 7

Lower
Richardson
Lake

105

Nulhegan River

Errol

Island
Pond

Spectacle
Pond

Visitor
Center

Bloomfield

North Stratford

Umbagog
Lake

NEW HAMPSHIRE

MAINE

Wenlock
Crossing

102 3

16

114

River

Stratford

Upper Ammonoosuc

Pontook
Reservoir

110A

Androscoggin River

to St. Johnsbury

110

Cedar
Lake

26

Guildhall

Groveton

W Milan

102

River

110

16

to St. Johnsbury

2

Lancaster

Berlin

2

VERMONT

NEW HAMPSHIRE

Connecticut

3

2

2

115

Littleton

3

White Mountains

93

Bethlehem

302

Mt. Washington

CANADA

Fort Kent

N B

QC

ON

ME

VT

Old Forge

N H

NY

MA

PA

CT

U.S.A.

149

North of the famous notches of the White Mountains lies Coös County, a chunk of wildland so full of character, the locals call it the North Country, which describes both its geographic placement and its Yankee spirit.

More than 90 percent forested, northern New Hampshire has ruthless weather, untrammeled mountains, vast woodlands, secluded lakes, and small, proud communities. With high mountain ridges separating them, two power-ful river systems begin their journey to the sea from this region: the 410-mile mighty Connecticut flows to Long Island Sound, and the 168-mile Androscog-gin traces its way to the Gulf of Maine. The NFCT traverses dozens of miles in each of these two watersheds as it winds its way through New Hampshire's northernmost county.

Some scientists speculate that 600 million years ago the land that is now the state of New Hampshire was part of the African continent. They point to geologic differences along the two sides of the Connecticut River, which reveal evidence of a massive continental collision and separation. More recently, about 20,000 years ago, glaciers pushed into these river valleys. Toward the end of this last ice age, 12,000 years ago, melting ice left piles of sediments in the valleys that now form riverside beaches. Boulders, stones, and sediment were moved in the glaciers' path, and today these same stones appear in the lines of rock walls along many farmers' fields across the state. The famous New Hampshire and Vermont poet Robert Frost wrote about these walls of stone in his poem "Mending Wall."

Northern New Hampshire habitats are as diverse as the landscape. Begin-ning at the peaks of the mountains, high-elevation spruce and fir forests are home to American martens, spruce grouse, and Bicknell's thrush. Hardwood and mixed-wood forests at lower elevations support black bears, fishers, ruffed grouse, and white-tailed deer that find shelter in the dense swamps during the harsh winter months. Peregrine falcons and bald eagles also make their homes in New Hampshire. Farm fields and meadows bordering the river sup-port foxes, coyotes, woodchucks, and nesting Canada geese. Wetlands created by beaver dams provide habitat for mink, otters, snapping turtles, and great blue herons. Local hunters still maintain the traditions of their forefathers and head out to the woods in search of deer, moose, and wild turkeys.

Originating near the historic border of the northern frontier, the rivers of the Great North Woods have seen many changes that have shaped the settle-ment pattern of human habitation for both Native Americans and Europeans.

Historically, the rivers have served as both a source of transportation and a locus for family life. About 9000 to 10,000 years ago, Paleo-Indians inhabited

Paddlers can launch from comfortable campsites in Mollidgewock State Park to search for moose and beaver. (Photo courtesy of Matt Burnett Guiding)

this region. Some of these first peoples were probably early ancestors of today's Abenaki, who have inhabited New England for thousands of years.

When French trappers migrated up the Connecticut River to the North Country during the first period of contact, they found the Abenaki living in riverside villages, where they hunted, fished, and grew crops. The local tribes often worked with French and English settlers, but cooperation grew tense as trade became intrusive and ancestral lands were threatened. The French and Indian War broke out, and English settlers built forts for protection. Fort at No. 4, along the Connecticut River in Charlestown, New Hampshire, is a reconstruction that today functions as a living history museum. Though many Abenaki left the area due to these conflicts, many remained, often escaping persecution by "hiding in plain sight," blending in with the settlers. Today, Abenaki celebrate their traditions at powwows like the annual spring gathering on the Dartmouth College Green, not far downstream on the Connecticut River.

In the 1700s the most important crop coming from the North Country hills was timber. As early as the 1730s the British Royal Navy scouted these woods for tall, straight pines for masts on their ships, marked the best trees with the king's arrow-shaped blaze, and floated them down the rivers.

Tales from the logging era are legendary. According to some, there were days when stretches of the Connecticut and Androscoggin were so blanketed with logs that the water disappeared. During winters, loggers lived in remote camps, where trees were cut, skidded out, and piled on frozen waterways until the ice melted in the spring. During the late 1800s the demand for lumberjacks grew and French Québécois and Irish woodsmen arrived. Later, European immigrants came by train directly from Ellis Island to work at the logging camps or at the pulp mills in Groveton and Berlin. A classic book written by Robert Pike, *Tall Trees, Tough Men*, chronicles this colorful era. By the early 1900s, the growth of the railroad made river transportation less important and the largest trees in the watershed were gone. The last great log drive occurred in 1915, but it wasn't until 2007 that the last working pulp mill along the NFCT, the Wausau mill in Groveton, closed, ending an era that shaped the culture of today's communities.

The advent of the Industrial Revolution provided other opportunities for the North Woods. Specifically, it generated a wealthy class of urbanites looking for a way to escape the grime of the city in exchange for the clean outdoors. The railroad made the journey easy, and New Hampshire's grand hotels drew early vacationers north. Tourists, writers, artists, and adventure seekers headed out initially for summer excursions to the lakes and mountains, then later for the winter snow and skiing. The Balsams, one of the few examples of grand hotels left standing today, was part of an early movement to capitalize on the natural beauty of the Coös County area.

New Hampshire's North Country is working to reinvent itself after the closing of the mills by again bolstering tourism. Scenic and cultural byways have been developed to promote visitation to the region where deep-rooted traditions still prevail. In the spring the maple syrup boils. Farmers markets crop up throughout the summer. The 170-mile-long Cohos Trail (see "The Cohos Trail" sidebar, this section) and nearby Appalachian Trail, to which the Cohos connects, attract hikers from all over the world all season long. Each fall, hunters and anglers head to the woods, while spectacular foliage attracts leaf peepers from New England and beyond. In the winter, cold days are still opportunities for snowshoeing, ice fishing, rabbit hunting, snowmobiling, and conversations around potbellied stoves.

The region's rural New England character continues to be preserved today. Steep-roofed homes, town granges, and historic church towers grace the Main Streets of its small towns where residents still turn out once a year to vote at the town meeting, maintaining the independence and self-sufficiency that have come to characterize Coös County communities.

People enjoyed the waterways of the NFCT long before it became a mapped water trail. (Photo courtesy of Steve Barba)

NFCT MAP 7: GREAT NORTH WOODS

Connecticut River to Umbagog Lake

The Northern Forest Canoe Trail (NFCT) passes through New Hampshire along three major rivers. In the west, the Connecticut River (*Kwanitekw*, meaning "long river") flows gently south. The river's sweeping oxbows and broad sandy beaches make enticing breaks from paddling. In the center, the Upper Ammonoosuc (*Namaosauke*, meaning "small, narrow fishing place") is a quick-moving shallow river overhung by forests in the shadow of the Percy Peaks and visibly populated with the wildlife of Coös County. In the east, the mighty Androscoggin River (*Anasagunticook*, meaning "river of rock shelters") cuts its convoluted way across the spiky boreal forest in a sometimes placid, sometimes gushing mass of whitewater.

On its own, each river provides a moderate two-day trip with the opportunity for riverside camping along its banks. As a Thru-Paddling trip, connecting these rivers for a downstream paddle may prove logistically challenging. The Connecticut and the Androscoggin Rivers run from north to south, while the Upper Ammonoosuc runs from east to west. Paddlers wishing to connect the Upper Ammonoosuc and Androscoggin rivers in one trip must portage several miles following New Hampshire Route 110A (see "Connecting Watersheds: The Route 110A Carry" sidebar in Section 3 for details).

Each of these three naturally and culturally significant rivers provide exceptional paddling opportunities for NFCT visitors. See NFCT Map 7 and the NFCT website for additional trip planning and navigational details.

CONNECTICUT RIVER

The wide, gently flowing Connecticut River joins the NFCT at the Nulhegan confluence at Bloomfield, Vermont. Bounded by agricultural fields with distant mountain views and a colorful history, this section offers a leisurely paddle with many sandy beaches formed by the river's meandering ways. Oxbows in the area reveal sediments that piled up when the last ice age waned. Although Vermont Route 102 parallels the river on the right, and an active railroad accompanies you on the New Hampshire side, few houses are visible from the river until you approach the final stretches of this segment.

The river serves as a migration corridor for birds, which fly south along its path to avoid brutal New England winters. Keep an eye out for flocks of resident Canada geese that loaf on the sandbars after feeding in nearby fields. Black bears also are known to swim back and forth across the river to take advantage of ripe field corn in late summer and early fall.

The aquatic habitats of the Connecticut range from sandy-bottomed to stony creek beds and support an abundance of both cold- and warm-water fish. The Connecticut River's northernmost sections nourish native brook and introduced brown and rainbow trout, as well as landlocked salmon. The dwarf wedgemussel, a federally endangered species, is found in greater numbers along the northern section of this river than anywhere else. Nonetheless, the population is sparsely distributed and mostly clustered in scattered mussel beds.

The Maine Central Railroad originally ran through this area in the late 1860s transporting goods, logs, and people throughout New England. As the Connecticut continues southward, watch for remnants of railroad craftsmanship, including granite culverts. Just past the NFCT Maine Central Trestle campsite, the river passes the Fort Hill Wildlife Management Area (WMA), owned by the

The Connecticut River slides in gentle S-turns as it meanders along sandy cliffs and past fertile farmlands. (Photo by NFCT)

BRUNSWICK SPRINGS

The Abenaki and subsequent residents used the water from nearby Bruns-wick Springs for its purported healing powers. Now owned and protected by a nonprofit Abenaki group, the springs are associated with a legend saying that anyone who tries to profit from the water will be cursed. The tale maintains that the original curse was cast during the French and Indian War when a wounded soldier, healed at the springs, tried to bottle the water for sale. In the ensuing argument, an Abenaki man and baby were killed. The story has it that the child's mother then cursed the springs. Years later, as the fame of the healing waters grew, hotels were built to take advantage of the healing waters, but all were eventually consumed by fire. Today little remains from the days of the grand hotels. The land is protected under a conservation easement, which ensures it will never be developed.

New Hampshire Fish and Game Department. The WMA is managed for a diversity of wildlife species, including waterfowl and upland birds, and an osprey nest platform located here can be seen from the water.

A little beyond the river segment's halfway point, you'll pass the steel-trussed Stratford–Maidstone Bridge (also known as the Janice Peaslee Bridge), an excellent place to end or begin a day trip. The area near the town of Stratford had a historically important role as one of the last outposts on the border with Canada. Stratford was originally called Woodbury and incorporated in 1773. During that time, the Connecticut River ran directly through the town and was used by Native Americans for trade. Beyond Stratford, the river continues to meander on its approach to Groveton, with distant views of Percy Peaks in the Nash Stream Forest to the east.

NFCT paddlers will end a trip here either by taking out in Groveton, following the Upper Ammonoosuc a short distance upstream, or continuing downriver on the Connecticut from the Upper Ammonoosuc confluence to Guildhall.

At the junction of the Upper Ammonoosuc and the Connecticut Rivers, a stone monument marks the possible site of Fort Wentworth. Built in 1755 by Roger's Rangers, the famed (or infamous) wilderness fighters, the fort was used during both the French and Indian War and the American Revolutionary War. Guildhall, settled in 1764, is the oldest community in Vermont's Northeast Kingdom.

The NFCT manages two first-come, first-served campsites along the 20-mile Connecticut River section. Three additional free campsites are available when the put-in and take-outs are included. There are no services accessible from the water between North Stratford and Groveton.

CONNECTICUT RIVER PADDLERS' TRAIL

With hundreds of access points and over fifty primitive campsites, the Connecticut River Paddlers' Trail provides a unique experience to paddle more than 400 miles through the heart of New England. The source-to-sea trail includes a series of primitive campsites and river access points from its headwaters in New Hampshire's Great North Woods south to Long Island Sound. A variety of organizations, including the NFCT, works collaboratively in its development. With the support of the community, work continues to protect the river corridor, construct new campsites and portage trails, and expand the Paddlers' Trail from source to sea. For more information, visit the Connecticut River Paddlers' Trail website (see Resources).

UPPER AMMONOOSUC RIVER

A tributary to the Connecticut River, the quick, clear-flowing, and shallow Upper Ammonoosuc River (or "Upper Ammo") offers paddlers a remote feeling through densely forested and vegetated banks, even though roadways and an active railroad parallel the river. The railroad was originally formed by the St. Lawrence & Atlantic Railroad to establish service between Portland, Maine, and Montréal, Québec, as a strategic connection to the Atlantic Ocean. Railroad bridges cross the river several times. Despite its proximity to faster modes of transportation, the river corridor teems with wildlife. Moose, waterfowl, otters, and turtles can be seen while paddling.

At 39,000 acres, the Nash Stream Forest is New Hampshire's largest state forest and home to the Percy Peaks, which rise to the north between Stark and Groveton. Trails access both peaks, and on clear days, you may be rewarded with views of Mount Washington to the south, and Maine's Old Speck peak in the east. The Percy Peaks Loop Trail also connects with the Cohos Trail (see "The Cohos Trail" sidebar, this section). Wild blueberries can be gathered on the rocky summits at the top of North and South Percy Peaks, while birds such as red-tailed hawks and wood thrushes can be seen in the hardwood forest.

A highlight of this section is passing under two covered bridges. The historic Stark covered bridge was built in 1862 and has been included on the National Register of Historic Places. The covered bridge in Groveton was built in 1852 and is now used only by pedestrians.

The village of Stark was originally founded as Percy, but the town's name was changed in honor of General John Stark, who served in the American Continental Army during the American Revolution. Among other things, General Stark coined the New Hampshire state motto, "Live Free or Die." A statue of Stark sits to the left of the river next to the Stark Heritage Center. The town also has an elementary school, a town hall, and the Stark Union Church, but no store or market. To the right of the photogenic bridge is the Stark Village Inn bed-and-breakfast, a good midway stopping point for paddlers not interested in camping.

Nearby Devils Slide offers a challenging 1.6-mile roundtrip hike that brings you to the summit of this large vertical rock formation offering views of the Stark village below. Nesting peregrine falcons inhabit the cliffs. Christine Lake, nestled between mountains north of Stark, is protected by conservation easements and home to brown and brook trout, loons, ospreys, and bald eagles.

Along New Hampshire Route 110, 1.6 miles east of Stark, a roadside sign marks the location of Camp Stark, the former WWII prisoner of war camp. This was the only POW camp in New Hampshire. About 250 German and Austrian soldiers lived at the repurposed Civilian Conservation Corps site. The POWs provided labor for Brown Paper Company, which was having a hard time filling wartime pulpwood needs.

The Wausau Paper Mill in Groveton was the last operating paper mill along the NFCT—until it closed in December 2007. Most of the mill was demolished in 2012, leaving only a few of the newer buildings standing. The dam that bisects the Upper Ammo here is still used to generate electricity and is one of three obstacles within a 1.5-mile stretch of river in the Groveton area, each with signed portages of only a few hundred yards.

The village of Stark with its covered bridge is a popularly photographed landmark and a good halfway mark for trips on the Upper Ammonoosuc River. (Photo by John Klopfer)

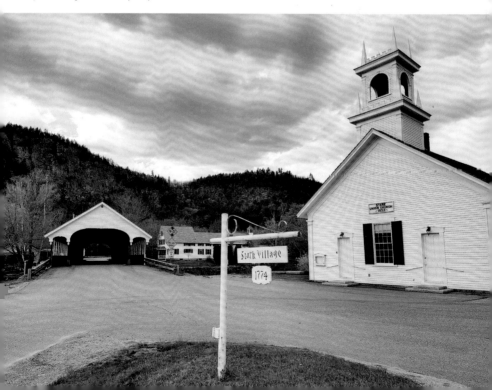

German POWs at "Camp Stark" provided labor for pulpwood needs during World War II. (Photo courtesty of M. Croteau)

Downstream of Groveton, osprey nesting platforms are present, and the river resumes its forested, wilder shorelines as it joins the Connecticut River.

Between West Milan and Groveton, three first-come, first-served campsites have been established by the NFCT, working in cooperation with local landowners. Each primitive site has a picnic table, sign-in box, and composting toilet. These amenities are carefully tended by a local volunteer who removes them from the riverbank and ties them to trees each fall so they aren't swept downstream in the spring freshet.

Many services are found in Groveton, and a country store is located in West Milan.

ANDROSCOGGIN RIVER

The Androscoggin River is Maine's third-longest river and was once a vital waterway for North Country loggers. Flanked by the rugged boreal forest, the Androscoggin is a gregarious river, easily accessed from numerous roadside pullovers. It has become a recreational haven for paddlers, whitewater enthusiasts, and anglers looking for trout.

The 168-mile Androscoggin waterway begins its journey above Errol from its headwaters originating from the Rangeley Lakes and drops more than 1500 feet on its way to its outlet at Merrymeeting Bay. The "Andro" joins the Kennebec River below Brunswick, Maine, before flowing into the Atlantic Ocean. It drains an area of over 3400 square miles in Maine and New Hampshire.

THE COHOS TRAIL

The Cohos Trail provides 170 miles of wilderness hiking from Crawford Notch in the famed White Mountains to the Canadian border at Pittsburg, New Hampshire. The trail passes through Nash Stream Forest near Stark and connects to the Appalachian Trail bisecting the state south of the NFCT. The Cohos links forty peaks, three watersheds, and more than a million acres of conservation forests and offers hikers the chance to experience the wonder of northern New Hampshire's landscape—from rugged cliffs to cascading waterfalls to major conservation and wildlife areas. It also parallels parts of the Connecticut River Paddlers' Trail at its northern end.

First proposed in 1978 by Kim Nilsen, a newspaper reporter, the trail finally started to become a reality in 1998, and the final section was completed in 2011. Those seeking an international adventure can continue on to the Sentier Frontalier's trails in the Eastern Townships of Québec, Canada (see Resources).

Geologists refer to the Androscoggin River's twisty course as a deranged drainage pattern. It was created 20,000 years ago when the entire New England landscape was covered by a 1-mile-thick layer of ice. As the ice receded, it left behind great piles of sand, pebbles, and rocks called moraines. The river exploited any opening it could find, cutting a helter-skelter course through the moraines. As the Androscoggin River winds its way to the sea, it still occasionally floods its banks in the spring.

New Hampshire's northernmost section of the Androscoggin River can be summarized as a series of short whitewater runs requiring good boat-handling skills (depending on flows) divided by longer areas of easy moving flatwater. Only Errol Rapids (Class II–III), the whitewater at Seven Islands Bridge (Class II), and the run below Pontook Dam (Class II+) are technical, and within this highlighted group, all are either avoidable or can be lined.

Much of the river here parallels NH 16, passing through what is known as the Thirteen Mile Woods—one of the most scenic drives in New England. Most of the Thirteen Mile Woods on the west side of the river is now protected from development by a conservation easement and is owned by the town of Errol. A Forest Legacy Program easement protects the forest on the east side of the river from development. The forests on both sides of the river are actively managed for timber products.

A canoe and kayak livery located riverside east of Errol offers camping, shuttle services, and canoe and rafting trips. Paddlers possessing the appropriate skill set and durable boat layups can start a whitewater run beginning below Errol Dam (Class II–III rapids); otherwise put in at the quieter waters of Braggs

The wide Androscoggin River is habitat to many fish species including brook, brown, and rainbow trout, smallmouth bass, northern pike, fallfish, bullhead, and yellow perch. (Photo by Phoebe Backler)

Bay below the NH 26 bridge and rapids. A footpath beyond the NFCT kiosk provides access to a gravel beach and informal launch area. A concrete launch ramp is also available immediately below the bridge, where there is fast current and Class I–II rapids.

Between Errol and Pontook Dam, the river is punctuated by sections of rapids in between easy miles of moving flatwater. Headwinds may present the greatest obstacle here.

After passing Bog Brook and two final sets of easy rapids, the river slows down, stretching into a broad expansive reservoir. Relics from the logging drives linger in this area. What appear to be small rock islands in the river are the remains of boom piers. At one time chains of logs linked end to end were anchored by these structures. They enabled river drivers to channel marked logs to the correct paper mill. The boom piers were put in when the river was frozen. When the ice melted, the structure settled to the bottom of the river, leaving an anchor exposed.

This section can end here upstream of Pontook Dam or continue downstream when water levels are high. The river bottom below the dam is graveled and full of rocks. The current is fast at the put-in, and for the next 2 miles you will see continuous Class II–III whitewater during periods of high water or during dam releases. Dam release times are posted on a power company kiosk or at the SafeWaters website. This lower section is best run by paddlers with solid whitewater skills and boats. A boat launch and parking area is available at the Paul O. Bofinger Conservation Area.

Trailside camping in this section is limited to state-managed Mollidgewock State Park or at private campgrounds in Errol and near West Milan. Many services, including restaurants, an extensive sporting goods store, and an outfitter, can be found in Errol.

SECTION 1

Connecticut River: Bloomfield, Vermont, to Guildhall, Vermont

Bordered by agricultural fields, the wide and gentle Connecticut River offers a leisurely float along its sandy turns with plenty of places to stop for a picnic and a swim. Several free campsites are evenly spaced out. A short Class I–II run (in high water) at the start leads to a slow, placid river.

TRIP DISTANCE: 24.5 miles (22 miles if continuing to Groveton upstream on the Upper Ammonoosuc River)

TRIP DURATION: Allow 2 days

FLOW/SEASON: The Connecticut River maintains a reasonable flow most of the paddling season, though the first mile or two below Bloomfield, Vermont, can be scratchy at low water levels. Ascending 1.7 miles up the Upper Ammonoosuc River to Groveton can be challenging at any time of the season.

DIRECTION OF CURRENT: Connecticut River, north to south; Upper Ammonsoocuc River, east to west

PUT-IN: Debanville Landing, at the confluence of Nulhegan and Connecticut Rivers in Bloomfield, Vermont. Put in at field downstream of the iron bridge. Hand carry access. Overnight parking by NFCT kiosk on Vermont Route 102. GPS: 44.751425°, –71.632742°

TAKE-OUT: Guildhall, Vermont, river-right, above bridge or below the bridge. Hand carry access via trail to VT 102. Overnight parking available across from the county courthouse. GPS: 44.564802°, –71.558855°

MAP: NFCT Map 7, Great North Woods

PORTAGES (0): None

HAZARDS: Class I–II waves (in high water) at the confluence with the Nulhegan; quickwater or whitewater near the take-out(s) in Guildhall

OTHER ACCESS: North Stratford, New Hampshire: Hand carry access by the ballfield at the municipal park. Overnight parking. GPS: 44.748039°, –71.628114°, **Stratford–Maidstone Bridge:** Hand carry access. Overnight parking. GPS: 44.651925°, –71.56211°; **Groveton:** Hand carry access. NFCT Normandeau campsite and paddler access on the Upper Ammonoosuc. Overnight parking. GPS: 44.58996°, –71.520916°

CONTACT: Vermont Agency of Natural Resources; New Hampshire Department of Natural and Cultural Resources; Connecticut River Paddlers' Trail; NFCT Trip Planner
SERVICES: Small general stores and restaurants in Bloomfield and Guildhall in Vermont, and North Stratford and Stratford in New Hampshire; Groteon, New Hampshire, has a grocery store, restaurants, and lodging
CAMPING: Free first-come, first-served NFCT primitive campsites (Maine Trestle, Samuel Benton, and Normandeau); state-managed campsite (Belknap); Vermont River Conservancy campsite (Scott C. Devlin Memorial)

The NFCT enters New Hampshire by way of the Nulhegan River from Vermont at Bloomfield. Bloomfield is home to an NFCT kiosk and Debanville's General Store & Café where you can have some pizza, buy a fishing license, or purchase a pair of Walking Boss suspenders. The iconic suspenders are made in town and harken back to the region's logging glory. Belknap, a free, state-managed campsite is in the woods behind the NFCT kiosk. Just upstream of the confluence, the state also maintains the water-access-only campsites at Lyman Falls. Access the Connecticut River from the field in Bloomfield, Vermont, downstream of the VT 102 bridge.

Alternatively you can put in across the river on the New Hampshire side. The launch is located in the municipal park off Main Street on the south end of North Stratford. Put in downstream of the ballpark. The launch area has picnic tables and a signed parking area.

The river begins swiftly here (up to Class II in high water) and is flanked by flat floodplains and forested hills. Less than a mile downstream, the river forks unexpectedly. Stay to the right at this junction. The left takes you into the confluence of Kimball Brook, which can be shallow and littered with tangled down trees.

A short distance after the forks rejoin, on the New Hampshire side of the Connecticut, sits a wood-products mill that produced lumber, bobbins, and veneer over the last century, a reminder of the area's logging past. On the Vermont side, catching a whiff of sulfur signals the tapped source of Brunswick Springs (see "Brunswick Springs" sidebar in New Hampshire overview) decanting into the river from Silver Lake out of sight above you.

Just beyond the springs, the winding river has worn the banks into high, sandy cliffs where you may see the nesting holes of bank swallows. The only designated "natural" section of the entire 410-mile Connecticut River begins where Wheeler Stream enters from Vermont. No motorboats are permitted in this 9-mile stretch. The steel-truss Stratford–Maidstone Bridge, built circa 1885, marks the end of the natural area and is a popular take-out spot after a day trip from North Stratford.

A granite-block railroad trestle—a remnant of the historic railroad corridor—appears in the middle of the river between Brunswick Springs and the Stratford–Maidstone Bridge. The landmark sits near the NFCT Maine Central Railroad Trestle campsite, river-right. Land on the beach by the campsite sign and walk (north) up into the woods. The site has a picnic table, campfire ring, and an outhouse. The land around the site is agricultural, and on summer mornings you might hear a tractor and see a farmer working the fields in the early-dawn light. VT 102 rolls by out of sight on the hill above. Just downstream of the campsite is a long beach, another great spot to picnic, swim, or simply enjoy the quiet.

The NFCT Samuel Benton campsite is 2.4 miles below the Stratford–Maidstone Bridge on river-right. The site includes an excellent landing beach, picnic tables, a moldering privy, and ample room for tents.

If you arrive here on a weekend, you might want to visit the nearby Riverside Speedway and Adventure Park. Although the track itself cannot be seen from the river, the fence perched atop the steep banks is a good indicator. After a few more broad oxbows, the Upper Ammonoosuc River enters from the left.

Sandy beaches build up on the inside of river bends, forming nice picnic and swimming spots along the Connecticut. (Photo by Katina Daanen)

From the confluence of the Upper Ammoonsosuc, the NFCT route continues east. If you choose to end your trip in Groveton, taking out at the NFCT Normandeau campsite and access area, turn upstream here and paddle, line, or wade 1.7 miles to the signed take-out on river-left. The campsite is situated on a large, grassy clearing in a silver maple floodplain forest. It has a picnic table, fire ring, and privy. It is a beautiful spot with easy access to town but can be buggy.

Otherwise, continue following the slowly moving Connecticut River downstream. You'll pass the Vermont River Conservancy Scott C. Devlin Memorial campsite in this stretch, a water-access-only site that is part of the Connecticut River Paddlers' Trail. About 3.3 miles after the confluence of the Upper Ammonoosuc, exit the Connecticut River in Guildhall on the Vermont side before the bridge in quickwater. The portage trail with hand carry access here is steep. Follow the road a short distance to the parking area. Just below the bridge is a short, but significant, section of runnable Class II+ whitewater where the river has been restored at the former site of Wyoming Dam. If you run the rapids, a take-out trail is also located downstream of the bridge on the Vermont side.

SECTION 2

Upper Ammonoosuc River: West Milan, New Hampshire, to Guildhall, Vermont

The Upper "Ammo" is small, quick, and often shallow. Be aware that if you choose to paddle later in the season, your trip may require wading. Occasional farms and houses populate the surrounding shoreline above and below the picturesque village of Stark, while three mill-related obstacles impede the short stretch through the former industrial town of Groveton. The bottom winds through forested shorelines before joining the Connecticut River. Campsites are available throughout this section.

TRIP DISTANCE: 25.8 miles

TRIP DURATION: Allow 2 days

FLOW/SEASON: The Upper Ammonoosuc is best run earlier in the season or after rains. Otherwise, expect to walk through some shallow areas, especially between Stark and Red Dam.

DIRECTION OF CURRENT: East to west

PUT-IN: **West Milan, New Hampshire** at New Hampshire Route 110A turnoff, above an ATV bridge. Privately owned property managed by the adjacent country store. Hand carry access. Overnight parking only by permission of the store owner (fee). GPS: 44.594791°, –71.301001°

TAKE-OUT: **Guildhall, Vermont,** above bridge, river-right. Hand carry access by trail to Vermont Route 102. Overnight parking available across from the county courthouse. GPS: 44.564802°, –71.558855°

MAP: NFCT Map 7, Great North Woods

PORTAGES (3–4): **Stark Carry,** 0.9 mile (wheelable; only necessary in low water or if not running the Class I rapids); **Red Dam Carry,** 0.1 mile (not wheelable); **Brooklyn Dam Carry,** 0.1 mile (mostly wheelable); **Weston Dam Carry,** 0.1 mile (carry)

HAZARDS: Down trees may be present in constricted areas above Stark and around braided islands below Stark; Class I–II Stark Rapids; Class I Nash Stream boulder field; quickwater around braided islands

OTHER ACCESS: **Stark:** Above rapids, 1 mile north of Stark village on NH 110. Improved access with parking.

GPS: 44.610837°, –71.40064°; **Below Stark:** Road access at or near each of the portages; **Groveton:** Covered bridge (no overnight parking); **NFCT Normandeau campsite and river access:** Adjacent to Normandeau Trucking, 130 Lancaster Rd. (Main St.), Groveton. Long-term parking. GPS: 44.58996°, –71.520916°

CONTACT: New Hampshire Department of Natural and Cultural Resources; NFCT Trip Planner

SERVICES: Groveton is the largest town with restaurants, a grocery store, lodging, laundry, and library. There is a B&B in Stark and a general store and deli in West Milan.

CAMPING: Private Cedar Pond Campground on NH 110A, east of West Milan (fee). Free first-come, first-served NFCT primitive campsites (Cordwell, Frizzell, and Normandeau); Vermont River Conservancy campsite (Scott C. Devlin Memorial)

River access for this section is located near the junction of NH 110 and NH 110A in West Milan by the ATV bridge and country store. Camping is available 1.7 miles east of the put-in on NH 110A at privately owned Cedar Pond Campground (beach area, laundry facilities, camp store, and showers).

From the put-in you'll immediately paddle under two bridges. The river here is extremely narrow and shallow. Tree branches jut out from the banks, and log-jams can form islands. After 0.3 mile, you'll repass under NH 110 before moving away from the road. Civilization doesn't encroach upon the river for the next mile until it crosses under a railroad bridge and Hart Road Bridge (old NH 110).

NFCT Cordwell campsite is another half mile downstream on river-left, just above the next railroad trestle. The bank below the campsite is short but very steep, with no flat ground to land on; be prepared to tie your boat before you unload. This shady campsite has a picnic table, register box, and an outhouse.

Below the campsite, the river begins meandering through a broad floodplain. Sweeps of gravel may require boats to be dragged in low water, and small islands of rock and branches in the river may also force paddlers to navigate

A two-day journey takes paddlers through shaded forests, around sandy bends, and under two historic covered bridges on the Upper Ammonoosuc River. (Photo by Chris Gill)

quickly. As you approach the Bell Hill Road Bridge, the highway will again come into view on the left bank. Here the 170-mile Cohos Trail crosses the river.

When boulders in the river begin to increase, this marks the start of a mile of Class I–II rapids that must be lined or portaged in low water. The rocks and stones in this area are slippery and difficult to walk through. Stark access, river-left, provides a means of circumnavigating this segment by portaging along NH 110. The rapids (and carry) end at the historically preserved white covered bridge in Stark.

Downstream of Stark, the river remains shallow but is wider and freer from natural debris. After a mile, the river bends and then bends again sharply to the right. A rocky shoreline beach appears, marking the NFCT Frizzell campsite on river-right. The thinning forest and flat riverbank make this a good stopping point before North Side Road comes into view around the next bend. The campsite provides a picnic table, register box, and composting privy.

Nash Stream enters on the right, 3.5 miles downstream of the Frizzell campsite. The mouth of Nash Stream marks a short Class I–II rapid, which ends as the river passes under the Emerson Road Bridge. An informal take-out is on river-right, below the bridge, with parking alongside the road.

Braided islands below Emerson Road and a gravelly meander through a flat wash plain above Red Dam may require wading in low water. Backwater mill ponds above Brooklyn Dam and Weston Dam provide more reliable flatwater reservoir paddling.

Although Red Dam was dismantled in 2007, the presence of remnants still requires portaging or lining. Follow the signed carry trail through a fishing access area river-right. The banks adjacent to Hwy 110, river-left, are steep. Then, 0.75 mile later, exit at the DANGER sign upstream of the second dam, on river-left. Portage down Brooklyn Street to an improved access area. Stone steps lead down the wooded slope to the put-in at the base of the dam.

Paddle under the covered pedestrian bridge. Services for Groveton can be accessed here from the town park where an NFCT kiosk is also located.

One more short carry gets you around Weston Dam. Take care during periods of high water releases; this put-in may be in turbulent water. The NFCT Normandeau campsite and access is on river-left, 0.3 mile below Weston Dam. The site has a picnic table, privy, fire ring, register box, and an aquatic invasives Clean, Drain, and Dry station for paddlers traveling upstream from Connecticut River waters.

After the industrial development of the riverbanks in Groveton, the lower river feels secluded and peaceful. The Upper Ammo now curves back and forth slowly across its final 1.7 miles to the Connecticut confluence. With 3.3 miles more of paddling down the placid Connecticut River, you arrive at the take-out, river-right, above the Guildhall Road Bridge in quickwater. Follow the steep trail up to the road and parking area. Just below the bridge is a short, but significant, section of runnable Class II+ whitewater where the river has been restored at the former site of Wyoming Dam. If you run the rapids, a take-out trail is also located downstream of the bridge on the Vermont side.

SECTION 3

Androscoggin River: Errol to Pontook Reservoir Dam

The powerful and deep Androscoggin River runs through boreal forests and offers both challenging whitewater and placid sections along the way. Class II–III rapids at the start can be skipped, but regular Class I–IIs keep the trip exciting all the way to the quiet impounded water behind Pontook Dam. New Hampshire Route 16 parallels the river, providing easy access In multiple locations.

TRIP DISTANCE: 17.5–20 miles

TRIP DURATION: Allow 1–2 days

FLOW/SEASON: The Androscoggin holds water well even in late summer. From Errol to Pontook Reservoir, 1500–3000 CFS is recommended. The rapids below Pontook depend on the dam release (schedule posted on-site and on the Safe-Waters website) and are a series of boat-shredding ridges and ledges when the dam is not releasing.

DIRECTION OF CURRENT: North to south

PUT-IN(S): Boat launch at the NH 26 bridge, Errol. Two access points—one below the bridge mid-rapid and another in the pool below the rapids. Overnight parking. GPS: 44.778137°, –71.133917°; or to run Class II–III Errol Rapids, put in at the **riverside access and picnic area off NH 16 above Errol**. Hand carry access. Privately managed parking by Northern Water Outfitters. GPS: 44.782827°, –71.128961°

TAKE-OUT: Pontook Reservoir Dam, NH 16. Concrete boat ramp. Large parking lot. GPS: 44.633946°, –71.249456°

MAP: NFCT Map 7, Great North Woods

PORTAGES (0–2): **Errol Dam Carry**, 0.2 mile (wheelable; only necessary if arriving upstream above the Errol Dam); **Pontook Dam Carry**, 0.1 mile (wheelable until trail; only necessary if continuing below Pontook Reservoir Dam)

HAZARDS: Class II–III rapids above NH 26 bridge; half a dozen Class I–II areas of rapids including Class II+ rapids at Seven Islands Bridge; Pontook Reservoir Dam; Class II–III continuous whitewater below Pontook Dam

OTHER ACCESS: **Androscoggin River state boat launch:** Off N. Mountain Pond Rd., Errol. Hand carry access from the parking lot to the base of the dam. Overnight parking. GPS: 44.785997°, –71.124184°; Additional access points from NH 16; **Mollidgewock State Park Campground:** 1437 Berlin Rd., Errol. Hand carry access. Overnight parking. Day-use fees. GPS: 44.738127°, –71.143607°; **Androscoggin Wayside Park:** GPS: 44.740523°, –71.181252°; **Seven Islands Bridge:** GPS: 44.71415°, –71.173812°; **Pontook Reservoir Dam** (downstream): GPS: 44.632601°, –71.24882°; **lower pulloff:** Above NH 110A intersection. GPS: 44.617223°, –71.240332°; **Paul O. Bofinger Conservation Area:** Boat launch below rapids and NH 110A intersection. GPS: 44.6144838°, –71.2222195°

CONTACT: New Hampshire Department of Natural and Cultural Resources; NFCT Trip Planner

SERVICES: Errol has outfitters, lodging, supplies, and restaurants.

CAMPING: Private Northern Waters Outfitters in Errol (fee); Mollidgewock State Park Campground and remote campsites (fee); private Cedar Pond Campground on NH 110A (fee)

There are several put-in options on the Androscoggin in Errol, including hand carry access below Errol Dam, the boat access at the NH 26 bridge (graced by an NFCT kiosk), and within the calm waters of Braggs Bay. NFCT paddlers arriving from Umbagog Lake and continuing downstream (or Thru-Paddlers coming upstream) will need to portage 0.2 mile around Errol Dam via the Androscoggin River state boat launch.

Whitewater enthusiasts will want to enter in the pool below the dam, where a quick paddle across Indian Bay brings you to the top of the Errol Rapids. The

The Androscoggin's regular rapids, easy access, and forested shorelines make it a classic North Country river. (Photo by NFCT)

NH 16 riverside access is adjacent to a white US Geological Survey gauge station, which is a great spot to scout the river. The road on river-right takes you through a camping area operated by Northern Waters Outfitters that Thru-Paddlers use as a 0.5-mile portage. At the NH 26 bridge, you can also get a good view of the Class II–III Errol Rapids. For paddlers choosing to avoid this much whitewater, put in 150 yards downstream of the NH 26 bridge in Braggs Bay.

From Errol, the river begins its journey in a stretch of calm water. Lining the river are the spear-like spruce and fir trees of the Thirteen Mile Woods. Three miles of slow water lead to Mollidgewock State Park, which offers tent sites, fire rings, outhouses, and water spigots. The primitive Moose Crossing and Osprey campsites farther downstream (but above Androscoggin Wayside Park) are part of the campground; stop first at the state park to inquire about openings at either of these sites before occupying.

Leaving the campground, the river presents a stretch of Class II rapids and riffles, but after that it slows once again. Androscoggin Wayside Rapids offer some big waves and turbulent eddy lines. If you tend too far left, the river bottom shoals up, and on river-right are several large boulders known as "canoe eaters." The last major landmark of this leg is Seven Islands Bridge. The main channel here has a very fast current. There can be large standing waves downstream of the bridge. Eddies are present downstream of a riverside access area.

As the river flattens into marshlands, you are approaching the Pontook Reservoir. The wide waters may require more paddling effort, especially in windy conditions. Stay well away from the head of Pontook Dam as you approach the

CONNECTING WATERSHEDS: THE ROUTE 110A CARRY

New Hampshire Route 110A is used as a 4.2-mile portage allowing paddlers to connect trips between the Androscoggin and Upper Ammonoosuc rivers. Paddlers who are continuing a whitewater run downstream from the put-in below Pontook Dam can exit the Androscoggin at an informal NH 16 roadside access, river-right, opposite a large island. Carry 0.3 mile south on NH 16 to the junction of NH 110A. Follow NH 110A 3.9 miles to the put-in on the Upper Ammonoosuc River upstream of the ATV bridge. The carry passes by privately owned Cedar Pond Campground.

Thru-Paddlers will follow the same route—in reverse. After following NH 110A to the intersection of NH 16 from West Milan, they can then choose from two options. The first option is to continue following NH 16 another 1.6 miles by foot, putting in above Pontook Dam. A second option is accessing the 0.3-mile Androscoggin River Rapids Carry, where paddlers then begin an upstream journey to the base of Pontook Dam. The start of the Androscoggin River Rapids Carry can be seen beyond a guardrail where the signed trail leads through the woods to the river.

To help prevent the spread of invasive aquatic species, all paddlers should practice Clean, Drain, Dry protocols when entering new watersheds. See the Planning a Trip section for more information.

cement boat launch and take-out river-right, near the road. This parking area has a bathroom.

EXTENDING YOUR TRIP: BOFINGER CONSERVATION AREA AND BEYOND

This trip can be extended by continuing downstream below Pontook Dam, where releases of water provide a thrilling whitewater run followed by miles of flat quickwater. During a release, 2 miles of challenging Class II–III rapids, known as Pontook Rapids, churn through the deep valley. The run is rocky with a lot of shallow eddies. Eddying out to plan your route through the rocks is an important tactic in this section. If there is insufficient water, the rapids will be too shallow and rocky to run. Check the times of the releases of water, which are posted at the dam and on the SafeWaters website.

A riverside path beside the dam (0.1 mile) leads to the put-in. The base of the dam here is a popular place for anglers, but be careful not to paddle upstream toward the dam, as the hydraulic at its base is dangerous. At the end of the 2-mile whitewater run, NH 16 comes back into view, river-right. Take out at

Bald eagles abound around Umbagog Lake and throughout Maine. (Photo by Mike Lynch)

the informal riverside access and location of the NH 110A Carry, or continue another 0.7 mile downstream of the portage sign, passing under utility lines that span the river, to take out at the Paul O. Bofinger Conservation Area. The land here is owned by the New Hampshire Fish and Game Department, which has ample parking along with a toilet.

The Androscoggin River offers many more miles of paddling beyond the Bofinger Conservation Area all the way to Brunswick, Maine. Suggested trip descriptions and downloadable maps can be found on the NFCT website. More information about paddling the entire Androscoggin River is available through the Androscoggin River Watershed Council, which also produces a trail guide.

Next page: *The Allagash Wilderness Waterway is one of the few places where you will find elm trees that escaped succumbing to Dutch Elm disease that spread elsewhere in the United States.* (Photo by Mack Truax)

Maine

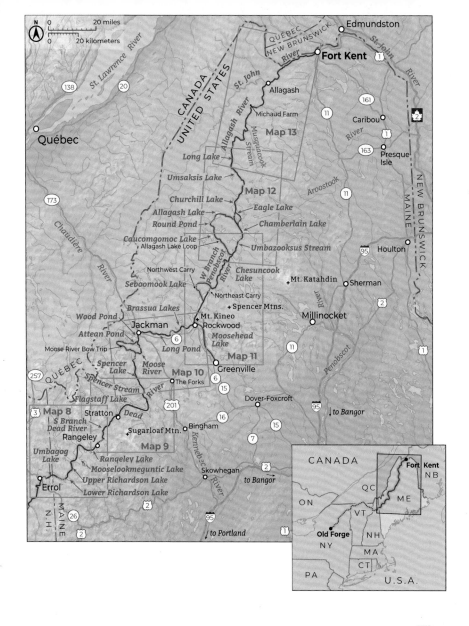

The Northern Forest Canoe Trail (NFCT) traverses some of the most scenic, wild, remote, and rugged landscapes that the state of Maine has to offer.

When traversing northern Maine—whether in a boat, a car, or even flying over in a small plane—it is hard not to feel a sense of awe at the sheer expanse of forested landscape. Northern Maine holds 10.5 million acres of unorganized territory (unincorporated townships with no local government), generally unpopulated. This green and watery vastness—extending across most of Maine, from the border with New Hampshire, northeast to the Canadian border at Fort Kent, and to Millinocket in eastern Maine—is in fact the darkest area on the East Coast according to satellite images taken at night.

Mingling with these woodlands is an abundance of freshwater—13.5 percent of the state is covered by water. Three out of the five largest lakes in the state—Moosehead, Chesuncook, and Mooselookmeguntic (one, three, and four, respectively)—are found along the NFCT. Maine has a little something for all paddlers—from the expansive Flagstaff Lake and the challenging Rapid River to the wildlife-rich Allagash Wilderness Waterway and the meandering Moose River.

This melding of water and forest led to a logging industry of epic proportions. In the mid-1800s Bangor, Maine, reigned as the lumber capital of the world, a nod to the state's most valued natural resource at the time. The timber harvesters' ethos was immortalized by literary talents such as Henry David Thoreau and Fannie Hardy Eckstorm.

During the latter half of the nineteenth century, a declining supply of old-growth pine coupled with America's westward expansion weakened Maine's national influence. Yet the state's contribution to logging technology and culture was unmistakable, as its inventions from the peavey to the bateau to driving dams and booms were picked up by the western operations.

Today, forestry and logging represent the third-largest resource-based economy behind farming and fishing in a state where tourism has become the primary economic engine. A select group of private lumber and investment companies still own the majority of the unorganized territory (roughly half the state). In addition, the State of Maine, Native tribes, municipalities, non-profit conservation organizations, sporting camps, families, and many others have owned, used, altered, restored, valued, and exchanged the land numerous times, even as it remains lightly settled and one of the most forested states in the nation. Public recreation access to these lands has been granted by most of these landowners as a specific permission. As a result, generations of Mainers are connected to the outdoors and consider this vast acreage a piece of their

Flagstaff Lake features beautiful scenery and plentiful campsites. (Photo by Katina Daanen)

heritage. So, when you paddle across Flagstaff Lake, or down the Moose River, or along the Allagash, you are navigating through a patchwork of private and public lands where you will find a diversity of objectives but also a shared commitment to the value of healthy, productive forest ecosystems.

Beyond paddling, visitors can expect superb wildlife viewing—moose and bald eagles abound—great swimming and hiking, and interesting cultural and natural history, from waterfalls and fossils to nineteenth-century farms and abandoned lakeside locomotives.

When it comes to fishing, Maine draws anglers from all over the United States who try their luck at catching its brook trout and wild landlocked salmon. Maine is the only eastern state with extensive native brook trout that reproduce in the wild. Fishing licenses are available at outfitters and sporting goods shops throughout the state.

The following overview will introduce you to some of Maine's highlights. Whether you paddle a few miles or a few weeks, a trip along the NFCT in Maine connects you with the footsteps and paddle strokes of old.

RANGELEY LAKES REGION

The Rangeley Lakes include Rangeley, Mooselookmeguntic, Upper and Lower Richardson, and Umbagog (pronounced um-BAY-gog, meaning "shallow water") Lakes and are the primary headwaters of the Androscoggin River.

Before the coming of landowner Squire James Rangeley, the region was known as the Androscoggin Lakes. In general, the Androscoggin Valley and its headwaters region were settled much later than the river valleys to the south and north. The Rangeleys did not see their first year-round settler until 1817.

Since the 1860s this forested lake land in westernmost Maine has drawn visitors seeking legendary angling and inspiring vistas. The mountains and open water of the Rangeleys grant peace of mind to all who choose to venture to this scenic region. The well-oxygenated cool waters of these lakes support a fishery that has attracted sport anglers for over 160 years.

Mooselookmeguntic, derived from a Wabanaki word meaning "moose feeding place," is known for its wild brook trout and landlocked salmon fishery—the lake has not been stocked since the 1970s. The Upper Dam Pool is fabled among anglers, as it has borne some of the largest trout caught in the region. Upper Dam was originally built in 1852–53 to ease the passage of logs downstream. As a result, the lake level was raised 12 to 14 feet, connecting Mooselookmeguntic and Cupsuptic Lakes. A reconstruction of the dam was completed in 2016.

If you paddle to Students Island on Mooselookmeguntic Lake, the perimeter trail will surely tempt you with a chance to stretch your legs. The north end of the island was the site of the once-popular Birches resort, built in 1885 and destroyed by fire in 1925. Fredrick C. Barker, a longtime resident of the Rangeley area, owned the Birches. As a young man, Barker worked in the Bemis logging camp and on the Rapid River log drive before turning to guiding when he

The cold, fertile water of the Rapid River flowing between Lake Umbagog and Lower Richardson Lake is famous for producing trophy brook trout. (Photo by Will Jeffries)

ARTIFACTS

Artifacts from the Archaic period (9000 to 3000 years ago) have been found at over half a dozen sites along the shoreline of the Richardson Lakes. Archaeologists have found tools such as a comb-backed ulu (a knife) and a gouge, connecting the region with thousands of years of human use. The Upper Dam region is the source of one of the oldest pieces found in the Rangeleys, Paleo-Indian (11,500 to 9000 years ago) chert. Chert was also found along the shore of neighboring Aziscohos Lake at a site where migrating caribou were ambushed millennia ago. In the 1800s, dams submerged an unknown number of regional sites and a window into the past. If you happen upon an artifact, please respect the desires of the modern Wabanaki people by not removing cultural objects.

became an early proponent of the Rangeley Lake Boat (see "The Rangeley Lake Boat" sidebar in Map 8, Section 1). He eventually launched a successful steamboat and sporting camp business on Mooselookmeguntic. In 1903, Barker published *Lake and Forest as I Have Known Them*, a well-crafted, humorous account of his life in the Rangeley region.

Once known as *Mollychunkamunk* ("stream in a deep ravine") and *Welokennebacook* ("bay and cove place"), respectively, Upper and Lower Richardson Lakes, and the Narrows, were separate lakes before Middle Dam connected the three in 1883. The lakes are stocked with landlocked salmon, brook trout, and lake trout, with salmon being the most routine catch.

If you happen to visit the Richardsons during a dry spell, you may see the stone foundations of the old Richardson farm—submerged in 1883—visible at very low water near Metallak Island. The lakes' namesake, Maine native George Frost Richardson, was a lumberman turned land speculator. Wood from the Richardson barns was reportedly used in the construction of Anglers' Retreat at Middle Dam, ancestor to Lakewood Camps, which now provides lodging on the lakeshore.

Today, much of the land surrounding these lakes has been protected by conservation organizations, including the Rangeley Lakes Heritage Trust, an organization dedicated to safeguarding the waters that provide year round recreational opportunities. Their mission is conserving and stewarding the natural and historical resources of the Rangeley Lakes region for the benefit of future generations.

Tucked between Lower Richardson and Umbagog Lakes is the Rapid River—a play-boater's paradise and one-time home to author Louise Dickinson Rich, who lived and wrote from Forest Lodge overlooking the Rapid River in the 1930s and '40s. The home is now privately owned and not open to the public. Over her career, she wrote dozens of magazine articles and twenty-four

INTERNATIONAL DARK SKY PLACES

The International Dark Sky Places (IDSP) program was founded in 2001 to encourage communities, parks, and protected areas around the world to preserve and protect dark sites through responsible lighting policies and public education. Nearby Katahdin Woods and Waters National Monument was designated an International Dark Sky Sanctuary in 2020.

Encompassing a region of over 5400 square miles, the largely forested land of the North Maine Woods lies beneath what may be the last remaining truly pristine night skies in the United States east of the Mississippi River. The Rangeley Lakes area, positioned halfway between Montréal and New York City, has some of the most accessible—and darkest—skies in the East.

Consider planning a trip to the area during the new moon and astronomical twilight to enhance the viewing experience. To obtain a clear skies forecast, visit the Clear Outside website (see Resources) and enter a latitude and longitude.

books, including the still-popular *We Took to the Woods*—the first in her Forest Lodge series. Her witty tales of the characters and the charm of their isolated neck of the Maine woods—accessible only by water in her day—soon picked up a national audience. During a decade of residence at Forest Lodge, Dickinson Rich experienced myriad events including witnessing one of the last river log drives in the East, a canoe trip around the Rangeleys, and the obsessive yet endearing "white water crowd" that overtook the Rapid River each Fourth of July to race their collapsible kayaks.

The rocks and water that make the Rapid River a favorite for whitewater enthusiasts also grant the watercourse legendary status among fly-fishing aficionados for the river's wild brook trout run, which has faced competition from nonnative smallmouth bass since the late 1990s when the bass worked their way upriver from Umbagog Lake.

Umbagog Lake is serene—less so on summer weekends—and wildlife rich, forming a watery border between Maine and New Hampshire. Anglers need to be aware of the state line and have the correct fishing license on hand. The density of fish species in the lake has drawn people for millennia.

The Umbagog National Wildlife Refuge—and the lake's labyrinth of wetlands that make up the confluence between the Magalloway and Androscoggin Rivers—will give you a chance to see any of the numerous species that call the refuge home: mergansers, goldeneye, black ducks, loons, warblers, bald eagles, ospreys, mink, otters, muskrats, beavers, bobcats, fishers, marten, deer, black bears, and moose. Paddle its waters at dusk and lay an ear toward the mystical "Umbagog band," the bullfrog cacophony that log drivers of the 1800s referred to as without comparison across Maine.

MAINE **179**

Molls Rock, 3 miles from the mouth of the Rapid River on Umbagog Lake, is named after Molly Molasses, who used the site with her husband, Chief Metallak, in the late 1700s and early 1800s. Spend a night on the rocky bluff and add your footprints to a long list of visitors, from Paleo-Indian hunters, who have used this location over the past 11,000 years, to nineteenth-century loggers. In the 1900s, archaeological digs near Molls Rock revealed tool fragments, white quartz scrapers, and over a dozen projectile points from the Archaic period. Archaeological digs and subsequent looting have upset many modern-day Wabanaki, who believe that buried cultural objects should remain on the land. The Androscoggin River begins north of Molls Rock, its current slowly meandering westward toward Errol, New Hampshire.

The towns of Rangeley and Oquossoc in Maine, and Errol in New Hampshire, offer many services for the outdoors recreational enthusiast, and Rangeley also serves Appalachian Trail hikers. The Appalachian Trail crosses Maine Route 17 at the Height of Land, a Rangeley Lakes National Scenic Byway roadside overlook with expansive views of Mooselookmeguntic and the Richardson Lakes. Campsites abound, but most are fee-based and require reservations.

FLAGSTAFF LAKE AND THE DEAD RIVER

Flagstaff Lake holds the distinction of being the largest human-made lake in the state of Maine. The 18,000-acre lake was created in 1950 when a 20-mile stretch of the Dead River was flooded by the construction of Long Falls Dam. Old photos of the village of Flagstaff show a low-lying river valley of meadow and forest dotted with homesteads and defined by a snaking river. The small population was tight-knit, engendering a community-oriented self-reliance. People helped one another: one generator ran the town, one tractor plowed all the gardens, and six cars met the needs of a town 130 strong. Swimming at the Flagstaff Pond beach was popular, as were picnicking and canoe trips along the Dead River. Hunting for deer and moose was important as a source of winter food, as was canning summer garden items such as blueberries and peas. In the winter, skiing and sledding down Jim Eaton Hill on handmade skis and cardboard were exhilarating. Beginning in the early 1900s, a log drive arrived, clogging the river each spring with a mountain of wood.

Following the original course of the Dead River brings you near the former village of Flagstaff between School House Point and Jim Eaton Hill. On a still day when the water is drawn down, you may get the chance to glimpse an eerie sighting of this submerged rural town. Photos, artifacts, and a memorial exhibit to the "lost" towns can be visited at the Dead River Area Historical Society in Stratton.

When the lake is calm, or drawn down, you may also notice a shimmering twist of current atop the surface revealing the Dead River channel of old; anglers tend to focus their efforts along the northern shore, east of Jim Eaton

Some residents of the doomed Flagstaff Village refused to let their houses be removed when the water began to rise. The reservoir was later lowered and the structures razed. (Photo courtesy of Dead River Area Historical Society)

Hill. An average depth of less than 15 feet leads to warm temperatures that create the right environment for a thriving pickerel fishery. The healthy spring smelt run supports brook trout and landlocked salmon as well.

In a valley that has witnessed seismic change in the past half century, the Bigelow Range has remained a constant feature of the landscape. Views from the lake are dynamic, with ever-changing vistas of the rounded and angular peaks. The pointed mass and spectacular views of the Bigelow Range reflecting across the breadth of Flagstaff Lake is a sight to behold. Here, the Appalachian Trail parallels the NFCT along the ridgeline of the lake's southern shore.

The upper Dead River is stocked with brook trout and has populations of rainbow trout and landlocked salmon. Try your luck! The river grows a little wider and marshy along the latter half of the paddle, as ridgeline views become more common. When the muddy bottom rises within sight, look for freshwater mussels. Here, the slow-moving river entices paddlers with a quiet meander en route to the awe-inspiring Grand Falls, the largest waterfall found along the NFCT.

The South Branch of the Dead River is a remote Trail section meandering between Rangeley and Flagstaff Lake and generally only navigable in spring. A rockbound freshet gives rise to a few Class III–IV rapids interspersed between segments of quickwater as the river tumbles through a scenic gorge and forested valley into Flagstaff Lake.

Quill Hill, a protected conservation area just 10 minutes from Rangeley, and adjacent to the South Branch, treats visitors to a scenic mountaintop drive culminating in a 360-degree panorama. The easement includes ADA-accessible viewing areas as well as hiking and outdoor recreational opportunities.

Stratton offers visitors many services, including lodging and dining options. Free camping options are plentiful on Flagstaff Lake. Some campsites require fire permits.

GREATER JACKMAN REGION

Spencer Lake is a true gem within the Greater Jackman region. Wrapped by mountains, the lake is an isolated getaway replete with sand beaches and nesting bald eagles. Expect to see loons, ospreys, great blue herons, kingfishers, and mergansers. If you're lucky you might spot a bobcat along the shore, and come evening keep your ears open for the haunting howls of coyotes.

The wider southern end of Spencer Lake is bound by layered ridges and features numerous coves worth exploring. Boulders of every size cap the sandy points. Search for limestone caves and keep a lookout for fossils. Anglers can hope for landlocked salmon, lake trout, and brook trout.

Little Spencer Stream and Spencer Stream (Class I–II) beckon the adventurous with a spirited and intimate experience. To the north of Spencer, the Moose River Bow Trip has long garnered visitors by combining scenic island-spotted ponds with a snaking flatwater river. Toss in a few Class I–II rapids and the ease of returning from where you launched—now that's the quintessential North Woods long weekend!

If whitewater is your thing, don't miss the rapids on the Moose River (Class II–III), between Long Pond and the Brassua Lakes, which offer some of the most challenging paddling along the NFCT.

The Moose River is divided up by three large water bodies. The first segment lies between Spencer Rips and Attean Pond. Here, the Moose meanders around Number 5 Bog. This unique feature comprises over 1400 acres of peat bog (one of Maine's largest bogs) and is home to rare orchids and a significant stand of jack pine. Depths of peat from 15 to 20 feet have been measured, signifying that the area was once a lake. The Maine Bureau of Parks and Lands owns and manages the bog and river shoreline.

As the deep, tannin-colored river meanders north, Catheart Mountain comes into view to the east. Beaver trails slide to the waterline, and near the bank you'll hear swarms of insects buzzing about the thicket. Soon, the trees are replaced by alders and silhouettes of long-dead trees as the edge of Number 5 Bog spreads east. Birdlife abounds—expect to see warblers, flycatchers, owls, woodpeckers, thrushes, herons, and sparrows.

The Moose enters Attean Pond through reeds and lily pads. Birches and tall pines rise from the boulder shores of islands in the south arm. Most of your view remains unimpeded by development. With easy access from Attean Landing, this island-studded lake nestled amid rugged mountains is also popular with anglers. Only a few camps—and Attean Lake Lodge's cluster of cabins located

SPENCER LAKE POW CAMP

Little remains of the WWII camps that once housed German prisoners of war in this area. In 1944, about 4000 German prisoners were allocated to Maine. Four camps were established, including one near Spencer Lake in Hobbstown Township. The prisoners supplied workforce labor on farms and to the Hollingsworth & Whitney paper company by filling logging jobs left vacant by American men who went to war.

The Spencer Lake POW Camp, located in the woods off Spencer Road, had capacity for 250 prisoners, though at one point it housed 310 men. It closed in 1946. The camp gained media attention when eighteen-year-old Franz Keller and two other young prisoners escaped during the early spring of 1945. They were captured five days later and sent back to the camp. In the 1950s, Keller returned to the United States as an engineer contracting with NASA on the Apollo missions. He later became a US citizen.

Only structural evidence scattered among the encroaching spruce forest hints at the camp's historic past. An engraved granite marker stands at the spot near an apparent cooking structure. The memorial was part of a service learning project coordinated by schoolchildren from the Forest Hills School eighth grade class of 2007 in Jackman.

on Birch Island, the lake's largest island—are visible. Attean Lake Lodge is a historic, rustic sporting camp that has been owned by the same family since 1900. Expect to see motorized fishing and pontoon boats.

Attean Pond and Wood Pond are connected by the briefest of Moose River mileage. In the spring, expect to see grackles and red-winged blackbirds. In the summer of 2008, smallmouth bass were caught here, signifying the continued advancement of this nonnative species into the Kennebec watershed.

As you enter Wood Pond, the distant low-lying horizon contrasts with the sheer end of Sally Mountain that butts up against the pond's western shore. White birches stand out from an otherwise dense green forest. The banks become more developed the closer you get to Jackman.

Once you reenter the Moose River out of Wood Pond, alders, birches, and maples highlight a marshy shoreline beyond Jackman. Lawns, docks, and rope swings mix with animal trails, beaver lodges, and lily pads all the way to Long Pond. Expect a wide range of birds, from kingfishers to raptors and warblers to whip-poor-wills. The river's negligible current makes it easy to retrace your paddle strokes at any point.

Diving swallows, croaking frogs, and marsh grass welcome you to Long Pond where a low-lying shore of mixed wood creates a narrow, elongated pond. As you cross the pond, you'll notice a transition from a marshy shoreline spotted with cabins to one less developed and pebble strewn. Moose frequent the reedy west end and the coves along the north shoreline.

Jackman is the last large Trail town offering a wide variety of services including lodging, camping, restaurants, outfitters, groceries, and laundry. Private and public campsites are evenly spaced out throughout this section.

MOOSEHEAD/PENOBSCOT REGION

Moosehead Lake (*Mousinibes*, meaning "moose lake") is one of the largest naturally occurring freshwater lakes in the United States and has functioned as a North Woods crossroads for thousands of years. Wild lake trout thrive in Moosehead, as do wild and stocked landlocked salmon. Moosehead also boasts one of the finest lake populations of brook trout in the state, producing some catches weighing more than four pounds.

Formed by volcanic rock, unmistakable Mount Kineo is the defining feature of Moosehead Lake, standing more than 700 feet above the boulder shore. Peregrine falcons are frequently spotted along Kineo's sheer face, and from the summit's fire tower you can see back along the NFCT to Flagstaff Lake and the Bigelow Range. Looking south at Mount Kineo from Norcross Point in the Northeast Cove, note how the northwest faces slope gently to shore whereas the southeast sides are notably precipitous. This alignment was caused by the southeasterly movement of the Laurentide Ice Sheet that covered the region until around 12,000 years ago. In fact, many regional lakes have a northwest-southeast orientation as a result of the same force.

The Maritime Archaic people as well as the modern Wabanaki were attracted to the rhyolite of Mount Kineo, using this igneous rock rich in silica to fashion tools and weapons. Since the early nineteenth century, the region has witnessed a long line of river drivers, sportsmen, literary adventurers, and vacationers. When you drop down Indian Hill into Greenville traveling north on ME 6/15, the mountains and lake spread out before you. The view inspired Henry David Thoreau, on the cusp of his second trip north in 1853, who described it as "a suitably wild-looking sheet of water, sprinkled with small, low islands, which were covered with shaggy spruce and other wild wood,—seen over the infant port of Greenville, with mountains on each side and far in the north" (excerpt from his essay "Chesuncook," in *The Maine Woods*).

From the northern end of Moosehead Lake, paddlers will enter remote waters via one of two historic carries. The Northeast Carry has been a connector between the Kennebec and Penobscot watersheds for centuries. During the log drive era, an ox-driven tramway was built across it to haul supplies to West Branch logging camps. Authors Henry David Thoreau, Lucius Lee Hubbard, and Thomas Sedgwick Steele arrived at the Northeast Carry via steamer from Greenville, and Thoreau arrived by canoe on his third trip in 1857. At the turn of the twentieth century, a 1000-foot pier extended into the lake to help steamers avoid the shallows. The white farmhouse near the launch is a former store and inn from this era.

The Northeast Carry follows a gravel road for 1.5 miles, then continues onto a dirt track ending at the put-in on the West Branch Penobscot River, at Penobscot Farm, the location of a once bustling logging camp. Now only well-hidden fence posts and barbed wire remain from an era long past. The Northeast Carry allows you to bypass expert-level whitewater that you would encounter on the West Branch if you used the Northwest Carry.

The 2-mile Northwest Carry passes by the Seboomook Wilderness Campground and Store to connect between Moosehead Lake and Seboomook Lake before heading east on the West Branch Penobscot River. This area was home to boarding houses during the logging era and, most notably, a prisoner-of-war camp during World War II where 250 members of Field Marshal Erwin Rommel's famous Afrika Korps were interned. Use the Northwest Carry only if you intend to paddle Seboomook Rapids, a series of twelve Class II–III ledge drops.

The West Branch of the Penobscot River (*Kettetegwewick*, meaning "the main branch") links lakes large and small—Seboomook, Lobster, and Chesuncook—where spruce-fir forests dominate the landscape and human settlements are sparse to nonexistent. During the 1800s logging boom, the Penobscot River was king, driving more logs than any other river in Maine. Logging began on the West Branch in the late 1820s, and during its heyday, more than 100 dams held water to aid in driving logs. The West Branch flows into Chesuncook Lake,

At the turn of the nineteenth century, Chesuncook Village was home to more than 200 full-time residents. The village is listed on the National Register of Historic Places, and the church hosts both a museum and seasonal worship services. (Photo by John Klopfer)

ANCIENT TRAVELERS

Moosehead Lake has been a North Woods destination for thousands of years. The lake was a crossroads for Native travelers utilizing any one of the major river systems: the Kennebec, the Penobscot, and the St. Lawrence. A felsite (or rhyolite) deposit on Mount Kineo was also used by the Wabanaki for generations to make tools and weapons. Artifacts made from this 425-million-year-old light-green stone have been found throughout Maine as well as in New Brunswick, Nova Scotia, and Vermont. Mohawks, who were members of the Iroquois and enemies with the Wabanaki until around 1700, went on raiding trips to the Moosehead region via the St. Lawrence River to attain valued Kineo felsite.

Other natural resources also drew ancient people to Moosehead. Shoreside birch was prized by the Wabanaki as raw material for canoes, baskets, and homes, and an abundance of game and fish made the region a vital hunting ground.

Maine's third-largest lake at 26,200 acres. It reached its current size in 1916 when Ripogenus Dam was built.

As you pass the marshy entrance to Caucomgomoc Stream, at the north end of Chesuncook Lake, peer over your shoulder to take in the 20-mile expanse of the lake to the south. If you've packed your fishing rod, landlocked salmon are the species of choice on Chesuncook Lake.

Chesuncook Village, a former logging community, was incorporated in 1838—about ten years after log drives began in the region. It was once a thriving town that included a general store, hotel, post office, and lumber mill. By 1920, 247 people lived here. The historical logging era ended in 1971 when the last log drive was towed down the lake by the Great Northern Paper Company. Today, about fifty seasonal "camps" remain, some tucked away in the woods, mostly clustered around a single road. Less than a handful of people still call it home year-round.

In 1973, Chesuncook Village was placed on the National Register of Historic Places. A small museum, housed in the restored church, which also hosts summertime nondenominational Sunday morning services, contains interesting history about the community and its logging past. When the Ripogenus Dam was enlarged, rising water levels on Chesuncook Lake forced the relocation of the cemetery that had been situated on a point. Today, that point still bears the name Graveyard, but the final resting place for village inhabitants and transient loggers alike is now located on higher ground, on a hill just outside of town. Several of the older headstones contain no dates, and some only a single name—thin stone edifices documenting the lives of lumberjacks lost during nineteenth-century river drives.

THOREAU ON CHESUNCOOK

Writer Henry David Thoreau visited Chesuncook during his 1853 and 1857 trips. When Thoreau spent the night in Chesuncook Village in 1853, he saw cattle grazing on a meadow shore, and at the village landing he noted a scow for hay and several bateaux pulled aground between the stumps. Thoreau wrote about a log house accented with moss and lichen and "roofed with spruce-bark," a "handsome" barn, a cellar where they stored moose meat, and a blacksmith shop. He estimated that 100 acres were cleared for haying and a garden, and mentioned a shaggy dog whose nose was full of porcupine quills. The Wabanaki still passed through, and Thoreau wrote that in the winter the village filled with 100 lumberjacks. Thoreau summed up logging as "a war against the pines" and reflected as he walked the Chesuncook shore that "the woods were as fresh and full of vegetable life as a lichen in wet weather . . . but unless they are of white-pine, they are treated with as little respect here as a mildew." The Thoreau-Wabanaki Trail has been mapped as a heritage paddling resource for those interested in tracing Thoreau's 1857 route.

While Chesuncook Village is now home to only a few hardy year-round residents, it marks the last vestige of civilization between Rockwood, 37 miles behind you on Moosehead Lake, and the town of Allagash, 96 miles ahead.

Lobster Lake, the West Branch, and Chesuncook Lake all treat paddlers to a horizon capped by the gray mass of Maine's highest peak and the terminus of the Appalachian Trail: Mount Katahdin.

Campsites are plentiful throughout this section, and first come, first served; however, all but those on Moosehead Lake are fee-based. Maine Bureau of Parks and Lands manages the Penobscot River Corridor that includes the West Branch and Seboomook, Lobster, and Chesuncook Lakes, while North Maine Woods oversees Umbazooksus Stream West and East campsites. Camping and entry fees are collected for all sites by North Maine Woods at checkpoints as you drive through the area. See "North Maine Woods Checkpoints and User Fees" sidebar in the Map 11 chapter overview for more information.

ALLAGASH WILDERNESS WATERWAY

Like much of northern Maine, both ancient glaciers and human history have shaped the Allagash Wilderness Waterway (AWW) landscape. From whittling devices to spear points, tools and weapons from the Paleo-Indians have been found along the shoreline of Eagle Lake, confirming human influence since the retreat of the glaciers.

Historically, Chamberlain Lake was the primary headwater lake to the Allagash River, but during the logging era, dams and channels were constructed, altering the flow of Allagash waters. In 1841, Penobscot loggers blocked the natural outlet of Chamberlain Lake at Lock Dam, the point where all water from the Chamberlain/Telos Lake watershed flowed north into Eagle Lake. When Lock Dam was built, water was redirected through the Telos Cut, a dug channel connecting Telos Lake with Webster Lake, accommodating the movement of logs south to markets in Bangor.

Over the decades, Lock Dam was modified several times. In 2018, the dam was rebuilt by the State of Maine, which marked the first time since the early 1960s that the flow in Martin Stream, the connection between Chamberlain and Eagle Lakes, became much closer to a normal stream, providing significantly improved habitat for native fishes.

Remnants from the past (from homesteads to logging equipment) still linger along the waterway to satisfy visitors' curiosity—including two massive locomotives that rest where they were parked in 1933 between Chamberlain and Eagle Lakes (see "The Tramway Carry" sidebar in Section 3, Map 12 chapter). Farther downstream, near the Cunliffe Depot campsite, the remains of two Lombard log haulers can be found. These steam-powered vehicles hauled up to fifteen sleds laden with timber and resembled a boxy pickup with a rear-tread drive and a pair of ski-like runners in front. This Maine-born invention was the first patented track-driven vehicle, to which all successors, from snowmobiles to tanks, owe a debt of gratitude. They appeared on the Allagash in 1908 and

The Northern Forest Canoe Trail calls to a sense of adventure and a desire to immerse oneself in the natural world and test personal limits. (Photo by John S. Read)

were responsible for the early demise of the Eagle-to-Chamberlain tramway. A lighter and more agile gasoline-powered Lombard soon evolved, and the vehicles remained a part of the logging scene along the Allagash for twenty-five years, until the early 1930s.

Designated as America's first federally protected, state-managed Wild and Scenic River system, the AWW stands alone as the most recognized paddle route in the state. The 92-mile-long waterway connects remote lakes and rivers in northernmost Maine. Overnight visitors are required to register and pay for camping through North Maine Woods when arriving by car or presenting themselves at a ranger station when arriving by water. NFCT paddlers enter the AWW at Chamberlain Bridge or by way of the infamous Mud Pond Carry.

Imagine having the option of paying to get your gear toted on the Mud Pond Carry. In 1957, Frank Cowan, the last in a long tradition of toters, gave up his post on isolated Umbazooksus Lake. A hundred years earlier Thoreau had met a blind fellow, Jules Thurlotte, who lived on the carry and had once made a career of hauling gear. Thurlotte relied on his back, whereas in 1880 Ansel Smith brought in a team of oxen to do the grunt work. In later years, a horse-drawn wagon was used. Today's adventurers must traverse the unmaintained, wet, and muddy Mud Pond Carry by foot.

With a maximum depth of 154 feet, Chamberlain Lake's cool, well-oxygenated water provides ideal habitat for brook and lake trout. In 2006, a state study using radio transmitters showed that Chamberlain Lake brook trout return home to specific tributaries for spawning each October. Very few studies have been done in Maine focusing on lake-specific populations of brook trout.

Numerous good spawning tributaries, such as Smith Brook, make Eagle Lake's 9500 acres (maximum depth 124 feet) ideal habitat for wild brook trout. The upper Allagash watershed is noted as being the only northern Maine drainage that doesn't contain yellow perch, a warm-water species that negatively affects brook trout. Dissolved-oxygen levels in Churchill Lake have decreased since the 1950s, making it a less suitable habitat for wild lake trout.

As you near Round Pond, be sure to keep your eye out for stately elm trees. Of the estimated 77 million elms in North America in 1930, over 75 percent had been lost by 1989. The isolation of these stands likely saved them from the ravages of Dutch elm disease. The tall, radiating branches shade a grass-and-fern understory in a fashion that feels distinctly Southern. Silver maples and more American elm trees stand like ancient sentinels at the approach to 30-foot Allagash Falls, another highlight of this section.

Regardless of where you began your AWW adventure, all paddlers are expected to check out of the wilderness area, stopping to report at the ranger station at Michaud Farm upstream of Allagash Falls. In the 1920s and '30s, Michaud Farm served as a base camp for logging crews. J. T. Michaud, a lumber baron, established the farm to grow grain for his workhorses and vegetables for the work crews.

ALLAGASH GEOLOGY

The bedrock of northwesternmost Maine, including the Allagash region, is predominantly sedimentary rock known as the Seboomook Group, which consists of dark-gray slate and light-brown sandstone. The moderate topography of the Allagash landscape combined with the uniform bedrock result in a relatively linear river that flows northeasterly along folds in the bedrock. Tributaries intersect with the main stem at right angles to form a trellis pattern. Elsewhere in Maine, where the geology is more diverse, rivers form a radial pattern in response to varied bedrock that lacks a consistent grain. Allagash Falls is a prime spot to view the bedded layers of sandstone and slate. Notice here the pockmarked and dish-shaped surfaces created by erosion. For more information about Allagash geology, read *Glaciers and Granite: A Guide to Maine's Landscape and Geology* by David L. Kendall or visit maine.gov and search for geology.

Recreation followed logging, and sporting camps developed along the waterway served the emerging needs of hunters and anglers. After the creation of the AWW in 1966, and to help preserve a wilderness corridor, most buildings and other structures were removed. However, Maine guide Henry Taylor and his wife, Alice, were allowed to continue to operate their sporting camps between Michaud Farm and Allagash Falls into the 1980s. After Henry Taylor's death, the camps fell into a state of disrepair. In 2004, a volunteer group received Bureau of Parks and Lands approval to restore one of the Taylor Sporting Camp cabins.

Within walking distance of Taylor Camps lie the deteriorating remnants of the Moir Farm homestead. The hay barn that Thomas Moir built in 1874 was based upon the Acadian vernacular design that features a steeply pitched roof. Thomas was a descendant of George Moir and Lucinda Diamond, who cleared the land in 1837 and were among the earliest white settlers in the region. Their arrival coincided with a declining presence of the Wabanaki along the Allagash. Descendants of Moir and Diamond can still be found residing in the town of Allagash.

Only two other historic sporting camps, Jalbert's and Nugent's, now owned by the State of Maine and leased for operation, remain. Their presence within the wilderness provides an added measure of safety for boaters on Chamberlain Lake and Round Pond.

The AWW provides the paddler with a pleasant combination of flatwater, quickwater, and whitewater (Class I–II) in a wild setting rich in human history. Trips can be easily tailored to fit a variety of distances and schedules, from a few days to over a week. Although not included as part of the NFCT mileage, the Allagash Lake Loop provides a true challenge for the most adventurous

WESGET SIPU POWWOW

Wesget Sipu is a Mi'kmaq phrase that translates to "fish river." The historical range of the Wesget Sipu people spans the St. John Valley, from the town of Allagash to Grand Falls, and includes the lower Fish River watershed. The people have had a presence in the St. John Valley for 8000 to 10,000 years.

Riverside Park, located at the confluence of the St. John and Fish Rivers in Fort Kent, is the eastern terminus of the Northern Forest Canoe Trail (NFCT) and represents a historic trading ground where the local band of Maliseet and Mi'kmaq exchanged goods with tribes from southern Maine and Canada. The Wesget Sipu people of the Mi'kmaq tribe—whose tribal registry is around 500 strong and whose language blends French, Mi'kmaq, and Maliseet—host an annual powwow in July at Riverside Park. The powwow, which is open to the public, brings together members from a dozen tribes throughout the United States and Canada and features traditional ceremonies, dances, and drumming as well as vendors showcasing regional skills such as snowshoe-making and trapping.

paddlers. This jewel of a lake also provides an alternative put-in for a trip down the AWW.

Campsites are first come, first served, fee-based, and plentiful throughout the waterway. No services are available until reaching the town of Allagash.

ST. JOHN RIVER

The St. John River is known by the Wesget Sipu people as *Woolastook*, or "beautiful river," and is derived from a Maliseet word. At 418 miles in length, the St. John River drains the top third of Maine, the second-largest watershed (26,000 square miles) on the eastern seaboard. After rising in remote northern Maine, it becomes the border between the United States and Canada before passing entirely into New Brunswick and later dumping into the Bay of Fundy. During the early twentieth century, the St. John watershed was the last in the state to lose its vestiges of old-growth pine. An assortment of unique plant life grows here, including Furbish's lousewort, which is found nowhere else on the planet.

The steeply banked St. John is wide, and often a good distance separates the tree line from the channel—a result of the annual torrent of ice and meltwater scouring this gravel-and-boulder river dale. In 2008, the Dickey gauge on the St. John logged a record high of 91,700 CFS. (At the same time, the US Geological Survey [USGS] gauge at Michaud Inn on the Allagash recorded 38,400 CFS, the highest level in its ninety-eight-year history of operation, topping the previous record set in 1961 by more than 10,000 CFS.) Highly eroded cliffs and reinforced sections of Maine Route 161 paralleling the river speak to the power of this watercourse.

This broad, island-dotted river treats paddlers to a mix of Class I–II rapids, quickwater, and flatwater through a rolling wooded and agricultural valley. Canada will be on your left. Stick to the right shoreline to avoid any international incidents—it is illegal to land on the Canadian side without going through customs.

Don't be surprised if you encounter French-speaking anglers who outfit their canoes with motors and fish for muskie. The first St. John muskie was caught in 1984. The nonnative species entered the watershed from Canada via the Northwest Branch of the St. John and has since contributed to a devastating drop in local landlocked salmon and brook trout populations. St. John muskie are known to reach upward of thirty pounds. Fort Kent is home to the Fort Kent International Muskie Derby, an annual summer event that started in 2003.

The final kiosk, sign-in box, and eastern terminus are located in Riverside Park. Fort Kent offers many services, including restaurants, camping, and a motel located about a mile west of Riverside Park, near the historic northern terminus of US Route 1, a highway originating in Key West, Florida.

Loons are more often heard than seen, their eerie, beautiful calls floating long distances across the water. (Photo by Mike Stavola)

NFCT MAP 8: RANGELEY LAKES REGION

Umbagog Lake to Rangeley Lake

Recognized for their beauty and diverse wildlife since the 1860s, the Rangeley Lakes—Rangeley, Mooselookmeguntic, Upper and Lower Richardson, and Umbagog Lakes—offer one of Maine's premier paddle trips. Expect outstanding paddling, swimming, fishing, and bird-watching. Ice-out is generally late April to mid-May. Blackfly season usually runs from the end of May through the end of June.

Because the Rangeleys are the primary headwater lakes for the Androscoggin River, NFCT Map 8 details the waterway in an east to west direction despite the fact that lakes are the predominant water feature. Traversing these headwaters consists of two very different experiences: large lakes offering flatwater paddling, numerous campsites, and glorious vistas in every direction, and the narrow and rocky Rapid River spilling from Lower Richardson Lake, which attracts whitewater enthusiasts from across the Northeast on high-water days.

Winds in the Rangeleys generally come from the west or northwest and can generate dangerous chop. Use caution, and travel with at least one experienced paddler. Keep close to shore and cross at a narrows when possible. Conditions are often calmer in the morning and evening.

Plan on four to five days for experiencing this entire section as a one-way trip, or break it up into smaller segments—exploring each of these lakes on their own by beginning or ending a trip from one of the campgrounds or state boat launches. The only things to slow you down will be when the fish are biting, the chance of wind, a portage, or just the sweet rapture at the natural wonders that surround you.

Public and private campgrounds as well as remote, water-access-only campsites abound throughout the area covered by NFCT Map 8. However, all but two are fee-based and by reservation only. The only two free first-come, first-served state-managed campsites are located on Mooselookmeguntic Lake between Upper Dam and the Maine Bureau of Parks and Lands boat launch on the mainland's south shore, opposite Toothaker Island. Rangeley Lake State Park offers

BIG FISH

The speckled brook trout put Rangeley on the map in 1863, when George Shepard Page, an East Coast sportsman, returned home from a fishing trip in the Rangeleys and gave some of his prized specimens (seven- and eight-pound brook trout) to newspaper friends in New York. Word spread, and the trout rush was on. The region soon became synonymous with trout as anglers continued to catch the occasional ten-plus-pound fish into the late 1880s. Until 1914, the Rangeley region held the world record for the largest brook trout landed by a fisherman at twelve and a half pounds. In contrast, the Adirondacks had never produced a brook trout larger than five pounds.

Page later cofounded the Oquossoc Angling Association (OAA), noted as one of the earliest fishing organizations in the country, and supervised the building of the fish hatchery on the Rangeley River. In the mid-1870s, the OAA introduced landlocked salmon to the Rangeley area to bolster the sport fishery. They also stocked trout and later introduced smelt as a forage fish alternative to the dwindling blueback trout (a key food source for brook trout).

The decline of fish—due to overfishing, habitat degradation from logging, and the eventual loss of the blueback trout—combined with the Great Depression caused a lull in tourism in the 1920s and '30s. Tourism rebounded after World War II, yet the era of the big fish was gone. Modern-day trophy fish average four to six pounds. Regulations, along with catch-and-release practices, have kept the fishery in good standing since the 1990s.

camping on Rangeley Lake. Stephen Phillips Memorial Preserve manages all reservable campsites on Mooselookmeguntic Lake. All campsites on the Richardsons are managed by South Arm Campground and must be reserved in advance. Most campsites on Umbagog Lake are part of the New Hampshire–based Umbagog Lake State Park system. Northern Waters, an outfitter out of Errol, New Hampshire, manages a group of remote sites at the mouth of the Rapid River.

The hospitable towns of Rangeley and Oquossoc, Maine, and Errol, New Hampshire, offer shuttle options as well as a range of services including lodging, dining, and tap houses. When visiting Rangeley, peek into the lobby of the historic Rangeley Inn, where an old black bear stands guard. The inn is a landmark from the heyday of grand hotels and sporting camps that reigned in the Rangeley Lakes region from the 1880s to the 1930s. Or stop by the Maine Forestry Museum, located a few miles north of Rangeley on Maine Route 16 where hundreds of artifacts, tools, equipment, and heavy machinery from regional logging operations are on display. Each July, the museum sponsors multiple

Camping is part of the fun for many paddlers. (Photo by Joe Klementovich)

events that celebrate the region's timber heritage, including the popular two-day Logging Festival and Parade.

Also allow time in your itinerary to visit the Outdoor Heritage Museum in Oquossoc. Collections are fashioned after a 1900s taxidermy shop, and exhibits bring to life the area's rich past through the voices of characters—such as champion fly tyer Carrie Gertrude Stevens, Registered Maine Guide Fly Rod Crosby, and taxidermist Herb Welch—who helped define the Rangeley Lakes region as an unparalleled destination for outdoors people. Errol is home to L. L. Cote, the region's largest sporting goods store.

See NFCT Map 8 and the NFCT website for additional trip planning and navigational details.

SECTION 1

Rangeley Lake

With easy access to paddling, hiking, birding, and fishing, this section offers paddlers opportunities to combine activities, such as hiking, looking for wildlife in lovely South Bog, or—water levels permitting—ending this trip with a Class I–II run down the Rangeley River. The most populated of the region's lakes, Rangeley is noted for having an excellent spring fishery.

TRIP DISTANCE: 7–10 miles

TRIP DURATION: Allow a half to full day

FLOW/SEASON: Spring, summer, fall. However, Rangeley River is a spring run—it becomes bony by mid-June.

DIRECTION OF CURRENT: Rangeley River, south to north

PUT-IN: Rangeley Town Cove Park, off Maine Route 4 at the end of Park Rd. in Rangeley. Improved launch. No overnight parking. GPS: 44.964403°, –70.646042°

TAKE-OUT(S): Oquossoc Town boat launch on ME 4 in Oquossoc. Hand carry access. No overnight parking. GPS: 44.966052°, –70.768434°; add 3 miles by running the Rangeley River to take-out at **Haines Landing** at the end of Carry Rd. in Oquossoc. Overnight parking. GPS: 44.962336°, –70.794872°

MAP: NFCT Map 8, Rangeley Lakes Region

PORTAGES (0–1): Rangeley Dam Carry, 0.5 mile (wheelable; only necessary if paddling the Rangeley River); or **Carry Road Carry**, 1.5 miles (wheelable) between the Oquossoc Town boat launch on Rangeley Lake and Haines Landing on Mooselookmeguntic Lake following Carry Rd. (only necessary for paddlers wishing to connect trips between the two lakes)

HAZARDS: Wind and chop on the lake, Class I–II rapids on Rangeley River

OTHER ACCESS: Rangeley Lake State Park (day-use fee). Overnight parking. GPS: 44.934203°, –70.706966°

CONTACT: Maine Bureau of Parks and Lands; Rangeley Lakes Heritage Trust; NFCT Trip Planner

SERVICES: Rangeley is a larger town with lodging, restaurants, groceries, a golf course, laundry, a library, an outfitter, and a health care clinic. Oquossoc has groceries, restaurants, an outfitter, and lodging.

CAMPING: Rangeley Lake State Park (fee)

The NFCT route travels from the boat launch at the Rangeley Town Cove Park, following the lake's northern shore and sweeping west, to the boat landing at the ME 4/Carry Road ridge in Oquossoc. Rustic cabins and camps pepper the shoreline.

Several side trip options can make this trip much less linear. The Rangeley Lakes Heritage Trust offers free maps that detail area hiking trails noted below. Hatchery Brook Preserve and trails, accessed from City Cove, appear first after departing Rangeley. Hunter Cove, and its gateway to the Hunter Cove Wildlife Sanctuary, is another 3 miles west. To enter the sanctuary, pass under the bridge and continue 0.5 mile to the eastern shore. The sanctuary offers birding and hiking trails. Continuing along the lakeshore beyond Hunter Cove, find access to Bonney Point's upland wooded trails in Smith Cove.

Weather permitting, paddle across the wide lake to Rangeley Lake State Park. The Rangeley Lake State Park boat launch is another great option to start

THE RANGELEY LAKE BOAT

The Rangeley Lake Boat was designed by the Oquossoc Angling Association in 1869 for use in the expansive lakes of western Maine. A utility rowboat built to be stable in chop and handle a few anglers, the lapstrake double-ender, generally 17 feet long and made of cedar, was popular from the later nineteenth century to after World War I, when demand for outboards added a transom to the design. The Rangeley, likely patterned after a St. Lawrence skiff, had several unique design features. It was lighter weight and smaller, and it could outmaneuver its bateau-like predecessor. Enclosed oarlocks and oars equipped with leather shoulders allowed the guide to focus on his client (called a "sport") and avoid shipping the oars in the heat of a good catch. Additionally, round seats were built into low-lying thwarts, permitting a sport to sit comfortably and cast without compromising the stability of the boat. Use of the Rangeley Lake Boat spread across Maine and beyond. Today, boat shops from Maine to Washington State still build the design.

or end your paddle. From here it's 3.75 miles to the take-out, the boat launch at Oquossoc.

South Bog, and its islands, is another area conserved by the Rangeley Lakes Heritage Trust. In the wetlands of South Bog, you'll mingle with loons, mergansers, black ducks, and wood ducks. Keep an eye out for a nesting pair of bald eagles. Habitat restoration has helped return a spawning population of brook trout to South Bog Stream (fly-fishing only). To stretch your legs, follow a 2-mile hiking trail loop that leads from the mouth of South Bog Stream with moderate gain or continues on to South Shore Drive. Your nostrils will fill with the earthy scents of an upland forest as you're rewarded with views while retracing the route of your paddle.

If you want to paddle the Rangeley River, where landlocked salmon and brook trout spawn, take out at the Oquossoc boat launch and portage west 0.25 mile on ME 4/Carry Road, then turn right on Hatchery Road. You'll find the put-in downstream of the bridge that leads to the hatchery. Expect about 1 mile of continuous Class I–II rapids (bony by mid-June) until the confluence with the Kennebago River at Indian Rock. Paddle into Mooselookmeguntic Lake and around a peninsula to the south to reach Haines Landing.

Paddlers who want to connect sections, but can't or don't want to run Rangeley River, will need to portage 1.5 miles following Carry Road to Haines Landing, where the Trail resumes on Mooselookmeguntic Lake.

SECTION 2

Mooselookmeguntic Lake and the Richardson Lakes

Long considered the domain of hunters and anglers, Mooselookmeguntic is Maine's fourth-largest lake and the grandest of the Rangeleys. Undeveloped western and southern shores combined with the lake's expanse give it a wilderness feel. The Richardson Lakes' long, serpentine expanse is also free of development, allowing captivating conifer-clad mountains that rise from the rocky shorelines. The Richardsons' sandy spits and beaches are quite popular with boaters. Paddle each lake individually or use the carry to connect the lakes for a longer trip. Whether you paddle to picnic, fish, or camp, these lakes will not disappoint.

TRIP DISTANCE: 16.5–21 miles

TRIP DURATION: Allow 2–3 days

FLOW/SEASON: Spring, summer, fall. Good fishing is temperature dependent, but locals suggest a general range of 600–800 CFS at Upper Dam's gauge for fishing.

DIRECTION OF CURRENT: n/a

PUT-IN: Haines Landing at the end of Carry Rd. in Oquossoc.

Overnight parking. GPS: 44.962336°, −70.794872°

TAKE-OUT(S): Note: **Middle Dam** is an ending point only if you are continuing a trip from the Richardsons. GPS: 44.778542°, −70.920358°; **South Arm Campground boat launch**, South Arm Rd., Andover. Overnight parking. GPS: 44.752190°, −70.842923°

Sunset on Lower Richardson Lake (Photo by Katina Daanen)

MAP: NFCT Map 8, Rangeley Lakes Region

PORTAGES (1): Upper Dam Carry, 0.2 mile (wheelable)

HAZARDS: High winds and big waves

OTHER ACCESS: Cupsuptic River/Lake: State of Maine public boat launch off Maine Route 16. Improved access with overnight parking. GPS: 45.01431°, –70.850017°; **Upper Richardson Lake, Mill Brook boat launch:** This launch works well for using ME 16 to shuttle back to Oquossoc or Rangeley. Overnight parking. GPS: 44.90685°, –70.90712°

CONTACT: Maine Bureau of Parks and Lands; Rangeley Lakes Heritage Trust; NFCT Trip Planner

SERVICES: Oquossoc has groceries, restaurants, an outfitter, and lodging. Private campground on the south shore of Lower Richardson Lake has a general store, boat rentals, laundry, and hot showers. Lodging (cabin rentals) is available north of Middle Dam.

CAMPING: The state manages two campsites on the southern shore of Mooselookmeguntic Lake that are free of charge and first come, first served. Camping at the remote sites on Mooselookmeguntic (managed by Stephen Phillips Memorial Preserve) and the Richardsons (managed by South Arm Campground) and private South Arm Campground requires reservations and a fee. Contact information is listed on NFCT Map 8 and the website.

Winds on these big lakes may shape your traveling plans. Prevailing winds are from the west/northwest on Mooselookmeguntic Lake. Weather from the south means a storm is brewing. Northwest winds are known to whistle down

The moment the magic appears after waiting out a rainstorm on Mooselookmeguntic Lake. (Photo by John Klopfer)

BALD MOUNTAIN FIRE TOWER TRAIL

Before casting off from Haines Landing, consider heading south on Bald Mountain Road to the 1.8-mile hiking trail that leads up the exposed peak of the same name—a former ski hill. The moderate climb rewards hikers with a panoramic view from an old fire tower overlooking the beam of the lake.

Upper Richardson's length, roiling the surface to oceanic proportions. Plan a windbound day into your trip, and if good weather prevails, use the extra day to explore.

Once on the water, reaching the Stony Batter campsite from Haines Landing is an easy paddle. There you'll find a sandy shore tucked under a canopy of tall trees—a lovely spot for a swim. The numerous islands (Lunch, Griffin, Shelter, Farrington, and more) that fill the wide cove below Stony Batter Point are ideal for exploring and picnicking. If time and weather permit, stop at Students Island further south to hike the perimeter trail, or plan to spend the night here, reserving a campsite at one of many options.

If continuing to Upper Richardson Lake, paddle from Students Island across the lake to Black Point and glimpse a view of Mount Washington, the tallest peak (6288 feet) in the Northeast. Continue to Upper Dam and portage left, passing the commemorative plaque marking the homesite of Carrie Gertrude Stevens, the renowned fly-fishing legend. **Note:** Ending or beginning a trip from Upper Dam is logistically challenging. Upper Dam can only be reached by driving remote backcountry roads through Rangeley Lakes Heritage Trust conserved lands. Overnight parking is not permitted.

If birding is a priority, make the short paddle across Upper Richardson from Upper Dam to Cranberry Cove, where herons and loons thrive; be aware that the cove is fragile habitat, so tread lightly.

Camping beneath the pines at Whitney Point will give you a superb vantage to watch the sun set over undeveloped conservation lands—a classic western Maine moment. Other favorite campsites among paddlers include Metallak and Pine Islands, which both feature sand beaches. After Pine Island, pass through the Narrows, where the lake shrinks to a channel and the wooded banks grow steep. The sandy spit at the Narrows campsite offers another great spot for a swim.

If you're continuing to the next Trail section, paddle across Lower Richardson to reach Middle Dam. Find the portage trail around the Rapid River just south of the white farmhouse—the former dam keeper's residence. Due to its remote location, Middle Dam should not be considered a trip-ending point. Otherwise, continue paddling to end this trip at the South Arm boat launch and campground, another 4.5 miles south of Middle Dam.

SECTION 3

Rapid River and Umbagog Lake

The Rapid River is considered one of the best places in America to catch a trophy brook trout. Expert whitewater kayakers will find enticing Class III and IV rapids, but this area is portaged by all other paddlers, following the historic Carry Road. The winding, swampy outlet that makes up the mouth of the Rapid River connecting to Umbagog Lake is a good spot for seeing moose. Adventuring in the Umbagog National Wildlife Refuge will expose you to a meandering, undeveloped shoreline that provides habitat for a wide range of birds and mammals.

TRIP DISTANCE: 12.7–17.7 miles

TRIP DURATION: Allow 2 days

FLOW/SEASON: The Rapid River is runnable all season at 600–2000 CFS. (Low water = 1000 CFS, medium water = 1400, high water = 2300 CFS.) Flow is controlled from Middle Dam. Regularly scheduled recreational dam release dates can be found on the SafeWaters and American Whitewater websites.

DIRECTION OF CURRENT: Rapid River, east to west

PUT-IN(S): Middle Dam is a starting point only if you are continuing a trip from the Richardsons. GPS: 44.778542°, –70.920358°; **Mill Brook boat launch** provides the best logistics (using Maine Route 16) for shuttling but requires you to paddle the length of Upper Richardson. Overnight parking. GPS: 44.90685°, –70.90712°; **South Arm Campground boat launch**, South Arm Rd., Andover, provides the quickest access to Middle Dam by water, but the shuttle drive is longer from Errol. Overnight parking (fee). GPS: 44.752190°, –70.842923°

TAKE-OUT: Androscoggin River state boat launch, off N. Mountain Pond Rd., Errol. Overnight parking. GPS: 44.787388°, –71.120935°

MAP: NFCT Map 8, Rangeley Lakes Region

PORTAGES (1–2): Rapid River/ Carry Rd. Carry, 4.2 miles (without a break), or 0.75 mile (then a break to paddle Pond in the River) then 2.5 miles (all options not easily wheeled)

HAZARDS: Class III and IV rapids on the Rapid River; high wind and waves on Umbagog Lake

OTHER ACCESS: Steamer Diamond boat launch: New Hampshire Route 16. Overnight parking. GPS: 44.791616°, –71.108364°; **Magalloway River:** Access on NH 16. Overnight parking. GPS: 44.857314°, –71.053002°; **Umbagog National Wildlife Refuge:** NH 16. Overnight parking. GPS: 44.832315°, –71.07521°; **Umbagog Lake State Park:** NH 26. Overnight parking (fees). GPS: 44.70228°, –71.055337°

CONTACT: Maine Bureau of Parks and Lands; New Hampshire

Department of Natural and Cultural Resources; Umbagog National Wildlife Refuge; NFCT Trip Planner
SERVICES: Errol has restaurants, lodging, camping, outfitters, and shuttle services
CAMPING: Cedar Stump campsites are managed by Northern Waters Outfitters, require a reservation, and charge a fee. Umbagog Lake State Park Campground and remote sites also require reservations and charge a fee.

Descending a hair-raising 155 feet over 3.5 miles—kayakers can experience technical Class III–IV whitewater tumbling through a cedar-and-ledge-lined corridor on the Rapid River. Waves can reach 4 to 6 feet in height in high water. Expect to find the river teeming with kayakers, rafters, and maybe a few skilled open-boaters when conditions are prime.

If you are arriving by water from the Richardsons (see Section 2 above), and you are not a whitewater paddler, this section begins with a portage. Otherwise your trip will commence from either the Mill Brook boat launch (recommended for shuttling) on Upper Richardson Lake or the South Arm boat launch on Lower Richardson Lake. From there you will paddle a number of miles before reaching Middle Dam and the location of the Rapid River/Carry Road portage.

Break up the arduous, not-always-easy-to-wheel, 4.2-mile portage into two sections by paddling 1.2 miles on Pond in the River. To reach this scenic, cedar-lined waterbody, tucked between ridge and mountain, turn left off Carry Road, about 0.5-mile after Middle Dam, and follow the rutted trail 0.25 mile to the put-in on Pond in the River. Remain on the old Carry Road if you want to continue portaging the entire 4.2-mile distance without the paddle break.

The Alligator, a steam tug relic from the log drive era that is rusting into the shoreline, can be viewed from Pond in the River. To find it, paddle into a small northeast cove just before reaching the take-out above the breached Lower Dam. At the take-out, a hillside picnic area displays a few logging-era relics above the structural remains of the old log sluice dam where exposed rebar poses a hazard. From the picnic area, you'll return to portaging, rejoining the old Carry Road for 2.5 miles, heading west.

As the incessant rip of the Rapid fills your ears, you'll climb a small bluff overlooking Lower Dam passing by Forest Lodge, the former residence of author Louise Dickinson Rich. The home is now privately owned and not open to the public.

Continue past a series of cabins before entering the woods accompanied only by the sounds of nature. Several side trails lead from the historic Carry Road portage to the river, providing fishing and whitewater boating access.

Treat yourself to a rest at Smooth Ledge, 1 mile before the end of the portage, where granite slabs slip beneath a spirited bend in the river—once a notorious sticking point for river drive logs. While gazing at the hypnotic rush, imagine the hydraulic force needed to push millions of tree trunks down this slim yet startlingly potent river.

Paddlers in Lake Umbagog National Wildlife Refuge stay alert for sightings of resident wildlife and waterfowl. (Photo by Sandy Tarburton)

Stay on Carry Road another 0.5 mile beyond Smooth Ledge. At the signed fork, keep left following a 0.5-mile unwheelable trail leading to the mouth of the Rapid River and the location of the Cedar Stump campsites. As you emerge from the Rapid River, the open expanse of Umbagog Lake rolls out before you. Umbagog is a shallow lake where even light winds can quickly produce waves.

Weather permitting, paddle across the lake to investigate the portion of Harper's Meadow that was designated the Floating Island National Natural Landmark in 1972. The ecological value of the area was further recognized in 1992 when over 20,000 acres were designated as the Umbagog National Wildlife Refuge.

The entrance to the Androscoggin River can prove elusive. Keep in mind that the outlet is to the south of the Floating Island area and about a half mile north of the Molls Rock headland.

Follow the wide, slow-moving river to the Androscoggin River state boat launch, just above Errol Dam, passing Steamer Diamond boat launch, another access point, on river-right.

EXTENDING YOUR TRIP: LOWER MAGALLOWAY RIVER

The lower section of the Magalloway River, below the dam at Aziscohos Lake, offers a variety of paddling experiences. Its upper reaches above Wilson's Mill provide exciting Class III–IV rapids during summer release dates. The lower part of the river runs through the Umbagog National Wildlife Refuge. For a day trip, launch at Wilson Mills and paddle south to a launch provided by the Umbagog Wildlife Refuge. For those seeking an easy overnight trip ending above Errol, there are campsites along the river and Umbagog Lake available with advanced reservation. See NFCT Map 8 for more trip details or download the Lower Magalloway River sample itinerary and map available through the NFCT Trip Planner tool.

NFCT MAP 9: FLAGSTAFF LAKE REGION

Rangeley Lake to Spencer Stream

The Flagstaff Lake region offers an enticing array of paddling, from the seasonal thunder of the Dead River's South Branch to the expanse of Flagstaff Lake as it spreads north, to the placid meander of the upper Dead River. When your paddling muscles grow sore, try swimming, fishing, hiking, or bird-watching while soaking in the beauty of the surrounding mountains. Plan on five to six days to paddle all of the Map 9 waterways, or split the region into the segments suggested below.

Flagstaff Lake and the Bigelow Range are truly spectacular. The mountainous views from the lake are an endless delight, while sand-and-rock shores invite a swim at every point. Whether it's the sweet ephemeral green of spring, the warmth and brilliant colors of summer, or vibrant autumn hues reflected across the lake, every season has something to offer.

The Maine Natural Areas Program recognizes the ecological importance of the 36,176-acre Bigelow Preserve. Of particular interest are several midslope old-growth stands and several rare plants, including Boott's rattlesnake root and mountain sandwort. Hikers have long considered the preserve a destination, as the legendary Appalachian Trail graces the eastern ridgeline.

Flagstaff Lake's shallow waters can cause dangerous chop when routine winds from the west or northwest blow. Autumn drawdowns at Long Falls Dam can return the lake to a level akin to its original riverine course.

Beyond Flagstaff, Long Falls Gorge and Grand Falls along the upper Dead River are must-see stops. A trail to the Long Falls overlook and information kiosk can be accessed from either Long Falls Dam Road or the portage. Reaching Grand Falls requires a little more effort, but feeling the mist and thunder of this isolated 40-foot drop is a special reward.

If you attempt to paddle the South Branch of the Dead River, expect Class III–IV rapids through a pair of scenic gorges. This river is only navigational in spring or with heavy summer rains, and the flow makes a huge difference in

Branches of the Dead River are best suited for experienced whitewater paddlers. (Photo by Aaron Black-Schmidt)

the type of challenges you will encounter. Solid Class III whitewater skills are recommended in unloaded boats.

See NFCT Map 9 and the NFCT website for additional trip planning and navigational details. DeLorme's *Maine Atlas and Gazetteer* is highly recommended when accessing any of the more remote boat launches.

SECTION 1

South Branch Dead River

Once used as a route to drive logs toward the Kennebec River, the South Branch of the Dead River is a seasonal run that includes technical Class III–IV rapids split between an upper and lower gorge. ***Caution: Much of this section is for experienced paddlers only.*** Paddlers are required to execute a quick maneuver between rapids to access the carry trail above Fansanger Falls in the upper gorge. The lower gorge features dramatic exposed cliffs and Class III whitewater without a portage option. Even with proper whitewater skills, boaters need spring snowmelt or a good summer rainstorm to paddle the South Branch; much of the year, low water, down trees, and boulders make the descent scratchy or downright impossible. Check for adequate flow before attempting a paddle. A more detailed map of the river between Kennebago Road Bridge and the public boat launch on Maine Route 27 is available for download through the NFCT store (free to members).

TRIP DISTANCE: 22 miles

TRIP DURATION: Allow 1–2 days

FLOW/SEASON: Late April to mid-May. The stretch between Lower Dallas Bridge and Langtown Mill drains earlier than the lower river.

DIRECTION OF CURRENT: South to north

PUT-IN: Lower Dallas Bridge along ME 16. Overnight parking. GPS: 45.004664°, –70.57815°

TAKE-OUT: Stratton boat launch on ME 27. Improved launch. Overnight parking. GPS: 45.151922°, –70.446872°

MAP: NFCT Map 9, Flagstaff Lake Region

PORTAGES (1–3): Rangeley/Haley Pond Carry, 0.3 mile (wheelable; only necessary if continuing a trip from Rangeley Lake); **Gull Pond Stream/Dallas (Route 16) Carry,** 3.7 miles (wheelable after Gull Pond Stream trail; only necessary if connecting sections); **Fansanger Falls Carry,** 1.3 miles (wheelable)

HAZARDS: Class III–IV through Fansanger Falls gorge; Class III rapids between Cherry Run and Nash Stream in the lower gorge

OTHER ACCESS: Langtown Mill Bridge: ME 16. Hand carry access. Roadside parking. GPS: 45.066788°, –70.576407°; **Kennebago Rd. Bridge:** Kennebago Rd., off ME 16. Hand carry access. Informal parking area. GPS: 45.10472°, –70.525325°

CONTACT: Maine Bureau of Parks and Lands; Maine Forest Service; NFCT Trip Planner

SERVICES: Rangeley offers lodging, restaurants, groceries, internet, laundry, outfitters. Stratton has lodging, restaurants, and groceries.

CAMPING: The Halfway Hilton lean-to and campsite is found along the Gull Pond Stream portage between Haley Pond and the Maine Forestry Museum, and one primitive site is at put-in. Many free campsites are available a few miles beyond the take-out on Flagstaff Lake. Fire permits may be required.

Even if you are a skilled whitewater paddler, the first thing to know about the South Branch Dead River is that it is often . . . dead. This is a flashy river with great fluctuations based on snowmelt and rain. Typically by June water levels begin to drop significantly and remain low for the rest of the paddling season.

With enough water, this section begins at a bend along ME 16, 4.5 miles northeast of Rangeley, where the alder-lined South Branch Dead River passes quietly under the road. A primitive campsite, well-used by car campers, is located here near the put-in and is the only established campsite along the river.

The first two miles of the South Branch below the Lower Dallas Bridge provide an easy glide along a meandering sandy-bottomed stream before the river begins changing character. Trees and riparian shrubs line the narrow channel and quickly remove you from the noise of the road. The mile-long upper gorge appears after 0.5 mile of Class II rapids. *Caution: This stretch involves a series of four Class III–IV ledge drops that should only be attempted by experienced whitewater paddlers in unloaded boats.*

A portage assisting paddlers around Fansanger Falls begins at an easy-to-miss signed take-out, between rapids, above the gorge. A dirt road leads from the river to ME 16. Follow the highway for 0.5 mile before taking a left on Quill Lane (also signed as CM Logger), an old camp road. The trail back to the river appears on the left, shortly after the camp road rejoins ME 16. Put in between Class I–II whitewater.

Class II waves persist en route to Langtown Mill, and then the paddling eases onward to the Kennebago Road Bridge and for several miles below. In the 1950s, sections of the South Branch were bulldozed here to ease the passage of pulp logs. There are a few boulder fields to navigate, and with enough water, paddlers will find this section between Langtown Mill and Kennebago Road Bridges free of the technical whitewater that appears downstream.

The Bigelow Range provides a stunning backdrop to Flagstaff Lake as well as a unique opportunity to combine paddling and hiking. (Photo by Chris Gill)

CONNECTING WATERWAYS: THE GULL POND STREAM/DALLAS (ROUTE 16) CARRY

The Gull Pond Stream/Dallas (Route 16) Carry helps paddlers connect a trip between Rangeley and Flagstaff Lakes. From the town of Rangeley, put in on Haley Pond at the park (GPS: 44.964674°, –70.641517°), paddle across the pond to the signed Gull Pond Stream Carry take-out at the north end. The unwheelable 0.3-mile portage trail passes by a free campsite and lean-to, then through Maine Forestry Museum grounds, before reaching Maine Route 16. You will then portage 3.4 miles following wheelable ME 16 to the Lower Dallas Bridge put-in to begin paddling this section.

If the South Branch water levels are too low to paddle, you will either need to walk another 14 miles beyond the Lower Dallas Bridge to Stratton or get shuttled to Flagstaff Lake from Rangeley. Services for this section are listed on the NFCT website and online Trip Planner.

If you hold any concerns about paddling Cherry Run and the lower gorge, take out here, at the Kennebago Road Bridge, then portage 7 miles to the ME 27 public boat launch in Stratton. Solid Class III whitewater skills are a must. Lining is possible for all but one series of rapids. There are no established portage trails.

Get ready to tighten your seatbelts below Cherry Run and the lower gorge. The river erupts into a steady set of Class II–III for most of the next 2 miles, until Nash Stream. When catching your breath in an eddy, take a minute to appreciate the memorable views of water mixing with ledge, jagged cliffs, and steep, conifered banks.

A spit of sand and ledge below the Nash Stream outlet celebrates the relaxing of the tumult. The river widens to a marshy corner of Flagstaff Lake, where a lasting view of the Bigelow Range welcomes you. Paddle 1 mile to the ME 27 bridge and boat launch, where an NFCT kiosk provides local and regional information.

SECTION 2

Flagstaff Lake

Those lucky enough to paddle Flagstaff Lake will never forget the ever-present Bigelow Range that rises gracefully from the lake's sandy shoreline. While mingling with moose and bald eagles, you will be treated to unending views of the Bigelows. Swimming, fishing, and searching for remnants of the flooded village of Flagstaff are other popular activities.

TRIP DISTANCE: 19 miles

TRIP DURATION: Allow 2–3 days

FLOW/SEASON: Spring, summer, fall. End-of-the-season drawdown can reduce the lake level dramatically.

DIRECTION OF CURRENT: At low lake levels, the old current of Dead River is discernible in some places, flowing generally west to east

PUT-IN/TAKE-OUT: Stratton boat launch on Maine Route 27. Improved launch. Overnight parking. GPS: 45.151922°, –70.446872°

MAP: NFCT Map 9, Flagstaff Lake Region

PORTAGES (0): None

HAZARDS: Wind can stir up dangerous chop.

OTHER ACCESS: Northwest arm: Cathedral Pines Campground. Overnight parking. Fees. GPS: 45.188745°, –70.458392°;

West shore: Meyers Lodge, off Flagstaff Rd. Hand carry access. Overnight parking. GPS: 45.188486°, –70.416852°; **Southeast arm access:** Bog Brook boat launch, Bog Brook Rd. Hand carry access. Small parking lot. Overnight parking. GPS: 45.138204°, –70.17022°; **Northeast arm access:** Long Falls Dam boat launch, off Long Falls Dam Rd. Overnight parking. GPS: 45.221122°, –70.197205°

CONTACT: Maine Bureau of Parks and Lands; Maine Forest Service; NFCT Trip Planner

SERVICES: Stratton offers lodging, restaurants, and groceries.

CAMPING: Many free first-come, first-served, state-managed primitive campsites. One private campground charges a fee and prefers reservations. Fire permits may be required at some sites.

This section documents the distance of the Trail from the ME 27 bridge on Flagstaff Lake's southwestern arm, where a NFCT kiosk is located, to the Long Falls Dam Carry take-out on the northeastern arm. However, unless you are connecting Flagstaff Lake as part of a larger NFCT adventure northward, most paddlers will want to use the same boat launch to begin and end a visit to this stunning lake. There are a couple of remote boat launches on the east side of the lake as well as others located closer to services on the west side.

Before launching, consider visiting the Dead River Area Historical Society, in Stratton, where you can see an exhibit on the former village of Flagstaff and the flooding of the valley. Stratton offers many services, including lodging, restaurants, and a grocery store. Like Rangeley, the town also serves Appalachian Trail hikers.

From the boat launch on ME 27, head north into Flagstaff Lake, where the crisp line of the Bigelow Range comes into view. Privately owned Cathedral Pines Campground, located near the mouth of the North Branch Dead River on the western arm of the lake, might be worth a side trip (or another option for launching a trip). Spend an afternoon beneath the centuries-old red pines and relax at the public beach with a grand view of the Bigelows. Benedict Arnold reportedly stopped at this spot during his well-known 1775 attempt to capture

Bracing air, sandy beaches, and rugged mountains make Maine an exciting place to dip into the Trail. (Photo by Aaron Black-Schmidt)

the British-occupied city of Québec. Consider that some of these old-growth pines would have been mere saplings when he passed through.

More than a dozen free campsites can be found on both sides of the channel on Flagstaff Lake soon after passing the North Branch river outlet. Savage Farm campsite rests atop a rise covered in pine. The exposed ledge provides a terrific place for swimming. Round the point and pass a series of small islands off the southern shore. Near the mouth of a marshy inlet (popular with moose) look for a tiny sandbar island covered in Dri-ki—a local term for driftwood—the remnants of trees drowned in the 1950 flooding. Close investigation will reveal remnant tar from a preflood roadbed.

Further remains from the inundated village of Flagstaff can be found near School House Point, an island campsite northwest of Jim Eaton Hill. Look over your gunwale for a chance to spy the eerie sight of a submerged chimney or rooftop when water levels are low. The foundation of the schoolhouse, located on an island, is also in this vicinity. You'll find sun-bleached pieces of Dri-ki scattered between lakeshore boulders.

Stick to the northern shore in order to trace the original course of the Dead River. Only a few cabins break the uninterrupted deciduous and conifer shore passing by Jim Eaton Hill.

Hurricane Island is lined with large boulders and hosts two campsites equipped with picnic tables. A journal housed in the sign-in box at the east-end campsite makes for interesting campfire reading. The historic current of

PADDLE AND HIKE

If you enjoy mixing the pleasures of hiking and paddling, combine a paddle across Flagstaff Lake with a return hike over the Bigelow Range. Paddle from the put-in at the Maine Route 27 bridge to the Bog Brook boat launch. Stash your canoe in the woods and head south on Bog Brook Road to find the Appalachian Trail (AT), where you'll head west, deeper into the Bigelow Preserve. Over the course of this rigorous 18-mile hike, which is at times above tree line, you'll summit four peaks, the highest being West Peak at 4150 feet—one of ten 4000-footers in Maine. The view from West Peak will give you a bird's-eye look at your entire trip. Spend a night at the Horns Pond lean-to and relax beside one of the highest alpine tarns in the state. Don't forget your fishing rod, as this pond is stocked with fry that arrive via backpack! After the Horns you'll part ways with the AT and head west on the Bigelow Range Trail. In Stratton, follow ME 27 north for 2 miles back to the boat launch. Drive to Bog Brook boat launch to retrieve your canoe.

the Dead River flows past this little island, and when the waters are low in late summer, evidence of the former Hurricane Rips (rapids) may become visible again as undulations on the surface of the lake southeast (or downstream) from your campsite.

On the southern side of the lake, West Peak and Avery Peak rise into view, sloping without interruption to the shoreline. Paddler access at Round Barn offers an opportunity for a hiking break on the Safford Brook Trail, which feeds into the Appalachian Trail. Round Barn offers many campsites, and you may even find yourself setting up camp next to an Appalachian Trail thru-hiker (see the "Paddle and Hike" sidebar in this section, on how to combine a paddling-and-hiking loop of Flagstaff Lake). At the eastern end of the northern shore, a series of large boulders provides a nice rest stop for a picnic or a chance to relieve the heat of summer with a swim.

From this eastern edge of the lake, paddle south to reach the Bog Brook access, or paddle north to reach the Long Falls Dam boat launch take-out, east of the dam. If you are continuing downstream on the Dead River, head into the northernmost corner of the lake, where the take-out for the Long Falls Dam Carry portage trail is located, west of the dam. Don't be surprised if your heart skips a beat as the echo of the falls mingles with the vanishing tree line beyond Long Falls Dam!

EXTENDING YOUR TRIP: NORTH BRANCH DEAD RIVER

The North Branch Dead River flows south from the beautiful Chain of Ponds, near the Canadian border, more than 24 miles to Flagstaff Lake. Its mix of lakes, flatwater, and rapids provide variety, and due to several access points, the river can be done as either a two- or three-day trip or as a series of day paddles. While its rapids are generally too low to paddle after mid-June, most can be portaged or lined at low water. The river contains an interesting piece of American history.

In 1775, Benedict Arnold and around a thousand men paddled up the North Branch and the Chain of Ponds on their way to attack Québec. For the modern paddler, the river offers wonderful views of mountains, forests, and peaceful sections as well as excellent rapids for experienced paddlers. Visit the NFCT website for downloadable maps and more trip information.

SECTION 3

Dead River: Flagstaff Lake to Grand Falls

The upper Dead River is a winding, slow-moving riparian channel where fishing, bird-watching, and relaxing are encouraged. The thick shoreline leans in and draws your attention to what is close: dark water, maple leaves, cedar, animal trails, and birdsong. The river picks up its pace on its approach to the spectacular Class V 40-foot drop of Grand Falls. After viewing the falls, return to the put-in at Big Eddy campsites or portage around the falls to take out at the remote Dead River raft access.

TRIP DISTANCE: 7.5 miles

TRIP DURATION: Allow a half day, or full day roundtrip

FLOW/SEASON: Spring, summer, fall. During Dead River release days, water levels change dramatically. The release schedule is posted online at SafeWaters, but water may be released without notice at any time, so be prepared for quickening and rising water levels.

DIRECTION OF CURRENT: South to north

PUT-IN: Big Eddy campsites, Long Falls Dam Rd. Hand carry access. Overnight parking. GPS: 45.230556°, –70.196266°

TAKE-OUT: Dead River rafting launch site off remote Lower Enchanted Rd. from US Highway 201. Hand carry access. Overnight parking. GPS: 45.30054°, –70.221652°

MAP: NFCT Map 9, Flagstaff Lake Region

PORTAGES (1–2): Long Falls Dam Carry (only necessary if continuing from Flagstaff Lake), 0.5 mile (wheelable, following the road) or 0.6 mile (carry, following the river); **Grand Falls Carry**, 0.9 mile, first half follows a Maine Huts & Trails hiking and cross-country ski trail; second half follows woods roads (parts more easily wheeled than others)

HAZARDS: Remains of the breached Dead River Dam just upstream from Grand Falls; Class II rapids leading into Grand Falls; and Grand Falls itself, which *must* be portaged

OTHER ACCESS: None
CONTACT: Maine Bureau of Parks and Lands; Maine Forest Service; Maine Huts & Trails; NFCT Trip Planner
SERVICES: Whitewater rafting companies, lodging, and a brewpub are found in the Forks. Jackman, north of Lower Enchanted Road, offers lodging, restaurants, outfitters, groceries, and laundry.
CAMPING: Free first-come, first-served primitive campsites at Big Eddy (a favorite of RVers and car campers), Philbrick Landing (fire permit required), and NFCT Island of the Giants campsite

The put-in may be initially turbulent, especially during a dam release, but as you leave Big Eddy behind, the final swirls of Long Falls drift away. The Dead River corridor soon narrows as the densely forested banks move in. The easygoing current allows progress without paddling and the leisure to enjoy your surroundings. Deciduous and evergreen trees hang over the deep water. Wild iris and ferns line the bank, while wind rattles the poplar leaves and alder branches bob at the river's edge. Keep a watchful eye and ear for songbirds, loons, kingfishers, mergansers, and woodpeckers.

The sheer wooded face of Blanchard Mountain will pleasantly startle you as you round an early bend. If you're quiet, you may glimpse a bald eagle. The twisted trunks of old maples have a stately presence along the shore. Take a moment to peer up Halfway Brook (located on river-left) over wetland meadows and back toward the Bigelow Range.

Above the confluence with Spencer Stream the river plummets over Grand Falls, which *must* be portaged. Approximately 3 miles downstream of Halfway Brook, you will approach an island in the middle of the river, just before the historic old Dead River Dam. Paddle to the right of the island. The 0.9 mile Grand Falls Carry begins here at the Maine Huts & Trails dock, on river-right, which you can use for visiting the falls and/or for portaging around it. Maine Huts & Trails also operates an impressive backcountry lodge a mile away from the falls. For hut status and information, visit their website (see Resources).

From the dock, follow the hilly, woodsy trail to the Tom & Kate Chappell Footbridge. After crossing the bridge, the trail is more easily wheelable. Follow the signed portage route through a network of woods roads connecting camps to the put-in just below Grand Falls.

Until the 1950s, Dead River Dam created a deadwater that stretched back to Long Falls. The dam has now fallen into pieces. If you are a confident Class II–III paddler, in low water you can shorten the portage by paddling over the dam ruins (be aware of debris) and under the footbridge, taking out on river-left at the beach in a pool above the falls. ***Caution: There is no barrier blocking Grand***

The spectacular sight of Grand Falls rewards those with the determination to get to this remote spot on the Dead River. (Photo by Will Jeffries)

Falls. Follow the wooded trail to a dirt road, and take a left to join the high-water portage.

Stunning views of the falls can be seen from a steep side trail you can access from either end of the second half of the portage. From the cul-de-sac above the falls, notice the smooth channel of the nearest cascade that was an old log landing, which was dynamited to provide a snag-free path for logs dumped in the river here. Follow a trail to a cedar-studded ledge overlook that juts into the gorge below the falls. The sheer volume of water will leave you in awe.

Another memorable view of the falls develops as you pull out into the river and look upstream. The pool below Grand Falls is a popular fishing hole (catch-and-release only). As you head downstream, take the left channel around an island. You'll pass a spit of ledge good for picnicking at the confluence with Spencer Stream. Please note that overnight camping is prohibited here. Take out at a wide set of steps downstream of the snowmobile bridge, river-left. Do not miss this take-out! Downstream, the Dead River erupts into 16 miles of Class II–IV+ rapids. Raft companies and whitewater paddlers use these steps as their access to run the rapid-intensive stretch.

NFCT MAP 10: GREATER JACKMAN REGION

Spencer Stream to Moosehead Lake

The Greater Jackman region is diverse: it boasts remote lakes and meandering rivers along with exhilarating whitewater. The area has something to satisfy every paddler's desire. Whether you're looking for day trips or multiday adventures, the possibilities abound. Venture beyond paddling and enjoy great swimming, a scenic hike, superb fishing, exceptional bird-watching, and the rejuvenating stillness of the region.

Spencer Lake stands out as a must-see. Spend a few nights at this remote jewel wrapped by a mountainous shore to watch eagles, relax on sand beaches, and fish. The layered ridgeline rising from its shores gives you the sense that you are comfortably isolated. Privately managed camping is available by

Poling is used by long-distance paddlers who need to move their boats upstream. With some practice, it is the most efficient way to ascend rapids. (Photo by Alan Flint)

reservation. Campsites and a boat launch on Fish Pond are accessed by vehicles using remote logging roads. Spencer Lake Beach campsites are water-access only.

Whether poling or paddling, a trip down the cedar-lined Little Spencer Stream and Spencer Stream (Class I–II) is a delightful ride through a remote and less-visited landscape. Paddling these streams is best done in spring. This short segment becomes unnavigable without adequate water flow. Thru-Paddlers are often faced with the reality of picking their way upstream through boulder fields in order to reach Spencer Lake.

The Moose River Bow Trip, which overlaps with a segment of the NFCT, is a popular paddle that combines scenic vistas with a variety of pond and river flatwater and whitewater (Class I–II) paddling. The Bow Trip can be accomplished over a long weekend and conveniently ends where it begins.

Continue along the Moose River for the opportunity to paddle the lengths of Long Pond and the Brassua Lakes, reached after braving (or avoiding) the infamous Demo Bridge Rapid (Class III–IV) and the Class II–III whitewater that follows.

See NFCT Map 10 and the NFCT website for additional trip planning and navigational details. DeLorme's *Maine Atlas and Gazetteer* is highly recommended when accessing any of the more remote boat launches.

SECTION 1

Spencer Lake, Little Spencer Stream, and Spencer Stream

The Spencer system flows through a landscape that is mostly undeveloped and far from any town or major roads. Spencer Lake is a treasure and recognized as one of the most pristine lakes in Maine. Spencer Stream is best paddled in spring or after heavy rains. With adequate water, the descent of Little Spencer Stream and the last few miles of Spencer Stream provide a spirited (Class I–II) ride where tall trees crowd out the sky. Both Little Spencer and Spencer Streams are well suited to poling (snubbing when traveling downstream).

TRIP DISTANCE: 12–13.5 miles
TRIP DURATION: Allow 2 days
FLOW/SEASON: Spring, summer, fall for Spencer Lake. Little Spencer Stream and Spencer Stream are spring runs. A flow of 200 CFS is moderate; 350 CFS is recommended.

DIRECTION OF CURRENT: North to south
PUT-IN: Fish Pond boat launch at campground on Fish Pond Rd., off remote Spencer/Hardscrabble Rd. Overnight parking. GPS: 45.443708°, –70.30164°

TAKE-OUT: **Dead River rafting launch site** off remote backcountry roads. Hand carry access. Overnight parking. GPS: 45.30054°, –70.221652°

MAP: NFCT Map 10, Greater Jackman Region

PORTAGES (1): **Spencer Lake Dam portage**, 0.25 mile (not wheelable)

HAZARDS: South and north winds on Spencer Lake; Little Spencer Stream Class I–II

OTHER ACCESS: **Bridge off Spencer/Hardscrabble Rd**. Hand carry access to stream feeding into Fish Pond. Parking limited to the shoulder of the road. GPS: 45.459085°, –70.299894°

CONTACT: Maine Bureau of Parks and Lands; Maine Forest Service; NFCT Trip Planner

SERVICES: Jackman offers lodging, restaurants, outfitters, groceries, and laundry.

CAMPING: Privately managed campsites on Spencer Lake and Fish Pond are free but require reservations. Contact information is listed on NFCT Map 10. There is a primitive campsite off Spencer Rd., east of the Fish Pond bridge (fire permit required).

You can begin this trip from one of two locations. One option is to start at the stream feeding into Fish Pond at the Spencer Road bridge, 0.8 mile east of Fish Pond Road, which connects to the campground and the second launch option. The narrow stream meanders through alder thickets for more than a mile before flowing through reeds into the north end of Fish Pond. Spend a few minutes here listening and watching for the thrushes, warblers, and swallows that thrive in the marshy outlet.

If you launch from the campground on the western shore of Fish Pond, you'll soon be paddling beneath stark ridgelines that guide you through a narrows and onto Spencer Lake. Trace evergreen mountains and exposed rock outcrops that run the length of this secluded lake. As you paddle south, willow and wild iris crowd below gnarled cedar. On the eastern shore, you'll find three privately owned but free Spencer Lake Beach campsites situated along a sandy spit that peer out over the dramatic waters of the pond. If time permits, reserve an extra night or two here beneath the birch and pine.

The dam located on the far south end of the lake was rebuilt in 2006 to maintain historic water levels, thereby protecting wetlands, trout habitat, and blocking smallmouth bass from its waters. To portage, take out at the rocky shoreline, a few hundred yards left of the dam. From the small landing, follow the signed trail for 0.25 mile to a put-in at a shallow cove. Upstream paddlers should scout for the takeout in the first of the three small coves downstream of the dam. After putting in on Little Spencer Stream, take a few extra minutes to first paddle up to view the base of the dam, where an impressive piece of bedrock remains embedded in its downstream face. The

CONNECTING WATERSHEDS: SPENCER ROAD/SPENCER RIPS CARRY

Spencer Road (a.k.a. Hardscrabble Road) and Spencer Rips Road are used as a 5.5-mile (wheelable) portage for paddlers wanting to connect the NFCT route between Fish Pond and the Moose River. Backcountry roads are followed from either the Fish Pond Campground or from the bridge crossing over the narrow feeder stream flowing into Fish Pond on Spencer Road. The site of the Spencer Lake POW camp and memorial appears a short distance east of the bridge. Take a moment to poke around the woods, noticing the crumbling foundations once home to more than 300 German soldiers (see "Spencer Lake POW Camp" sidebar in Maine overview for the story of this historic encampment).

Spencer Rips Road, a lesser-used dirt road, intersects with graded Spencer Road. Spencer Rips Road turns into a one-lane track passing through preserved Nature Conservancy land that dead-ends at the Moose River. Two free first-come, first-served primitive campsites are located on either side of the Moose River. The river-right site is downstream of Class II Spencer Rips, adjacent to the put-in. The river-left site is upstream of the rips. To help prevent the spread of invasive aquatic species, all paddlers should practice Clean, Drain, Dry protocols when entering new watersheds. See the Planning a Trip section for more information.

Paddling resumes downstream on the Moose River, following the eastward route of the NFCT. See Section 2 below for details paddling the Moose River section to Attean Pond from Spencer Rips, where the NFCT joins the Moose River Bow Trip.

dam is built into natural cliffs, and a small island forms a nearly complete circle of granite around the pool.

As you enter Little Spencer Stream, weave your way between cedar- and moss-capped outcrops that poke into the channel. You'll encounter a series of three deadwaters, each followed by a set of Class I–II boulder gardens and rapids. Below the deadwater pools, the stream has a marshy quality, particularly at Parker Bog Brook outlet, where rhodora, sheep laurel (lambkill), and open views predominate. Watch for moose tracks along the sand and gravel bars.

Below Parker Bog Brook, Little Spencer Stream narrows into winding quickwater. Keep an eye out for old pulp logs that rest on the cobbled bottom. Maples, birches, and conifers enshroud the channel and mature cedars grow from dark, moist hummocks. Rushing water is your constant companion, occasionally interrupted by cobblestoned pools. A large lichen-covered outcrop slides into the water as Little Spencer Stream joins Spencer Stream.

Whether arriving after tracking Little Spencer Stream or by driving backcountry logging roads and putting in on Fish Pond, remote Spencer Lake is considered by some to be one of the Trail's most beautiful bodies of water. (Photo by Dawn Chernetzky)

The view up Spencer Stream is highlighted by a distant ridgeline, and the 2-mile ride to its confluence with the Dead River is quick and fun. Continuous Class I water keeps you moving, and the rock-strewn channel forces you to pay attention.

Pass under the snowmobile bridge and take out at a set of steps, used by raft companies, on river-left soon after Spencer Stream merges with the Dead River. **Caution:** Downstream, the Dead River erupts into 16 miles of Class II–V+ rapids.

From the snowmobile bridge, a network of trails leads to private camps and views of spectacular 40-foot Grand Falls. Please note that camping is prohibited anywhere at the Spencer Stream and the Dead River confluence.

SECTION 2

Moose River Bow Trip Alternative Route

The Moose River Bow Trip is a remote pond-and-river loop. Ease of logistics has made this scenic side trail from the NFCT a popular paddle—be prepared to see others, especially on weekends and holidays. The Moose River has some Class I–II rapids, all of which can be portaged. To view an interactive map, visit the NFCT Trip Planner or Maine Trail Finder and search for Moose River Bow Trip.

TRIP DISTANCE: 34 miles
TRIP DURATION: Allow 3–4 days
FLOW/SEASON: Spring, summer, fall
DIRECTION OF CURRENT: Moose River circuitous, southeast from Holeb Pond, then east, then north to Attean Pond
PUT-IN/TAKE-OUT: Attean Landing at the end of Attean Rd., off US Highway 201. Improved boat launch. Overnight parking. GPS: 45.58796°, –70.259777°
MAP: NFCT Map 10, Greater Jackman Region
PORTAGES (5): Holeb Pond Carry, 1.2 miles (not easily wheeled); **Camel Rips Carry**, 0.2 mile (not easily wheeled); **Holeb Falls Carry**, 0.4 mile (not easily wheeled); **Spencer Rips Carry**, 0.2 mile (not easily wheeled); **Attean Falls Carries** (two rapids separated by a short pool): Upper Falls Carry 0.1 mile; Lower

Falls Carry: 100 yards (not easily wheeled)
HAZARDS: Holeb Falls *must* be portaged. Be aware that dynamiting has created jagged rock along many rapids.
OTHER ACCESS: Spencer Rips, remote access from backcountry roads (Hardscrabble Rd./Spencer Rips Rd.) Hand carry access. Overnight parking well away from logging roads. GPS: 45.519821°, –70.295458°
CONTACT: Maine Bureau of Parks and Lands; Maine Forest Service; Maine Trail Finder; NFCT Trip Planner
SERVICES: Jackman has lodging, camping, restaurants, outfitters, groceries, and laundry.
CAMPING: Camping is free and first come, first served. Fire permits required.

As you leave Attean Landing, Sally Mountain unravels across the north shore of Attean Pond; you'll paddle in the shadow of its bald peak as you travel west. The far southern shore is dominated by Attean Mountain, noted by mixed tones of conifer and deciduous trees. Look for bald eagles and loons. You'll pass inviting beaches and designated campsites. You may choose to camp at Sally Beach campsite and hike to Sally Mountain's summit. Behind the largest beach, a 1.2-mile trail climbs to the exposed peak of Sally Mountain.

Dramatic ridgelines drop to either shore as you near the portage to Holeb Pond. The 1.2-mile portage trail begins to the left of the campsite at the head of Attean Pond's western arm. Alder-lined Holeb Pond is smaller and less traveled than Attean. Put in near large boulders and gaze at distant mountains.

Southwest of Holeb Pond's Birch Island, find Holeb Stream and paddle for a mile to the Moose River. During high water the Moose River can reverse the flow of Holeb Stream, hence the tangled delta at the stream inlet. Two small rapids form at Camel Rips where a ledge slides into the river near a popular campsite.

Finding the 0.3-mile portage around Holeb Falls will require attention. The river splits as a ledge rises from the shore and boulders fill the river. Take the

Big boulders dot the Moose River, near Spencer Rips. (Photo courtesy of Northstar Canoes)

left channel and, once through, take an immediate right. Paddle 0.5 mile, over two small drops, and after passing a stillwater on your left, take a left into an even narrower stream. Travel a short distance to the take-out. At the end of the portage, you can walk back upstream to see the falls, where the river loses 40 feet through this narrow chasm. It's worth the trip!

You'll encounter a small rapid at Mosquito Rips followed by a stint of smooth water until Spencer Rips, where the NFCT formally joins the Moose River. Spencer Rips can be portaged on river-right. Paddlers who have followed the 5.5-mile Spencer Road/Spencer Rips Carry will put in here at the hand carry access.

Large boulders, some the size of a Volkswagen Beetle, dot the river below Spencer Rips while Number Five Bog rests hidden behind a bank of spruce fir on river-left. Here you'll find the river is deep and the current lazy.

The river picks up speed as you approach Attean Falls. Attean Falls is a pair of rapids separated by a pool. The first set of Class I rapids can either be portaged (0.1 mile) or scouted on river-left if running. This portage trail continues another 0.3 mile, allowing you to bypass both rapids with a single portage, if desired.

The second set of Class I–II rapids is portaged (100 yards) or scouted on river-right (near a large pine and a nice campsite). Scout this rapid! Find a large boulder perched on shore for a bird's-eye view. Boulders funnel the current right and push a lot of water up against a large rock; canoes are often pinned here. The pool below is popular with moose.

Look for a rusty rail at the base of the scout rock. This piece is a relic from the era when a train carried boats around the rapids, thereby providing access to Spencer Rips and the road to private lodges on Spencer Lake.

As you paddle north from the outlet of the Moose River, the horizon is filled with Sally Mountain ridge. Lily pads and reed grass brush against your hull as you pass untrampled islands. Reconnect with your place of departure, Attean Landing, by watching for vehicles atop the northeast shore.

SECTION 3

Moose River, Wood Pond, and Long Pond

Wood Pond (a.k.a. Big Wood Pond), the Moose River, and Long Pond offer easily accessible paddling in a natural setting. Fishing, bird and wildlife watching, and swimming are also satisfying choices here. Use Jackman as a home base for day trips, or resupply here during a longer adventure.

TRIP DISTANCE: 21 miles

TRIP DURATION: Allow 2 days

FLOW/SEASON: Spring, summer, fall

DIRECTION OF CURRENT: West to east

PUT-IN: Attean Landing at the end of Attean Rd., off US Highway 201. Improved boat launch. Overnight parking. GPS: 45.58796°, –70.259777°

TAKE-OUT: Demo Rd. Bridge, off Maine Route 6/15. Hand carry access. Roadside parking on south end of bridge. GPS: 45.618185°, –69.967437°

MAP: NFCT Map 10, Greater Jackman Region

PORTAGES (0): None

HAZARDS: North/northwest winds generate heavy rollers on the ponds; Class I–II on Moose River leading to Demo Rd. Bridge

OTHER ACCESS: Jackman public boat landing: Off Mill Rd.

Improved launch. Small parking area. Overnight parking. GPS: 45.619775°, –70.257594°; **Pomerleau Park:** 536 Main St. Hand carry access. Day-use parking only. GPS: 45.629133°, –70.262745°; **Jackman Landing Campground:** 582 Main St. Private campground (fees). GPS: 45.634573°, –70.26305°; **Veterans Memorial Bridge Park:** US 201 bridge. Dock with improved hand carry access. Overnight parking. GPS: 45.637535°, –70.262183°

CONTACT: Maine Bureau of Parks and Lands; Maine Forest Service; NFCT Trip Planner

SERVICES: Jackman has lodging, restaurants, outfitters, groceries, and laundry.

CAMPING: Primitive campsites are free and first come, first served. Jackman Landing is a fee-based private campground (reservations preferred) with water access, laundry, and shower facilities.

Moose-spotting becomes easier and easier as paddlers head east along the Trail in Maine. (Photo by Steve Spencer)

From the put-in at Attean Landing, meander through a wide marshy tidbit of the Moose River connecting Attean Pond to Wood Pond. The southern expanse of Wood Pond rolls out before you. To reconnect with the Moose River north of Jackman, follow Wood Pond's eastern shore. You'll pass a public boat launch, a string of rental cabins and permanent homes, then Pomerleau Park, all of which are located within the greater Jackman area. The town itself stretches out for more than a mile along US 201 and offers many visitor services.

As you reenter the Moose River, Jackman Landing Campground appears on river-right before the bridge. Pass beneath the bridge and pull up to the dock on river-left at Veterans Memorial Bridge Park for easy access to a convenience store, hardware store, and library. After paddling a few miles beyond the US 201 bridge, the breeze through the poplars will drown out the sound of cars and lawn mowers.

The Moose River enters Long Pond through reeds and wetlands. Signs of civilization, including an active railroad and ME 6/15 trace the southern shoreline, but the northern shore is less developed. Look for signs of moose in the coves east of the upper narrows. The NFCT and Maine Bureau of Parks and Lands developed two primitive campsites along the northern shore. A nice beach marks the first site located in a cove immediately west of the lower narrows. The other site can be found 2.3 miles farther east. Near the end of the pond, along the southern shore, you'll find a series of large boulders that provide a nice resting spot for swimming, snacking, or fishing for brook trout. The pond returns to being a river in the southeastern corner.

As you leave Long Pond, alders grow from a dense shore along the Moose River. You'll paddle a few Class I rips, pass an island, and run a few more sets of Class I–II rapids. In low water, some rapids may require lining. Take out on river-left 25 yards above Demo Road Bridge, upstream of a series of boulders, including one large one with a hand-painted gauge. **Note:** Due to changes in the river channel, the index painted on the rock is no longer accurate. The carry trail leads up to Demo Road.

THE DEMO ROAD CARRY

Paddlers continuing to Little Brassua Lake are now faced with the choice of paddling 2.5 miles of Class II–III whitewater with under-used portage trails, or portaging on Demo Road for 3.4 miles to a put-in below the whitewater. The first 2.4 miles of the portage follow graded logging roads and are completely wheelable. Watch for logging trucks, who have the right-of-way. At the 2.4-mile mark, turn right to follow another (wheelable) logging lane for 0.75 mile. The last 0.3-mile path (not easily wheeled) leads through the woods to the river put-in.

SECTION 4

Moose River, Little Brassua, and Brassua Lakes

Several miles of challenging Moose River whitewater (Class II–IV) connect Long Pond with Little Brassua Lake. The Brassua Lakes feature accessible paddling in a remote setting. The view of Mount Kineo from the mouth of the Moose River is unforgettable!

TRIP DISTANCE: 15 miles
TRIP DURATION: Allow 2 days
FLOW/SEASON: Spring, summer, fall; rapids get bony in low water.
DIRECTION OF CURRENT: West to east
PUT-IN: Demo Rd. Bridge off Maine Route 6/15. Hand carry access. Roadside parking south of the bridge. GPS: 45.618185°, –69.967437°
TAKE-OUT: Rockwood public landing, 62 Village Rd. Improved boat launch. Overnight parking. GPS: 45.67699°, –69.738179°

MAP: NFCT Map 10, Greater Jackman Region
PORTAGES (1+): Demo Rd. Carry, 3.4 miles (see Section 3 above for portage details); or **Demo Bridge Carry**, 0.1 mile (not wheelable) to avoid the most difficult Class III–IV rapids, ledges, and hydraulics appearing under the two bridges + **Elbow Carry**, 0.3 mile (not wheelable) following a rough trail, river-right, by Stony Brook rapids; **Brassua Dam Carry**, 0.2 mile (not easily wheeled)

HAZARDS: Moose River rapids (Class II–IV)
OTHER ACCESS: Brassua Lake boat launch (Misery Cove). Overnight parking. GPS: 45.622051°, –69.835998°
CONTACT: Maine Bureau of Parks and Lands; Maine Forest Service; NFCT Trip Planner
SERVICES: Rockwood has a minimum of services. Jackman and Greenville have lodging, restaurants, groceries, outfitters, and laundry.
CAMPING: Campsites on the Brassua Lakes are free and first come, first served. Fire permits are required except at the NFCT Brassua Lake Island campsite, south of Poplar Hill.

The Demo Bridge Rapid (which passes under the two bridges) is a Class III ledge (up to Class IV in high water) that *must* be scouted. The rapid is formed as the river funnels through opposing slabs of ledge, which is then followed by a river-wide ledge and hydraulic. *Caution: Only experienced whitewater paddlers should consider running the Moose River between Demo Road Bridge and Little Brassua Lake.* Below the bridge, the river is rock-garden-infused wild water with occasional ledges. A series of Class II rapids opens things up. You need to stay alert, as the river is bony, pour-overs abound, and good scouting eddies are at a minimum. If in doubt, follow the 3.4-mile Demo Road Carry to put in at the confluence of Little Brassua Lake.

The 0.1-mile Demo Bridge Carry, a rough trail along the left river bank, helps paddlers bypass the challenging rapids and ledges under the bridges. Downstream, Class II–III rapids continue for another 2 miles.

About 1 mile downstream of Demo Road Bridge, below a bend, watch for a bubbling horizon, where Stony Brook enters. This denotes a Class III rapid with a ledge, standing waves, and nasty hydraulics. Scout or portage this rapid following the 0.3-mile Elbow Carry, river-right.

The next rapid is a tricky Class II where the river butts into a ledge and slides left. As the rapids ease, you are granted a moment to breathe and appreciate the wild, thickly vegetated shore where old pines rise to the sky.

Long Pond Mountain climbs from the southern shore as you enter Little Brassua Lake, peering across the belly of the lake toward eroded banks and ledge points. Road noise may carry from the southwestern shore, but the lake is undeveloped. Distant mountains (Ironbound and Boundary Bald) rise to the northwest as you approach the narrows between the lakes. Pass gray stumps with tangled root systems and listen to warbler songs.

The even slope of Poplar Hill fills the horizon as you enter Brassua Lake. An NFCT campsite is located south of Poplar Hill, within a cove on the east end of a small island. Brassua Dam will be visible to the southeast below flat-topped Blue Ridge. A row of cabins takes shape on the southeastern shore as you near the dam with the portage trail to the left of it. Put-in below the dam from a fishing access trail.

Brassua Lake in September. In autumn, when reservoir drawdowns expose more shoreline, it might be more challenging to find rewarding take-outs. (Photo courtesy of Northstar Canoes)

The Moose River is undeveloped immediately below the dam. Class I riffles carry you along, and you will likely see anglers casting for brook trout and landlocked salmon. The banks of the river soon become more developed with cabins, boats, and a marina.

The rugged cliff side of Mount Kineo will inspire pause as you round the final bend of the Moose River. In the distance lie Big Spencer and Little Spencer Mountains, and the expanse of Moosehead Lake spreading out, with its shorelines to the south and north beyond view. You'll find an upwelling of cabins en route to the Rockwood public landing, but you'll hardly notice the change, as Mount Kineo will command your attention. Paddle south to the take-out.

NFCT MAP 11: MOOSEHEAD/ PENOBSCOT REGION

Moosehead Lake to Umbazooksus Stream

Moosehead Lake has mesmerized visitors for centuries. Forested hills and mountains cloak this massive lake, which is dotted with more than eighty islands. At 74,890 acres and 40 miles long, Moosehead—headwaters to the Kennebec River—is the largest lake in Maine (and one of the larger naturally occurring freshwater lakes in the continental United States). You'll be impressed by the natural character of Moosehead despite the relative ease of accessibility and its long history of use. Paddle beneath mountains and explore the countless coves and backwaters on this surprisingly wild lake. Don't miss the sheer face of Mount Kineo, a scenic favorite!

A quick hop across the Northeast Carry to the Penobscot River watershed lands you on the West Branch of the Penobscot (often referred to simply as the West Branch). The West Branch provides a scenic and contemplative flatwater river paddle. Consider a side trip to investigate the sand-and-ledge shores of Lobster Lake and nearby Lobster Mountain. This claw-shaped lake is known for its geology and old-growth stands of red and jack pines on Big Island. If you're after whitewater, access the West Branch via the Northwest Carry instead for a fun ride down a series of Class II–III pool-drop rapids.

Chesuncook Lake offers distant views of the gray exposed face of Katahdin. The northern end of the lake encircles Gero Island, and the shorelines are rich with inlets and coves that make for great exploring. Chesuncook Lake is home to remote Chesuncook Village, once home to more than 200 permanent residents, but now only seasonal camps are left lining the main "street."

Allow five to six days to paddle this section, or divide the distance into the segments suggested below with fishing, hiking, swimming, and wildlife viewing always close at hand. Be aware that strong winds come up without warning and turn Moosehead into a tumultuous inland ocean, halting progress for even the most skilled paddlers. Put some extra time in your schedule and an extra book in your drybag to help pass windbound shore time.

NORTH MAINE WOODS CHECKPOINTS AND USER FEES

From Moosehead Lake north through the Allagash Wilderness Waterway (AWW), and along the St. John River, shuttle trips from put-in to take-out will likely take you through North Maine Woods checkpoints. North Maine Woods Inc. (NMW) is a group of landowners, primarily commercial timber companies, who work together to maintain roads for their logging operations and allow public access. When using these private roads, remember that commercial timber harvesting is underway on many of these lands and that logging trucks *always* have the right-of-way. It is a good idea to make sure you are carrying a spare tire when traveling on these rugged, remote roads in areas with poor or no cellular coverage.

In addition to the roads, NMW maintains many first-come, first-served campsites and other amenities for visitors, funded by entry and camping fees collected at the checkpoints along the road. You may also register online for land use fees north of Moosehead Lake for both North Maine Woods and state lands prior to arrival. The organization produces maps and informational publications to help you navigate and better understand the forests, rivers, and culture of this remote and beautiful area. Maine's Department of Agriculture, Conservation and Forestry also contracts with NMW for the collection of AWW and Penobscot River Corridor camping fees. Visit North Maine Woods online (see Resources) for more information.

See NFCT Map 11 and the NFCT website for additional trip planning and navigational details. DeLorme's *Maine Atlas and Gazetteer* is highly recommended when accessing any of the more remote boat launches.

SECTION 1

Southern Moosehead Lake: Greenville to Rockwood Alternative Route

Although not part of the Northern Forest Canoe Trail (NFCT) corridor, southern Moosehead Lake is easily accessible and offers many coves, bays, and islands worth exploring. The area provides top-notch fishing, swimming, hiking, and wildlife watching. Campsites are plentiful along the eastern shoreline and around Sugar Island. This alternative route joins the NFCT at Rockwood.

TRIP DISTANCE: 18.5 miles

TRIP DURATION: Allow 2 or more days; leave extra time for the possibility of being windbound

FLOW/SEASON: Spring, summer, fall. Ice-out on Moosehead can be as late as mid-May.

DIRECTION OF CURRENT: n/a

PUT-IN: Greenville Junction boat launch, 22 Maine Route 6. Improved boat launch. Overnight parking. GPS: 45.46270°, –69.62040°

TAKE-OUT: Rockwood public landing, 62 Village Rd. Improved boat launch. Overnight parking. GPS: 45.67699°, –69.738179°

MAP: NFCT Map 11, Moosehead/Penobscot Region

PORTAGES (0): None

HAZARDS: Northwest winds. Dangerous swells can appear without notice.

OTHER ACCESS: Greenville: Town-owned dock adjacent to the boardwalk and near the steamship *Katahdin* and NFCT kiosk. Hand carry access. Overnight parking. GPS: 45.46041°, –69.591573°; **Lily Bay State Park:** 425 Lily Bay Rd., Beaver Cove. Improved launches. Overnight parking. Entrance fee charge. GPS: 45.568588°, –69.56617° or 45.576286°, –69.550558° (Rowell Cove)

CONTACT: Maine Bureau of Parks and Lands; North Maine Woods; Maine Forest Service; NFCT Trip Planner

SERVICES: Rockwood has lodging and a marina but few other services. Greenville has lodging, restaurants, outfitters, groceries, laundry, and other shopping.

CAMPING: Campsites on Moosehead Lake are free and first come, first served. Fire permits are required for some sites. Fee-based camping is available at Lily Bay State Park.

Maine contains more miles of NFCT waters and more remote wilderness areas than any other state or province on the Trail. (Photo by Aaron Black-Schmidt)

Paddlers can access the water from several locales in the downtown Greenville area. As you paddle from the town harbor, mountains rise from the shore; expect to mingle with sea planes, motorboats, and the steamer *Katahdin*—a toast to the steamer era that thrived from the mid-1800s until the mid-1900s. Historically, steamers serviced the log drives and tourists.

Round the point of Burnt Jacket Mountain and head northeast if you want to explore Lily Bay. You'll be treated to an early view of Mount Kineo. In early summer, nesting loons are tucked away along the shore here. The Sugar Island campsites are popular with paddlers, and Lily Bay is known for its smallmouth bass fishery.

Continuing up the western side of the lake, you'll be surprised by a quiet, sparsely populated shore. As you poke beyond the masses of Deer and Sugar Islands, you'll face miles of open water stretching northwest beyond Spencer Bay to Mount Kineo.

When the wind whips, Lambs Cove provides a safe haven on the west side. A campsite on the small island within the cove can provide refuge for paddlers waiting for the weather to change. This section ends at the Rockwood public landing, where the route for the NFCT resumes.

SECTION 2

Northern Moosehead Lake: Rockwood to Northeast Carry

Moosehead's massive size is ever-present while paddling the north end. Past Farm Island, an open view unfolds—you'll see Moosehead's distant north shore lying atop a watery horizon. If northwest winds are present, paddling the western shoreline of Moosehead Lake offers the best protection. The Northeast Carry provides the safest and easiest access to the West Branch Penobscot River, while the Northwest Carry delivers expert-level whitewater thrills for several miles upstream of Penobscot Farm.

TRIP DISTANCE: 15.5 miles

TRIP DURATION: Allow 1–2 days

FLOW/SEASON: Spring, summer, fall. Ice-out on Moosehead Lake can be as late as mid-May.

DIRECTION OF CURRENT: n/a

PUT-IN: Rockwood public landing, 62 Village Rd. Improved boat launch. Overnight parking. GPS: 45.67699°, –69.738179°

TAKE-OUT: Northeast Carry. Hand carry access. Overnight parking. GPS: 45.868260°, –69.630574°

MAP: NFCT Map 11, Moosehead/Penobscot Region

PORTAGES (0–1+): Northeast Carry, 2 miles (wheelable; only necessary if continuing to the West Branch Penobscot River). Additional portages necessary if using the Northwest Carry (see "Northwest Carry Alternative" sidebar, this section).

HAZARDS: High winds and dangerous swells can appear without warning.
OTHER ACCESS: East Shore: Norcross Brook. Improved boat launch. Overnight parking. GPS: 45.84080°, −69.62530°; **West Shore:** Northwest Carry/Seboomook Wilderness Campground. Improved boat launch. Overnight parking. GPS: 45.879611°, −69.724583°
CONTACT: Maine Bureau of Parks and Lands; North Maine Woods; Maine Forest Service; NFCT Trip Planner
SERVICES: Rockwood has lodging and a marina but few other nearby services. A seasonal country store is 0.3 mile from the Northeast Carry boat launch. Seboomook Wilderness Campground at the Northwest Carry also has a seasonal store.
CAMPING: Campsites on Moosehead Lake are free and first come, first served. Fire permits are required for some sites.

During the summer, a boat shuttle travels between the Rockwood public landing and the Kineo Peninsula to connect people with the peninsula's hiking trails. A trailhead at the Mount Kineo boat landing takes off on old carriage trails that circumnavigate the peninsula and lead to a fire tower offering panoramic views of the lake.

There are several island campsites within a short distance from the Moose River outlet, but care must be taken in making the 2-mile passage. Winds and high waves can make this crossing treacherous. Hardscrabble Point is a lovely

Exposed bedrock in Big Duck Bay Cove on Moosehead Lake, the largest lake in Maine (Photo by Katina Daanen)

Northwest Carry Alternative

Use the Northwest Carry only when intending to paddle the whitewater of Seboomook Rapids, a series of twelve Class II–III+ ledge drops popular with whitewater experts on the West Branch Penobscot River without maintained portages. Follow the western shoreline of Moosehead Lake, passing Socatean Stream—Moosehead's primary brook trout–spawning tributary and a good moose habitat that makes for interesting exploring. Williams Brook is another scenic side venture.

Enter Northwest Cove, passing Seboomook Point campsite perched atop a ledge with a southerly view. It's a great place to watch a storm unwind.

When you reach the Northwest Carry, you'll find the Seboomook Wilderness Campground and Store. Take out here and portage 2.5 miles (wheelable) to the Seboomook Ledge campsite.

After portaging 0.2 mile around Seboomook Dam, prepare for your descent of the West Branch and its Class II–III+ whitewater. Most ledge drops should be scouted, especially when levels are greater than the 3-foot index chiseled into the rock at the dam. The river slows down after the Burbank campsites. This whitewater route rejoins the NFCT at the Northeast Carry put-in at Penobscot Farm.

cedar-spotted promontory. Camp in the meadow, where there is also easy access to Mount Kineo hiking and the fire lookout trail. Swim from the idyllic pebble beach and watch the sunset from beside a crackling fire. From here, paddle up either shore, leaving the bulk of the lake to your side.

If sticking to the eastern side, you'll follow a string of mountains that rise in succession from the cobble shore. This side is largely undeveloped and a joy to explore. You'll pass an occasional old farm, but the shore here is pleasantly wild; hear the wind rattle poplar leaves, and crane your neck at old pines.

The craggy face of Eagle Mountain overlooks Big Duck Cove. The inviting cove offers protection from wind where several campsites are located in the shadow of the mountain.

At Norcross Point, look south for the striking lineup of mountains that extends back to Blue Ridge toward the mouth of the Moose River. As you approach the head of Northeast Cove, you'll see a row of cabins and homes. To reach the Northeast Carry, head toward the white farmhouse (which was a store and inn when Thoreau visited the area) on the far left. There is a 100-foot hand carry between the gravel beach and the parking area.

The Northeast Carry is the most efficient (and safest) take-out if proceeding to the West Branch of the Penobscot. To reach the West Branch Penobscot River from Moosehead Lake, wheel along the Northeast Carry Road for 1.5 miles to a triangular intersection. Take the left fork but immediately *cross over* Seboomook Dam/Poulin Road (also known as Lobster Trip Road), continuing on a lesser-used dirt track. Follow this track for another 0.5 mile to put in on the West Branch Penobscot River, at the location of the former Penobscot Farm.

SECTION 3

West Branch of the Penobscot River and Chesuncook Lake

The West Branch Penobscot River is slow-moving and scenic. Expect occasional Class I riffles and a wild and undeveloped shoreline graced with distant views of Katahdin. The river emerges at the northern extreme of oblong Chesuncook Lake where the outlets of the West Branch, Caucomgomoc Stream, and Umbazooksus Stream create countless coves and backwaters that will entice an adventurous spirit. Fishing, swimming, wildlife viewing, and visiting historic Chesuncook Village will complement your paddling day. Campsites are evenly spaced out, fee-based, and first come, first served.

TRIP DISTANCE: 25.5 miles

TRIP DURATION: Allow 2–3 days

FLOW/SEASON: Spring, summer, fall

DIRECTION OF CURRENT: South to north

PUT-IN: Penobscot Farm. Unimproved, informal hand carry access. (*Note:* The 0.5-mile dirt track turn-off from Seboomook Rd./Poulin Rd. is best suited for high-clearance 4WD vehicles when gate is open. Parking permitted.) GPS: 45.894067°, –69.610702°

TAKE-OUT: North Maine Woods West campsite on Umbazooksus Stream, Umbazooksus Rd. (a.k.a. Longley Stream Rd.). Gravel boat launch. Overnight parking. Fees collected by North Maine Woods. GPS: 46.127334°, –69.372438°

MAP: NFCT Map 11, Moosehead/Penobscot Region

PORTAGES (0–1): Northeast Carry, 2 miles (wheelable; only necessary if continuing from Moosehead Lake)

HAZARDS: Class I riffles on the river; dangerous wind-driven waves on the lake

OTHER ACCESS: Fees collected by North Maine Woods at checkpoints. **Roll Dam Campground:** Hand carry access. Overnight parking. GPS: 45.917331°, –69.688469°; **Lobster Stream boat launch:** Hand carry access. Overnight parking. GPS: 45.892261°, –69.564666°; **Caribou Lake boat launch:** Hand carry access. Overnight parking. GPS: 45.837026°, –69.313873°; **Chesuncook Dam boat launch:** Improved boat launch. Overnight parking. GPS: 45.88210°, –69.23430°

CONTACT: Maine Bureau of Parks and Lands; North Maine Woods; NFCT Trip Planner

The West Branch of the Penobscot River is wide and (mostly) smooth from the Northeast Carry to Chesuncook Lake. (Photo by Aaron Black-Schmidt)

SERVICES: Seasonal country store along the Northeast Carry has limited supplies.

CAMPING: All campsites in this section are fee-based. Maine Bureau of Parks and Lands manages the Penobscot River Corridor that includes the West Branch and Seboomook, Lobster, and Chesuncook Lakes. North Maine Woods oversees Umbazooksus Stream West and East campsites.

Dip your boat into the West Branch at the historic site of Penobscot Farm, the once-bustling logging camp. Here the river is deep, with a gentle current, and lined by muddy banks. Kingfishers dart about. Cedar, tamarack, and spruce silhouette the shore, and birch lean toward the water. When the pebble bottom rises within sight, watch for freshwater mussels, the brilliant green of aquatic grass, and sunken pulp logs.

If time allows, consider taking a side trip up Lobster Stream to beautiful Lobster Lake. The outline of Lobster Mountain will lure you up this gentle stream. Expect to see moose and beavers. The narrow entrance into this tucked-away gem reveals a sand-and-ledge shore with spectacular views of Big Spencer Mountain. See more details below about extending your trip.

Rejoin the West Branch and continue along its unfettered course. Thoreau Island appears soon after passing under the Golden Road Bridge. This is a campsite where Henry David Thoreau was known to have stayed during his 1853 expedition with Penobscot guide Joe Attean and George Thatcher, a relative from Bangor. Tall pines rise from the grassy bank here. If you're quiet, you may pass a bald eagle perched high on boughs above.

You may have to navigate a few gravel bars as you approach the outlet of Ragmuff Stream. At Big Island take the right channel and ride a series of riffles.

Lower downstream, glide over pools with sloping ledges, passing by high, eroded banks. Islands begin to dot the channel as it widens and grows marshy beyond Little Ragmuff Stream. Landlocked salmon fishing is good along this stretch of river. Each fall salmon and trout migrate up the West Branch to spawn.

Soon the expanse of Chesuncook Lake and the rounded outline of Gero Island come into sight. To the south and east, the pale ridgeline of Katahdin pops onto the horizon.

Boom House campsite marks the place where logs were gathered to be boomed down Chesuncook Lake. Behind the campsite a trail leads to Chesuncook Village, which can also be accessed at the Graveyard Point landing, opposite Gero Island. A signed walk directs you from the landing to the little museum located in the restored church. The historic cemetery is a short walk away from the church following the sole road from the village.

Gero Island, an entire island managed by Maine Public Reserved Land, lies directly east of the West Branch's outlet and is worthy of exploration. A series of campsites and lean-tos here offers a lovely place to spend the evening. East of Gero Island, the Allagash Lake Loop originates from Caucomgomoc Stream (see Section 1 in the Map 12 chapter for details).

From Gero Island, the Trail continues northeastward into Umbazooksus Stream. Pass between Little Longley Stream cove and campsite on the mainland and Gero Island as you head into Umbazooksus Stream. These days, since the raising of the lake waters, Umbazooksus Stream is a bit of a misnomer—the long, narrow cove resembles more of an arm of Lake Chesuncook than a stream. North Maine Woods manages two campsites on either side of Umbazooksus Stream. This section ends on the west shore at the boat launch.

EXTENDING YOUR TRIP: LOBSTER LAKE AND LOBSTER MOUNTAIN TRAIL

Lobster Lake is a favorite among paddlers. Its claw-shaped shoreline is varied and punctuated by mountains. Dramatic outcrops, old-growth pine, sand beaches, and tucked-away coves invite exploration. Pass your time here swimming, fishing, hiking, viewing wildlife, and admiring the geology.

En route to the hike up Lobster Mountain (the trail leaves from the Jackson Cove campsite), you'll be awed by the view down Little Claw where the mountainous backbone of Lobster drops to the shore. The 2.5-mile moderate hike rewards you with a view of rugged Mount Katahdin to the east. A 500-foot conservation buffer protects the shoreline of Lobster Lake from further development, yet a few cabins, including a ranger station, exist here.

Anglers seek out the native runs of landlocked salmon, lake trout, and brook trout, and naturalists love the southern end of Big Claw, where several brooks enter the lake. Expect to see a range of species, from muskrat and moose to goldeneye and beaver. The diverse geology of the lake is unique in Maine. Look for marine fossils near Ogden Point and the unconformity exposed near the Northeast Cove campsite. More information about the geology of Lobster Lake can be found searching the maine.gov website.

NFCT MAP 12: ALLAGASH REGION (SOUTH)

Umbazooksus Stream to Umsaskis Lake

The Allagash Wilderness Waterway (AWW) may be the most recognized paddle route in Maine, and for good reason. Many Thru-Paddlers mark the AWW as the apex of their journey, counting more moose than people on the relatively leisurely final miles of the Trail.

The only state-administered Wild and Scenic River in the federal system, the Allagash has been used by people since the receding of the last glacier about 12,000 years ago. A trip along the Allagash offers a remote experience in a wild, scenic place, engaging your senses in the cultural and natural histories of the region. Remnants from the logging era are scattered all along the waterway.

Whether it's a tramway or a train, a boarding house or a bateau, the artifacts you see will give you the eerie sense of traveling through a living museum. Some of the tallest white pines in the state rise above Eagle Lake, and 400-million-year-old stone embedded with fossils of coral can be found on Chamberlain Lake. Artifacts discovered on Eagle and Churchill Lakes date back as early as the Paleo-Indians (11,500 to 9000 years ago).

The Allagash Wilderness Waterway embodies what paddlers often seek: wide waters, tall trees, quiet, and plenty of wildlife. (Photo by Dean B. Bennett)

Henry David Thoreau provided us with the first written account of the Mud Pond Carry in 1857. Today, the well-worn carry provides a way to connect with the footsteps of old. This unmaintained carry is on private land and not an official part of the NFCT. However, consistent with the landowner's policy of allowing public recreation, use of the carry by paddlers is permitted.

If you desire a rigorous adventure, try the Allagash Lake Loop, a less-traveled route that entails upstream travel (against Class I rapids) on Caucomgomoc Stream and remote Caucomgomoc Lake, with a 3-mile portage to Allagash Lake. Along with paddling this isolated waterbody, you can explore the ice caves, hike Allagash Mountain, swim from a ledge shore, or fish for wild brook trout. Exiting the lake along Allagash Stream involves riding Class I–II rapids and portaging around lovely Little Allagash Falls.

Throughout the area, expect stellar fishing, swimming, hiking, and wildlife viewing throughout the waterway. When planning your trip, check the AWW website, as numerous regulations apply, including restrictions on boat size.

See NFCT Map 12 and the NFCT website for additional trip planning and navigational details. DeLorme's *The Maine Atlas and Gazetteer* is highly recommended when accessing any of the more remote boat launches.

SECTION 1

Allagash Lake Loop Alternative Route

Remote Allagash Lake is the only nonmotorized waterbody in the Allagash Wilderness Waterway. There are only three ways into this precious spot, and all involve a degree of adventure. Visitors to the NFCT typically add Allagash Lake to their itinerary as part of a larger journey or as a means of avoiding the Mud Pond Carry. Be aware, however, that this is a tough route involving upstream travel, a 3-mile portage, and Class I–II rapids. The alternative route begins on Umbazooksus Stream and rejoins the NFCT on Chamberlain Lake. The loop includes Caucomgomoc Stream and Lake, Ciss Stream, and Allagash Lake and Stream. Expect solitude, great fishing, superb wildlife viewing, and scenic hiking.

TRIP DISTANCE: 36 miles (See "Closing the Loop" at the end of this section, which will add mileage to this trip.)
TRIP DURATION: Allow 3–4 days
FLOW/SEASON: The upper reaches of Caucomgomoc Stream and Allagash Stream are often low by midsummer. Check with an Allagash Wilderness Waterway (AWW) ranger to ensure adequate flow before heading into this remote area.
DIRECTION OF CURRENT: Caucomgomoc Stream, northwest to southeast; Allagash Stream, west to east

PUT-IN: North Maine Woods West campsite on Umbazooksus Stream, Umbazooksus Rd. (a.k.a. Longley Stream Rd.). Gravel boat launch. Overnight parking. Fees collected by North Maine Woods. GPS: 46.127334°, –69.372438°

TAKE-OUT(S): Route rejoins the NFCT and continues north. See "Closing the Loop" at the end of this section for take-out options.

MAP: NFCT Map 12, Allagash Region (South)

PORTAGES (3): Caucomgomoc Dam Carry, 0.75 mile (wheelable); **Allagash Lake Portage**, 3 miles (wheelable/not easily wheeled); **Little Allagash Falls Carry**, 0.3 mile (wheelable)

HAZARDS: Lake winds; heavy upstream current; Class I–II rapids

OTHER ACCESS: Fees collected by North Maine Woods at checkpoints. **Johnson Pond/Stream boat launch:** Hand carry access. Overnight parking. GPS: 46.315894°, –69.581775°; **Allagash Stream boat launch:** Hand carry access. Overnight parking. GPS: 46.33760°, –69.60460°

CONTACT: North Maine Woods; Maine Bureau of Parks and Lands; NFCT Trip Planner

SERVICES: Chamberlain Bridge and Allagash Lake ranger stations: Rangers can accept fees, provide information, and assist with emergencies. A privately owned lodge on Round Pond offers lodging and shuttle services. Visit the NFCT website for service contact information.

CAMPING: All campsites in this section are first come, first served, and fee-based. Maine Bureau of Parks and Lands manages the Penobscot River Corridor that includes Chesuncook Lake. North Maine Woods oversees Umbazooksus Stream West and East campsites. AWW campsites are administered by the Maine Bureau of Parks and Lands. Fees are collected at North Maine Woods checkpoints.

From the North Maine Woods West campsite on Umbazooksus Stream, paddle south to Chesuncook Lake and find the mouth of Caucomgomoc Stream to the southwest, just north of the West Branch of the Penobscot River. Paddle along the northeast shore of the stream as an intricate web of marsh spreads to the southwest. A ridge funnels you toward the small beach at the Canvas Dam campsite—the site of a dam constructed of wood and canvas during the log drives.

Black Pond is long and narrow, interspersed with reed grass and Dri-ki. A mix of deciduous trees and conifers lines the undeveloped shore. As the pond narrows, the bank grows steeper and the understory opens. You'll wind around an oxbow that is popular with moose.

When the stream transitions to Class I rips, you have a mile of upriver travel remaining. At the ledge falls look for a worn 0.75-mile portage trail on the left. Follow this path to a tote road and take a right. After a second right you'll find Caucomgomoc Dam and a primitive campsite.

Umbazooksus Stream is sometimes a paddle, sometimes a portage. (Photo by John Klopfer)

Layered rolling hills rise gently from the open water of Caucomgomoc Lake. The southern end of the lake is mostly undeveloped, and its diverse shoreline is worth exploring, as is fishing for landlocked salmon. Head north up the marshy outlet of Ciss Stream.

Ciss Stream winds through an expanse of marsh grass, lily pads, and gray trunks. The wildlife viewing is spectacular. Be prepared for diving swallows, soaring eagles, and grazing moose.

From Ciss Stream, paddle across Round Pond to the north end. There are two campsites here. The signed portage to Allagash Lake—a distance of 3 miles— begins from a road behind the northeast campsite. After the first 2 miles, you'll pass a gate with a fork in the road beyond. The left fork continues along the wheelable road to the ranger station. The right fork follows a rougher trail that is not as easily wheeled. Both forks end at Allagash Lake.

The wild solitude of Allagash Lake settles in as you stand on its ledge shore in the shadow of a craggy mountain. Choice activities abound on Allagash Lake. Swim from ledge points. Hike the 0.7-mile trail (it's steep) up Allagash Mountain, where the distant peaks of Mount Kineo and Mount Katahdin rise to the south. Bring your headlamp if you want to delve into the depths of the ice caves on the northwest shore. Fishing on the lake offers access to populations of wild brook and lake trout never influenced by stocking.

Exit the lake via cobbled Allagash Stream from the upper northeast corner. Quickwater and Class I rips lead to Little Round Pond. To the left of Little Allagash Falls (20-foot drop), a 0.3-mile portage trail passes through the campsites. Below the falls, expect three ledge-drop rapids. Avoid the first by following a narrow channel to river-right. The second should be portaged or lined. The third coincides with a small bridge. Definitely scout this rapid (or portage) on river-left.

The stream widens to a wildlife-rich outlet. Paddle past the decaying railroad trestle into Chamberlain Lake to rejoin the NFCT route. Look for Katahdin hovering atop the southeast horizon. As on all large lakes, strong winds and high waves are a potential danger. Follow the shoreline, and be prepared to land and wait out the weather if necessary.

CLOSING THE LOOP

This trip can also be turned into a closed loop by returning to the starting point at the North Maine Woods Umbazooksus Stream West campsite, reversing the instructions for the Mud Pond Carry in Section 2 of the Map 12 chapter. This option includes more than 15 miles of additional paddling and portaging.

Another option is paddle the length of Chamberlain Lake (13 miles) and take out at Chamberlain Bridge Ranger Station on Telos Road (GPS: 46.17060°, −69.20800°). Improved boat launch and overnight parking. However, paddlers will need to coordinate their own shuttle between the North Maine Woods Umbazooksus Stream West campsite put-in and Chamberlain Bridge take-out.

SECTION 2

Umbazooksus Lake and Mud Pond

The far northern end of Umbazooksus Lake once had a railroad pier built out over the water so that logs from Eagle Lake could be dumped directly into the lake to begin their journey south to the mills. From Umbazooksus Lake, you will follow the unmaintained 1.6-mile Mud Pond Carry, an ancient connector between the Penobscot River and St. John River watersheds. The mystique, difficulty, and history of this carry are reason enough for many to seek it out. Expect thick mud, knee-deep puddles, and a blowdown-clogged trail, ending at the equally boggy shorelines of Mud Pond. You'll appreciate the open waters of Chamberlain Lake by the time you reach them!

TRIP DISTANCE: 7 miles
TRIP DURATION: Allow 1 long day
FLOW/SEASON: Low water will require additional portaging on upper Umbazooksus Stream and expose a mudflat at the Mud Pond access. Umbazooksus Lake is navigable all season.
DIRECTION OF CURRENT: Umbazooksus Stream, north to south
PUT-IN: North Maine Woods West campsite on Umbazooksus Stream, Umbazooksus Rd. (a.k.a. Longley Stream Rd.). Gravel boat launch. Overnight parking. Fees collected by North Maine Woods.
GPS: 46.127334°, –69.372438°
TAKE-OUT: If not continuing north, following the route of the NFCT through the Allagash Wilderness Waterway (AWW), paddle south an additional 7 miles to take out at **Chamberlain Bridge.** Improved boat launch. Overnight parking. Fees collected by North Maine Woods and/or AWW rangers.
GPS: 46.17060°, –69.20800°
MAP: NFCT Map 12, Allagash Region (South)

PORTAGES (1–3): Umbazooksus Stream Carry, 0.3 mile (not wheelable; only necessary in low water); **Mud Pond Carry,** 1.6 miles (not wheelable); **Mud Brook Carry,** 0.4 mile (not wheelable)
HAZARDS: Lake winds; difficult footing on portage trail
OTHER ACCESS: None
CONTACT: North Maine Woods; Maine Bureau of Parks and Lands; Allagash Wilderness Waterway Foundation; NFCT Trip Planner
SERVICES: North Maine Woods manages road access to boat launches. User fees apply. Chamberlain Bridge ranger station: Rangers can accept fees, provide information, and assist with emergencies.
CAMPING: Campsites are first come, first served. North Maine Woods oversees Umbazooksus Stream West and East campsites, and AWW campsites are managed by the Maine Bureau of Parks and Lands. Fees are collected at North Maine Woods checkpoints or at AWW ranger stations.

From the North Maine Woods West campsite, Umbazooksus Stream soon narrows as it passes beneath the Longley Stream Road Bridge. You'll be headed against a mild current and likely have to portage above a small rocky bend. **Note:** During dam drawdowns or during periods of low water, this waterway will be rock-ridden and impassable.

The stream winds its way through an open valley where a wide span of meadow separates the channel from a forested ridge. Gray trunks reach from the meadow grass. The stream is green with aquatic grass and filled with bullfrogs. Umbazooksus Stream is a good place to practice poling. The stream narrows as it snakes toward Umbazooksus Lake. Umbazooksus Lake Dam was

The carry to Mud Pond is itself often a muddy slog, but its romantic reputation makes it a "must-do" for some trippers. (Photo by Erin Spencer)

decommissioned in the late 1990s, and the gates have been left open, technically eliminating the need for a portage. The current flowing from Umbazooksus Lake through this constricted passage can be surprisingly strong. Carry right around the dam, if necessary.

Umbazooksus Lake is oblong and undeveloped. The 1.6-mile Mud Pond Carry leaves from the north shore about a mile from the dam. A small boulder supports the suggestion of a cairn at a noticeable opening in the tree line where the gravelly (and sometimes watery) portage trail originates, but it is difficult to see these details from afar. Taking a bearing (it's about 19 degrees) is your best bet at accuracy. The GPS coordinates are listed on NFCT Map 12.

The infamous carry trail is a worn trough through a thick wood on private land that is not maintained. Expect to scramble over and under blown-down trees and to wade through thick mud and standing water in some areas. Early on you'll face a slight incline. Around the height of land, the understory opens, exposing tall trunks atop a carpet of ferns and trilliums.

As you near Mud Pond, the trail grows wetter with the possibility of walking through deep water created by beaver activity. A small clearing opens onto Mud Pond, a shallow oval pond with a marsh covering the western shore. A mudflat extends out from shore at the put-in. Try building a bridge of downed wood to get your boat and gear to water.

Paddling across Mud Pond, you'll find a small brook exiting from the north shore. This brook connects to the small cove on Chamberlain Lake, but the presence of beaver activity may reduce it to a trickle. Find the portage to the right of the brook. The 0.4-mile winter snow machine trail is strewn with rocks and roots but leads to a grassy meadow at its mouth in the cove.

Paddle across a cove heavy with old stumps and enter Chamberlain Lake and the AWW. The distance from Umbazooksus Stream West to the first campsite, Mud Brook, on Chamberlain Lake is 7 miles. To continue on the NFCT (see Section 3), head north into the lake; to end a trip at Chamberlain Bridge, paddle south 7 miles. This section can also be added as part of the Allagash Lake Loop Alternative Route, creating a multi-day trip that begins and ends at the North Maine Woods West campsite. See Section 1 above for more information.

SECTION 3

Chamberlain Lake and Eagle Lake

Chamberlain and Eagle Lakes provide a wonderful introduction to the Allagash Wilderness Waterway (AWW). Enjoy the quiet of these majestic headwater lakes. Fish for wild trout, swim in the cool water, or explore the numerous inlets and coves.

TRIP DISTANCE: 30 miles
TRIP DURATION: Allow 3–4 days
FLOW/SEASON: Spring, summer, fall
DIRECTION OF CURRENT: n/a
PUT-IN: Chamberlain Bridge, Telos Rd. Improved boat launch. Overnight parking. GPS: 46.17060°, –69.20800°
TAKE-OUT: Churchill Dam, Churchill Dam Rd. Improved boat launch. Overnight parking. GPS: 46.493469°, –69.288763°
MAP: NFCT Map 12, Allagash Region (South)
PORTAGES (1): Lock Dam Carry, 0.1 mile (wheelable); or Tramway Carry, 0.5 mile (not easily wheeled)
HAZARDS: Winds run the length of the lakes and create dangerous swells.
OTHER ACCESS: Indian Pond/ Stream on Indian Pond Rd. Hand carry access. Overnight parking. GPS: 46.272232°, –69.311602°
CONTACT: North Maine Woods; Maine Bureau of Parks and Lands; Allagash Wilderness Waterway Foundation; NFCT Trip Planner
SERVICES: Chamberlain Bridge, Lock Dam, and Eagle Lake all have ranger stations.
CAMPING: Campsites are first come, first served, and managed by the Maine Bureau of Parks and Lands. Fees are collected at North Maine Woods checkpoints or at AWW ranger stations.

Relics of the logging area are found along the Tramway Carry between Chamberlain and Eagle Lakes. (Photo by NFCT)

Put in at Chamberlain Bridge and paddle the thoroughfare to enter Chamberlain Lake. At 11,084 acres, it is the largest lake in the Allagash chain. As you reach open water, the gray mass of Mount Katahdin rises to the southeast.

From afar, notice a small island and the promontory of Ledge Point on the western shoreline. Keep an eye out for a few outcrops of 400-million-year-old fossilized conglomerate white-and-gray pockmarked stone. The fossilized corals are a remnant from when the region was part of a warmer clime south of the equator. (See "Allagash Geology" sidebar in Maine overview for more.)

On the east shore, opposite Rocky Cove, a stand of birch marks the clearing at Nugent's Camps. This rustic sporting camp has been entertaining guests since 1936. Above the camp, keep your eyes peeled for a slab of ledge that pokes into the lake and conceals a pebble beach.

Beneath birch and pine, south of a point 3 miles beyond the camp, grass grows on old docks that mark the Chamberlain Farm site, once a prominent lumber depot built in the mid-1800s. The farmhouse, the only building still

THE TRAMWAY CARRY

If you're interested in seeing relics from the logging era and are willing to take a longer portage, continue up Chamberlain Lake another 3.5 miles past Lock Dam to the 0.5-mile Tramway Carry. The carry is located in the northern end of Chamberlain Lake. Pass between two points into a marshy cove. Look for a channel through the reeds that leads to an opening in the tree line marking the beginning of the Tramway Carry.

A few steps down the carry trail will find you walking back through history where you can pause to check out artifacts and reconstructions from a bygone era. From the take-out on Chamberlain Lake, you'll first pass the boilers that powered the tramway, then a cable-and-track conveyor system that carried logs between Eagle and Chamberlain Lakes from 1903 to 1907. As you continue, notice the cable and track camouflaged beneath the forest where more than forty pulp cars lay decaying. At the Eagle Lake end, you'll be dumbstruck by the sight of two massive engines that still reek of oil. At one time, the Eagle Lake & West Branch Railroad extended 13 miles south from Eagle Lake to Umbazooksus Lake and transported logs from 1927 to 1933. After viewing the locomotives, cross over a railroad track, where a wild assortment of rusting steel—such as freight beds, flywheels, and a propeller—lie resting. The Tramway Historic District is listed in the National Register of Historic Places.

standing, is owned by Nugent's and has been used as a cabin since the 1940s. The most noticeable shoreside relic is the remains of a boom towboat that was abandoned in 1913.

Farther north along the east shoreline, Lock Dam offers several spacious campsites and the easiest access to Eagle Lake. The small stream provides reliable water levels and flow for canoeists entering Eagle Lake via Martin Cove. Paddlers may also choose to access Eagle Lake following the historically significant Tramway Carry (see "The Tramway Carry" sidebar, this section).

From the Lock Dam Carry put-in, paddle past marsh grass and over lily pads as you emerge into Martin Cove. From the southeastern end of Eagle Lake, button-shaped Pillsbury Island fills the horizon. Pass to the west of the island, with Bear Mountain standing tall on the mainland. The Thoreau campsite, near a dish of ledge on the island's north end, is popular with paddlers.

Smith Brook, tucked away to the northeast of Pillsbury Island, offers endless exploration and a chance to see moose, deer, loons, and ospreys. Head upstream to find unique pinkish volcanic rock.

Heading north, you'll soon face the open expanse of Eagle Lake. White birches highlight the eastern shore. Keep your sights on the rounded summits of First and Second Ridges on the Pump Handle Peninsula. Pump Handle campsite, on the northwestern end, has a pebble beach that is visible for miles. Spend the night here and be lulled by loons and barred owls. The Lookout Trail begins behind the site and climbs to an exposed ledge with a view that spreads to the south.

Opposite the peninsula, head up Soper Brook for a marshy jaunt. On the north side of the outlet, find an old-growth stand of white pine, among which is a sugar maple estimated to be 170 years old. Paddle until you bump into a small waterfall.

Round the elevated headland that holds the Zeigler campsite. Snare Brook, at the north end of Eagle, offers another marsh to explore, where an early morning visit could reveal a moose, a heron, or even a black bear.

The northwest shore of Round Pond is cloaked in marsh. Expect to see loons and mergansers. Soon, you'll spot the thin steel line of Johns Bridge on the horizon.

Paddle under Johns Bridge and head into the marshy thoroughfare that leads to Churchill Lake (3720 acres). You'll pass reed grass, lily pads, and pale stumps. The thoroughfare is popular with moose, loons, ospreys, and bald eagles. The sandy spit of Scofield Point is ahead on your left.

Churchill Ridge is a defining feature on the lake, rising from its northern shore; head toward its westerly shoulder. The abrupt southern face of the ridge is a by-product of glaciation.

As you paddle between the High Bank and Jaws campsites on your way to Heron Lake, a sandy strip reaches from the western shore. Don't be surprised to see a great blue heron standing guard here.

Heron Lake is small. Listen to the rustle of poplar leaves as you swing around a bundle of stumps. Marsh grass on the northern shore is a popular feeding ground for moose. Paddle toward a dock to the left of Churchill Dam to take out.

SECTION 4

Allagash River: Churchill Dam to Umsaskis Lake

During the 1800s, Churchill Lake was reputed to grow the largest white pine in the state of Maine. The headwater lakes narrow at Churchill Dam, where the Allagash erupts into Chase Rapids, a 4-mile stretch of steady Class II water. End your day at Umsaskis Lake, where a layered ridgeline surrounds a boulder-and-ledge shore.

TRIP DISTANCE: 12 miles
TRIP DURATION: Allow 1–2 days
FLOW/SEASON: Churchill Dam releases water from 8:00 AM to 12:00 PM to maintain Chase Rapids. Below 500 CFS = low, 600–2000 CFS = recommended, 3500+ CFS = high.

DIRECTION OF CURRENT: South to north

PUT-IN: **Churchill Dam**, Churchill Dam Rd. Improved boat launch. Overnight parking. GPS: 46.493469°, −69.288763°

TAKE-OUT: **Umsaskis Lake Thoroughfare boat launch**, American Realty Rd. Hand carry access. Overnight parking. GPS: 46.614113°, −69.39361°

MAP: NFCT Map 12, Allagash Region (South)

PORTAGES (1): **Churchill Dam Carry**, 0.1 mile (wheelable)

HAZARDS: Chase Rapids are 4 miles of Class I–II rapids

OTHER ACCESS: None

CONTACT: North Maine Woods; Maine Bureau of Parks and Lands; Allagash Wilderness Waterway Foundation; NFCT Trip Planner

SERVICES: Shuttle service around Chase Rapids can carry gear, boats, and people for a fee.

CAMPING: Camping is first come, first served, and fee-based at designated sites within the AWW. Fees are collected at North Maine Woods checkpoints or at AWW ranger stations.

From the take-out above Churchill Dam, portage 0.1 mile along the road to put in just above Chase Rapids. Be sure to arrive before noon if you want to run the rapids. Flow is regulated May 1 through the end of October with daily water releases that provide a Class II run. However, the ranger will shuttle you and/ or your gear for a fee if you want to avoid Chase Rapids or paddle the rapids with an empty boat.

Allow extra time for a visit to the Churchill Depot History Center, adjacent to the ranger station on river-left, where you will see exhibits on the bustling logging community of Churchill Depot—including bateaux, a belly dump wagon, and a Sheffield Velocipede Car. The old building looming above the put-in on river-left is the boardinghouse, built in the 1920s.

Paddling away from the put-in, you'll hear the rumble of Chase Rapids and see a frothy horizon line. Land on the small island to scout the first drop. Experienced boaters generally boat-scout the remainder of Chase Rapids. The 4-mile stretch to the former Bissonnette Bridge site involves about twelve sets of Class I–II rapids, separated by quickwater or pools. The river is boulder strewn and requires your close attention to dodge rocks in favor of tongues.

Around Harrow Brook the tumult breaks for a moment to give you a chance to appreciate the conifer-and-birch-clad shore, where cedars lean in and pines tower over all else. At the turn of the twentieth century, Chase Rapids marked one of the last places that Maine's historic caribou herd was seen.

One last rapid drops you above the former Bissonnette Bridge. Pull ashore here to pick up gear if portaged by the ranger. Below Bissonnette it's a quick ride to Umsaskis Lake. You'll have to navigate a few riffles and gravel bars while you watch for moose, grebes, and jumping fish.

A golden evening in the Allagash. (Photo by Will Jeffries)

The river widens to a marsh that leads to Umsaskis. The tree line pulls away, and a variety of channels emerges. Soon a ridgeline appears guiding you to the lake.

Umsaskis Lake feels like a small oasis. Sheltered by an assortment of pointed ridgelines, the shore is characterized by a mix of boulders and marshes. The Ledges campsite offers a pebble beach for swimming and a ledge perch topped with mature pines where the sunset view is second to none.

Wild brook trout fishing is exceptional here. The shallow marshy northern end of Umsaskis provides a good place to view wildlife. The Umsaskis Lake Thoroughfare boat launch is on river-left, upstream of the bridge.

NFCT MAP 13: ALLAGASH REGION (NORTH)

Umsaskis Lake to St. John River

Along its northernmost reaches, the Allagash Wilderness Waterway (AWW) continues to live up to its renown for scenic, wildlife-rich paddling. Intriguing remnants from early logging days appear along the route in the forms of a breached dam, rusted Lombard log haulers sitting on the edge of the forest, and campsites bearing the names of bygone homesteads and river driving legends.

The natural beauty of the Allagash encourages both contemplation and awe. Ringed by mountains, wildlife-rich Round Pond is a peaceful evening destination. Little visited since the logging days, Musquacook Stream is a vast network of wetlands worth exploring, and no trip down the Allagash is complete without a few moments spent in wonderment at Allagash Falls.

The wide St. John River drains the top third of Maine and as a result is the defining feature of the northern landscape. The scenic quality of this rolling agricultural valley and the seasonal muscle of its river will surprise you. Expect to feel its push when wrapped in whitewater. Ledge regularly pokes from the St. John's shore as a grassy floodplain mixes with its high, eroded banks.

Lake to river to pond to river again: The Allagash goes on and on and on.
(Photo by Dean B. Bennett)

The St. John is quickly becoming famous for its muskellunge fishing. Although the nonnative muskie has greatly reduced local salmon and trout populations, this monstrous fish has become popular because of its size and ability to fight when hooked.

Check the AWW website when planning your trip, as numerous regulations apply to the waterway, including restrictions on boat size.

See NFCT Map 13 and the NFCT website for additional trip planning and navigational details. DeLorme's *The Maine Atlas and Gazetteer* is highly recommended when accessing any of the more remote boat launches.

SECTION 1

Allagash River: Umsaskis Lake to Michaud Farm

Long Lake and Round Pond offer open-water diversity to the Allagash's blend of deadwater, quickwater, and Class I. Easy progress allows time to enjoy this scenic corridor. Idyllic Round Pond is popular for its wildlife viewing and hiking. Below Musquacook Deadwater, the river widens and grows shallow.

TRIP DISTANCE: 34 miles

TRIP DURATION: Allow 2 days

FLOW/SEASON: Spring, summer, fall. Below 500 CFS = low, 600–2000 CFS = recommended, 3500+ CFS = high.

DIRECTION OF CURRENT: South to north

PUT-IN: Umsaskis Lake Thoroughfare, American Realty Rd. Hand carry access. Overnight parking. GPS: 46.614113°, –69.39361°

TAKE-OUT: Michaud Farm Ranger Station. Hand carry access. Overnight parking. GPS: 46.95189°, –69.196278°

MAP: NFCT Map 13, Allagash Region (North)

PORTAGES (1): Long Lake Dam Carry, 0.1 mile (not wheelable)

HAZARDS: Headwinds on Long Lake can slow you down.

OTHER ACCESS: Henderson Brook Bridge on Blanchette Rd. Hand carry access. Overnight parking. GPS: 46.76364°, –69.30524°

CONTACT: North Maine Woods; Maine Bureau of Parks and Lands; Allagash Wilderness Waterway Foundation; NFCT Trip Planner

SERVICES: Ranger stations are located at Umsaskis Thoroughfare, Round Pond, and Michaud Farm. Rangers can accept fees, provide information, and assist with emergencies.

CAMPING: Camping is first come, first served, and fee-based at designated sites within the AWW. Fees are collected at North Maine Woods checkpoints or at AWW ranger stations.

Despite being remote, the Allagash is surrounded by working timberlands, as this bridge for logging trucks shows. (Photo by John Klopfer)

Pass under the Umsaskis Thoroughfare Bridge and note the debris lodged under the steel crossbeams from the occasional spring days when the river rises to meet the bridge. Squeak between reed grass and alders to reach Long Lake. A forested ridge marks the southeast corner of this narrow lake that stretches for several miles. Cedars grow from a cobble shore, and the campsites have gravel beaches. Sandy spits highlight the northern end of the lake. Look for the sandy delta below a ridge where Chemquasabamticook Stream enters. Early morning visits here allow you to mingle with moose, deer, and waterfowl.

Passing through the marshy narrows leading to Harvey Pond, keep a watch on the grassy bank for freshwater mussel middens that are the work of mink, muskrat, or otters.

You'll see a horizon line and hear tumbling water as you approach the aging Long Falls Dam. Built in 1907, this dam was originally 700 feet long. Most folks use the 0.1-mile portage trail on river-right through the campsite, though under favorable conditions, it's possible to line by rock-hopping along the shore, river-left. *Caution: Spikes still protrude from the old timbers and are capable of piercing fragile hulls, which makes lining or paddling potentially dangerous.*

You'll encounter a few riffles above Cunliffe Island as hackmatack and spruce fir grow from shore and old birch and cedar lean toward the water. Several miles of quickwater pass, broken by occasional riffles. The channel snakes between rows of tall trees, and on a clear day the sun will brighten the layered shore and distant ridges.

As you round an eastward bend by Gamash Brook, a series of shoaly rips unwind. Soon, pass beneath Henderson Brook Bridge, another official access point to the AWW. Beyond the bridge, the river separates around grass and braided alder islands. Quiet water near the north channel is a good spot to see grebes, herons, ducks, and warblers.

Paddle by stately elms and maples as you pass below the high ridge that buttresses Round Pond. Moose tend to congregate at the inlet of the pond. If you spend the night camping on Round Pond, keep an ear out for howling coyotes and hooting barred owls.

Be sure to allow time to hike the trail up Round Pond Mountain. The Allagash River can be seen snaking its way through the wilderness below you as you follow the 2.5-mile trail leading up to a decommissioned fire tower.

Exit the pond through a set of Class I rips. Expect a series of riffles over the next several miles. As you round a bend past Croque Brook, the north slope of Round Pond Mountain drops to the shore.

A mature stand of silver maples marks the mouth of Musquacook Stream. The view up the stream reveals conifer-thick hills rising above a grassy wetland. The headwater lakes of the Musquacook watershed were dammed for log driving in the early 1900s. Below Musquacook Stream, several miles of deadwater unwind along the Allagash. Expect to see moose.

As Five Finger Brook pours into the channel, you'll pass one among several upcoming washes of eroded riverbank. In lower water, gravel bars begin to intensify here. A long-held practice on the lower Allagash, coined the "Maine guide stance," has the stern paddler standing up to gain a better perspective on the river ahead. Try it. It works!

A hundred yards upstream of the Cunliffe Depot campsite, river-right, and just south of a small waterfall, find a path up the grassy bank that leads to two abandoned Lombard log haulers.

You won't miss Michaud Farm Ranger Station, situated at the base of a long ridge on the river's edge. A set of Class I riffles drops you below the ranger cabin. The AWW asks that all paddlers sign out of the waterway here regardless of whether you are ending your trip or continuing on downstream.

SECTION 2

Allagash River: Michaud Farm to Allagash Village

The northern riverine forest below Michaud Farm and the dramatic 40-foot cascade of Allagash Falls are regional wonders. Taylor Camps and Moir Farm give you a window into the past of the lumber camps, settlers, and sporting camps that formed the Allagash community. Expect Class I and II riffles and whitewater. In low water the river becomes shallow.

TRIP DISTANCE: 17 miles

TRIP DURATION: Allow 1 day

FLOW/SEASON: Spring, summer, fall. Below 500 CFS = low, 600–2000 CFS = recommended, 3500+ CFS = high.

DIRECTION OF CURRENT: South to north

PUT-IN: Michaud Farm Ranger Station. Hand carry access. Overnight parking. GPS: 46.95189°, –69.196278°

TAKE-OUT: White Birch Landing, immediately upstream of Casey Rapids, town of Allagash. Private boat launch. Overnight parking. Launch fees. GPS: 47.083110°, –69.051295°

MAP: NFCT Map 13, Allagash Region (North)

PORTAGES (1): Allagash Falls Carry, 0.25 mile (mostly wheelable)

HAZARDS: Up to Class II rapids; Class V Allagash Falls (must be portaged)

OTHER ACCESS: Michaud Inn boat launch on Michaud Tote/Inn Rd. Hand carry access. Overnight parking. GPS: 47.070504°, –69.076777°

CONTACT: North Maine Woods; Maine Bureau of Parks and Lands; Allagash Wilderness Waterway Foundation; NFCT Trip Planner

SERVICES: Michaud Farm is a ranger station. Rangers answer questions and help with emergencies. The town of Allagash has lodging, camping, outfitters, and a diner.

CAMPING: Public campsites are first come, first served. Maine Bureau of Parks and Lands manages campsites within the AWW, and North Maine Woods manages sites outside of it. Fees are collected at North Maine Woods checkpoints or at AWW ranger stations. Fee-based camping at private White Birch Landing in the town of Allagash. Contact information is listed on the NFCT website.

Below Michaud Farm the river winds around a series of braided islands. A short distance downstream of the Taylor Landing campsite, a restored Henry Taylor Camps cabin sits overlooking the river from atop a high bank, river-right, behind one of the islands. Salvaged items from deteriorated camp structures, including components dating from the 1930s, have been incorporated into one refurbished log cabin that is open to the public. A crumbling remnant of Moir Farm, an old hay barn, is located nearby.

When the growl of the falls drifts upstream, look for a well-marked 0.25-mile portage on river-right in a grassy opening. Allagash Falls remains merely noise as the trail dips into the woods. You'll pass campsites on the right as rusty-needled paths sprout left toward the falls. When the boardwalk ends, follow a spur to the left to view the 40-foot falls. The waterfall slides over upturned slate through a series of scenic drops. Trees lean in from the edge of the ravine.

Put in at a pool at the base of the falls in quickwater. Below the falls the river widens and is spotted with rocks and occasional islands. You'll spend your time searching for the deepest channel.

Allagash Wilderness Waterway campsites are well marked and well maintained. (Photo by NFCT)

On this final stretch, steep ridges climb smoothly above the boulder-and-ledge shore. Around McGargle Rocks you'll hit a series of Class I rips as a finger of ledge runs along the left shore. Light-green deciduous leaves are in constant contrast to the forest green of conifer.

Another series of Class I–II rapids forms around Twin Brook Ledges, a slate outcrop that denotes the formal end of the AWW. The river begins to parallel Michaud Tote Road here.

A US Geological Survey (USGS) flow gauge is located near a set of Class I rips and the Michaud Inn boat launch. You'll begin to see homes as the shoreside forest turns young. Near the final bend, a worn trail leads up the steep bank to Two Rivers Lunch, a popular dining spot for locals and paddlers alike. Be sure to arrive before 3 p.m. The diner is open only for breakfast and lunch.

One last Class I rip (Casey Rapids) drops you at the Maine Route 161 bridge. In the early 1900s, Thomas Pelletier ran a ferry service here before the first wooden bridge was built in the 1940s. In later decades his daughter, Evelyn McBreairty, would welcome paddlers to "Pelletier Point" and regale them with tales from the Allagash River's working past. Evelyn passed away at age ninety-four in 2012.

The take-out for this section is at White Birch Landing (located on private property), river-left, at a bend on the peninsula about 0.2 miles before reaching the ME 161 bridge.

SECTION 3

St. John River: Allagash Village to Fort Kent

The St. John River carves a wide channel through a rolling agricultural valley. Having survived numerous dam proposals, this free-flowing segment of the St. John provides a memorable tour through the rural north. Expect quickwater topped off with a series of Class I–II rapids. This section ends at the Northern Forest Canoe Trail's (NFCT's) eastern terminus. **Note:** Landing on the Canadian shore is illegal. For border crossing information, see the Planning a Trip section.

TRIP DISTANCE: 28.5 miles

TRIP DURATION: Allow 2 days

FLOW/SEASON: The upper St. John is considered a spring run, yet if the Allagash River is good, you should be able to paddle the St. John; 3500+ CFS = runnable.

DIRECTION OF CURRENT: Southwest to northeast

PUT-IN: White Birch Landing, upstream of Casey Rapids, town of Allagash. Private boat launch. Overnight parking. Launch fees. GPS: 47.083110°, –69.051295°

TAKE-OUT: Riverside Park, 40 Dufour St., Fort Kent. Improved boat launch. Overnight parking. GPS: 47.255623°, –68.594976°

MAP: NFCT Map 13, Allagash Region (North)

PORTAGES (0): None

HAZARDS: Intermittent Class I–II rapids

OTHER ACCESS: Hartt Landing off Maine Route 161 on St. John River. Overnight parking. GPS: 47.19446°, –68.848395°

CONTACT: North Maine Woods; Greater Fort Kent Area Chamber of Commerce; NFCT Trip Planner

SERVICES: The town of Allagash has lodging, camping, outfitters, and a diner. St. Francis has an outfitter/campground, diner, and country store. Fort Kent has many services including groceries, lodging, and restaurants.

CAMPING: Fee-based camping at private White Birch Landing in the town of Allagash and Pelletier's Campground upstream of the confluence with the St. Francis River. Free camping at the Fort Kent Blockhouse. Contact information is listed on the NFCT website.

Navigate the maze of grassy islands that fills the confluence of the Allagash and St. John Rivers at the town of Allagash. Green hills to the north and a steep eroded bank to the south welcome you to the grand St. John River. Ridgeline tones are neatly segmented as the lower-elevation deciduous trees give way to the higher-reaching conifers. Watch for bald eagles, beavers, and waterfowl. As you near the outlet of Pelletier Brook, several gravel bars

ST. JOHN VALLEY HERITAGE TRAIL

The St. John Valley Heritage Trail is a rail-to-trail system in the former Fish River Railroad corridor, which was later taken over by the Bangor & Aroostook Railroad (B&A), a rail line that once transported goods and passengers across northern Maine. The trail is now managed by the Bureau of Parks and Lands.

Running between Fort Kent and St. Francis, this 17-mile trail passes through sections of thick woods and, at times, along the south bank of the St. John River. In the summer, the hard-packed gravel is shared by pedestrians and bicyclists.

About five miles west from the Fort Kent trailhead is a lean-to that can be used as a shelter or picnic site. Although the trail parallels Maine Route 161 for several miles, the mixed forest remains quiet and serene.

Nearing the trail's end in St. Francis is a historic railroad turntable preserved by St. Francis Historical Society. At one time, St. Francis was the end of the line for the B&A Railroad. The B&A turntable was made in 1904 and was used until the 1980s to turn an entire locomotive around. For more information visit maine.gov and search under multi-use rail trail for St. John Valley Heritage Trail.

mingle with ledge and rile the waters, creating up to Class II situations.

Class I–II Cross Rock Rapids develop below a knob of ledge marked with an old rusty logging chain. The upper St. John witnessed its final river drives in the 1940s, when trucks overtook the river as a means to move logs.

At Golden Rapids (Class I–II) the current squeezes between ledge and island, creating a set of standing waves. A second rip develops as the river returns to a single channel.

After a few miles of flatwater, you'll encounter another island as a sandy bank rises to river-left. Class I–II Rankin Rapids forms at the end of the island. On either shore forested ridges cradle a wide channel of grass and boulders.

Named for pioneering botanist and botanical artist Kate Furbish, Furbish's lousewort is found only on a 140-mile stretch of the St. John River and nowhere else. (Photo courtesy of Maine Natural Areas Program)

The youngest person known to have completed a Thru-Paddle celebrates with his parents at the eastern terminus kiosk. (Photo courtesy of the Bognet family)

A few more riffles roll over gravel bars as you approach Pelletier's Campground. If you're spending the night here, you'll be surprised by the clear and vibrant night sky that lends itself to stargazing. Downstream of the campground, islands covered in grass, conifers, and ledges denote the confluence with the St. Francis River.

Keep river-right, remaining on the US side of the St. John. From here to Fort Kent, the river is broad, passing through agricultural and timbered lands and flanked by ME 161. Interesting ledges and glacial rock formations line the shore closer to Fort Kent, and one last set of Class I whitewater greets you after a series of braided islands about six and a half miles from the finish. From here the river fluctuates between areas of quickwater, spinning circles of current alongside your hull, and moving flatwater. In low water, the river will be scratchy.

As the homes and businesses of Fort Kent take shape beneath layered hills, you'll pass under the green international bridge to New Brunswick, Canada. The sand and gravel boat launch just below the confluence with the Fish River is Riverside Park, where an NFCT kiosk marks the eastern terminus.

Fort Kent offers many services. Allow a little extra time on the way into town to visit the historic Fort Kent Blockhouse (see Resources). The state-owned two-story structure is built of square-hewn cedar logs, some of which measure over 19 inches in width, and the site is listed on the National Register of Historic Places. Camping is available nearby.

Thru-Paddler's Overview

Introduction by Nicole Grohoski, the first female Thru-Paddler (2006)

The Northern Forest Canoe Trail (NFCT) became an official water trail, complete with maps and signage, in the spring of 2006—the same year that Tom Perkins and I became the first pair to Thru-Paddle the current Trail (Donnie Mullen had completed an earlier route in 2000). For seven weeks, we paddled and portaged the same traditional trade routes used by Native Americans, First Nations, and early European settlers while traveling through the current working landscapes of the Northern Forest. This region, rich in human history and tradition, and abounding with natural wonders, is truly extraordinary to experience by paddle.

One might ask—and many have—"Why did you want to paddle the Trail?" This is an understandable question that I often ponder without really knowing the answer. I can say that, for me, the appeal of a trip like this lies in finding a daily rhythm away from the hustle and bustle of the "real world." Life is broken down into its simplest necessities—eating, sleeping, and moving from place to place, powered only by your own strength.

Since I had never paddled for more than five consecutive days on a canoe trip before, and I possessed few whitewater skills, I knew that I had much to learn prior to and during the trip. I also knew that common sense, humility, and pure determination would be just as important as a collection of paddling skills. While your level of proficiency will determine the ease with which you travel the NFCT, your level of motivation will affect your ability to complete it.

On the morning of my birthday, about halfway into the trip, I woke up knowing that we had a 3-mile portage ahead of us on a road that turned out to be unwheelable. Things perked up when we met a true Maine character who had been living on the secluded Rapid River for over forty years—good stories, advice, and free granola bars! We looked forward to an easy afternoon cruise on the Richardson Lakes, only to find ourselves bobbing up and down over large swells but determined to make headway all the same. We took a break on the shore's sunny beaches and spotted moose tracks among the driftwood (no moose, but we were lucky to see a complete rainbow). We found ourselves on a secluded island, with no mosquitoes, a clear sky, and a hearty dinner of mac and cheese followed by a birthday surprise for me: just-add-water blueberry cheesecake. While a day like this can be experienced by anyone traveling on the Trail, it is the succession of days and weeks of extraordinarily diverse circumstances that makes a Thru-Paddle remarkable.

The landscapes I experienced, the natural and cultural communities that enveloped me in their familiarity, the understanding of the historical significance of these routes, and the challenges and joys brought by the ever-changing waters were worth every minute, hour, and day of the forty-nine that I spent on the Trail.

END TO END

Thru-Paddling the NFCT is a challenging endeavor that requires considerable preparation beforehand and perseverance during the journey. It involves crossing large lakes, paddling upstream, and portaging for long distances. The trip is not for everyone, but for those dedicated enough to take on the challenge, it's an adventure that will provide inspiration and memories for a lifetime.

The most efficient Thru-Paddling direction is following the NFCT route west to east, which requires paddlers to ascend, or portage around, 162 upstream miles. Thru-Paddling from east to west involves more than 270 upstream miles including *beginning* your trip paddling the St. John and Allagash Rivers for the first 90 miles against a current. You'll also be more likely to encounter prevailing westerly winds. To date, the only person known to have Thru-Paddled "the wrong way" is Peter Macfarlane. After completing a "traditional" twenty-eight-day solo Thru-Paddle in May and June 2013, five years later he took on the task of Thru-Paddling the Trail in reverse—starting in Fort Kent, Maine. Despite the added challenges, Peter still finished a completely self-propelled adventure in twenty-eight days, arriving in Old Forge, New York, on June 10, 2018.

The following pages offer a brief overview of things to consider when planning an end-to-end expedition, but it is in no way complete. For comprehensive Trail advice and navigational directions, prospective Thru-Paddlers should pick up a copy of *The Northern Forest Canoe Trail Through-Paddler's Companion*, by Katina Daanen, who completed Thru-Paddles in 2011 and 2021. This resource documents the Trail in its entirety—from the western terminus to the eastern terminus—and covers everything from the perspective and unique needs of a Thru-Paddler, or anyone else looking for more tactical advice on following NFCT maps or using the FarOut app. The guidebook includes trip planning tips, information about challenging Trail segments—including navigating the rivers requiring upstream paddling—as well as detailed descriptions for every portage.

NFCT, Inc., celebrates and recognizes all paddlers who complete the entire Trail. Thru-Paddlers (self-propelled, integrated, and integrated downstream)

Wind and chop on the many large lakes along the Trail can impede travel. Smart paddlers allow extra time in their itinerary for short or zero-mileage days. (Photo by Aaron Black-Schmidt)

who follow the trail as a single expedition, and Section-Paddlers who complete the Trail over the course of several trips over multiple paddling seasons, can apply for recognition at the NFCT website.

SEASONAL CONSIDERATIONS

The season in which you decide to paddle will most likely be determined by your schedule. This century, ice-out on Moosehead Lake (one of the latest ice-outs across the NFCT) has fluctuated between April 15 and May 12. Late-season paddlers will encounter fewer bugs but also less reliable river levels. The ideal season and flow for downstream travel is noted in each section description earlier in the book.

Trip Duration

The NFCT has been completed in as few as twenty-one days (with three people paddling a Wenonah Minnesota III canoe in 2012) and as many as fifty-five days when traveling west to east. The time that it will take each boat to paddle the length of the Trail depends on many factors, including water conditions (levels and flow), weather, physical preparedness, group size, rest days, where you decide to camp, your ability to minimize portage trips, and your decision to accept or decline portaging help from passing motorists. Your personal reasons for paddling the Trail are also important to consider—your trip will be shorter if your goal is to set a speed record than if it is to bird-watch or fish.

Paddle for a couple of hours or a couple of decades on the Northern Forest Canoe Trail . . . The wonder never fades. (Photo by John Klopfer)

Nicole Grohoski and Tom Perkins began in the second week of May 2006 and finished the last week of June. With seven rest days (including a three-day wait for weather to change before crossing Lake Champlain), the journey took forty-nine days. They benefited from high water (except when traveling upstream) and avoided dragging boats through or portaging around shallow areas. They were also graced with warm swimming weather for a good portion of the trip and were able to avoid some of the bugs for which Maine is infamous.

Alexander Martin, who paddled from late April to the end of May 2007, comments, "We started during ice-out and ended just at the start of blackfly season, getting ourselves mixed up in a bit more of the former than of the latter. Despite all the rain, freezing-cold weather, and swollen rivers we encountered, this may be the optimum season for hitting the Trail as a Thru-Paddler."

Peter and Mariana Du Brul paddled from mid-August to early October in 2007 and experienced less rain and fewer bugs as well as more easily poled or lined upstream sections. However, many downstream sections were too shallow to paddle and, when reflecting on dragging the boat along the river bottom and walking on slippery rocks, Peter writes, "This was really the only time we could have come, but if I'd known it would be so bad I'm not sure we would have." On the other hand, international adventurers Zoë Agasi and Olivier Van Herck paddled the same time of year in 2018 and list several reasons they think beginning a trip in August was best: fewer bugs, an abundance of ripe berries and apples, warmer water with less current to fight going upstream, and having the Allagash almost entirely to themselves.

Beginning a Thru-Paddle on the Trail any earlier than April or later than September would be inadvisable due to weather conditions in the Northern Forest;

however, a six-month, paddle-friendly time range should provide ample opportunity to determine your ideal paddling conditions and desired pace, and thus allow you to plan your trip timeline.

ON THE TRAIL

The decisions you make on the NFCT will be informed by maps, apps, books, and common sense. Once your life becomes confined to a 17-foot vessel, it is one primarily defined by weather, water conditions, and your motivation. A Thru-Paddle is a journey that you create. Some days might be maddening; others will be magnificent. Two logistical challenges for the Thru-Paddler, once on the Trail, are navigation and the number and length of the portages required to complete the journey.

Navigation

Part of the Thru-Paddling experience that differs significantly from that of a Section-Paddler is the direction of travel. NFCT maps and this official guidebook describe all river segments in the downstream direction, but if you are conducting your Thru-Paddle as an NFCT-designated Self-Propelled trip in one continuous west–east direction, this means traveling 162 miles upstream. Thus, you will need to interpret some of these map descriptions for upstream travel. (Integrated Thru-Paddlers complete the entire trail in one journey, but use shuttles in order to paddle some, or all, of the miles encountered upstream, in downstream segments.)

Navigating upstream travel can be confusing because it is often unclear which branch or channel to choose. One piece of helpful advice for paddling upstream in a marsh with many channels: look at the plants on the river bottom to see from where the current flows.

Significant segments of upstream travel include:
- Missisquoi River and its North Branch, Vermont and Québec: 73.3 miles (NFCT Maps 4 and 5)
- Clyde River, Vermont: 30 miles (NFCT Map 6)
- Upper Ammonoosuc River, New Hampshire: 22 miles (NFCT Map 7)
- Androscoggin River, New Hampshire: 19 miles (NFCT Map 7)
- Spencer and Little Spencer Streams, Maine: 6 miles (NFCT Map 10)

While competent river-reading and map-reading skills will help you navigate difficult sections of Trail, good judgment and a willingness to turn around and try again are also important.

Portaging

The NFCT includes 70-plus miles of portaging (65 individual portages in all), mainly between watersheds and around hazards. The number of miles you actually traverse on foot depends on your efficiency (two trips of gear along a

There's fun to be found in portaging—you just have to know how to approach it. (Photo by Katina Daanen)

3-mile trail become 9 miles of walking) and water levels. The South Branch of the Dead River in Maine (NFCT Map 9) is often "dead" by early summer. Paddlers may find themselves portaging another 14 miles or more following Maine Route 16 to Stratton. A good set of portage wheels (almost indispensable for a kayak) can eliminate the need for multiple trips along roads and well-maintained trails; however, there are many portages that require overhead carrying.

If you haven't done a lot of portaging before your Thru-Paddle, taking a couple of short practice trips will give you a chance to try some different techniques and equipment, which can prevent a lot of frustration once you're on the Trail.

Weather

Weather patterns in the Northeast can be unpredictable and sometimes extreme. Be prepared mentally and physically for anything. Weather will affect the logistics of your trip in three important ways: water volume, wind, and lightning. You will have to decide if whitewater conditions are appropriate to paddle on a case-by-case basis. You may need to improvise portages based on high- or low-water conditions. Wind will often make crossing lakes unpleasant or dangerous. Plan your route carefully to maximize lee regions and avoid large waves. While less common, lightning will require you to take a break or set up camp early.

PADDLING AND BOAT-HANDLING SKILLS

Strong paddling skills are essential for a successful Thru-Paddle. Do not attempt the NFCT without being proficient at all types of paddling, navigation, rescue techniques, portaging, and camping. That being said, much can be learned through experience on the Trail. The NFCT affords plenty of opportunity to hone skills while covering 700 miles of varied types of water—from large exposed lakes, to whitewater, to shallow streams—and more than 70 miles of varied types of portage terrain—from paved roads, to muddy trails, to near bushwhacks.

Flatwater

The NFCT crosses the tenth-largest naturally occurring freshwater lake by area in the United States, Lake Champlain. This lake, as well as many other large lakes along the Trail, poses a significant challenge in most weather conditions. Because of low water temperatures during much of the paddling season and the difficulty of righting a capsized boat in open water, it is imperative to know how to control your boat in wind and waves and to know when the conditions necessitate staying on shore. In the unfortunate event of a capsize, single-boat Thru-Paddlers should be familiar with self-rescues (such as a flip or a shake-out) and multi-boat groups should feel comfortable with the boat-over-boat (T-rescue) technique. Contact the American Canoe Association (see Resources) for paddling technique and boating safety classes.

Moving Water

Downstream paddling on moving water is perhaps one of the most enjoyable ways to experience the Trail. With changing scenery, more abundant wildlife, and a bit of helpful current, your downriver paddling may seem luxurious compared to the other challenges of the Trail. Upstream paddling is more challenging, but your ability to read moving water, locate weaker currents, and recognize faint eddy lines will significantly reduce your efforts, as will keeping your boat parallel to the current.

Whitewater

The NFCT includes sections of whitewater ranging from Class I riffles to Class IV rapids, with portages around all falls and dams. (See "River Difficulty Ratings" in the Planning a Trip section for definitions.) Rapids should be run at your discretion, based on your experience and current water levels; it is always advisable to scout unfamiliar whitewater. Nearly all Class III and all Class IV rapids have established portage trails, and it is usually possible to line a boat along the shore or bushwhack to avoid paddling; adjacent roads sometimes provide another portaging option. For more serious whitewater, an empty boat is more responsive and easier to self-rescue in case of a flip so consider portaging your gear before running difficult rapids. Paddlers should be competent at swift-water rescue, freeing pinned boats, avoiding strainers, and handling gear-laden capsized or swamped boats.

Upstream whitewater paddling poses an additional challenge to Thru-Paddlers. In heavy currents, it is often necessary to carry or line boats; shallow areas will often require pulling or poling your boat. You will be able to eddy-hop up some rapids, though you should always be prepared to jump in and out of your boat in order to maintain ground against changing conditions. Upstream paddling is often tough going; be prepared to traverse fewer miles each day as you travel these segments.

Lining and Tracking
Your boat will need to be outfitted with painters (bow and stern lines) in order to ease it downstream (lining) or pull it upstream (tracking). You can line/track a boat alone or with a partner, keeping the boat aligned with the current, while being wary of slippery rocks. Agility and willingness to wade are necessary, as is maintaining a knot-free line. Lining and tracking can be difficult but are often necessary to avoid portaging or impossible upstream paddling.

Poling
If you're paddling the Trail in a canoe, you may want to consider bringing a strong and light wood or aluminum pole around 12 feet in length, preferably outfitted with a shoe for traction, in order to ascend shallow streams. Solo poling from just aft of the boat's center is the best way to learn the skill, but you can also pole from the stern with a bow paddler. A pole can either be planted on the streambed or used like a paddle; it can also be used when traveling downstream, in the practice of snubbing. It is best to be adept at this skill before embarking on the NFCT if you plan to rely on it.

GEAR AND EQUIPMENT
In addition to paddling skills, you will need appropriate equipment to complete a Thru-Paddle on the Trail. A synthesis of equipment considerations can be found in this section. (See also the Paddler's Checklist in the Introduction.)

Canoe or Kayak?
Both canoes and kayaks—and even at least one paddleboard—have successfully been used on Thru-Paddle trips. However, the gear demands and varied water conditions of the Trail make the canoe the most versatile boat of choice. (**Note:** The Allagash Wilderness Waterway (AWW) has rules governing boat sizes, particularly kayaks and paddleboards. Check with Maine Bureau of Parks and Lands for regulations.)

For traditional paddlers, a wood-and-canvas boat (with a repair kit) is a good choice; for those looking for a sturdy and durable boat, a modern material that includes ABS plastic, like T-Formex (or Royalex), is preferable. Other Thru-

Solid whitewater paddling skills and adaptability are necessary to complete a Thru-Paddle trip. (Photo by Chris Gill)

Paddlers use boats made of lighter materials like Kevlar and graphite, which will get beat up on boulder-strewn rivers.

A tandem boat should be around 17 feet in length (a solo boat would be a bit shorter), able to comfortably carry both packed gear and paddlers, and able to be portaged. A canoe needs to track well while still maintaining maneuverability in whitewater. You could paddle a decked canoe or one with a spray skirt, but consider the ease of getting into and out of a boat quickly when you are traveling upstream—you will need to walk or line your boat often and without losing ground in the process.

Once you have selected your boat, you will need to outfit it with the following:

- Painters about the length of the boat (or longer, if you are comfortable with the skill of lining)
- Additional line for tying down gear or freeing a pinned boat
- Flotation bags (if you plan to tackle the more challenging whitewater)
- Skid plates on the bow and stern (optional)
- A comfortable portage yoke for trails that cannot be wheeled
- Portage wheels
- Bailer
- Throw bag
- Repair hardware

Your boat will also need to hold drybags or other waterproof containers for camping gear, electronics, and food. And regardless of whether you choose to paddle a canoe or kayak, every paddler needs to wear a properly fitting, Coast Guard–approved personal flotation device (PFD).

Navigational Tools

At a minimum, every boater should carry NFCT maps and a compass. The guidebooks and NFCT FarOut app are intended to supplement the official maps, not replace them. A GPS tracking device, US Geological Survey (USGS) topographic maps, and/or *AMC River Guide* books for each state may also be helpful.

Paddles

Each paddler will need a paddle, and each boat will need a spare. A bent-shaft paddle increases the efficiency of each stroke, which will pay off over the distance of the Trail. However, you may choose a straight-shaft paddle for familiarity or aesthetics. Be sure that the paddle grip is comfortable and that the length is appropriate. A carbon-fiber paddle will also reduce your effort on flatwater, though you will need a more durable alternative for whitewater.

Camping

Although lodging is sometimes available along the Trail, you must be prepared to camp along many segments. Some campsites are on private land, some on public; NFCT maps and the *Through-Paddler's Companion* will provide the details about location, regulations, and use. Before you go, check the online NFCT Trip Planner to learn about campsites that have been established or closed since the maps were printed. Regardless, you must know how to set up your tent, cook, build a fire, hang a bear bag, treat water, and dispose of human waste, all while following Leave No Trace principles (see Introduction for principles, and Resources for Leave No Trace contact information).

For camping, you'll of course need all the basics listed in the Planning A Trip chapter. You'll also need:

- Tent with fly and ground cloth
- Tarp(s), for keeping gear dry and for making shelter
- Sleeping bag and pad
- Stove and cookware
- Extra rope
- Warm, dry clothing for camp

While unnecessary for the NFCT, other more traditional items—ax or hatchet, reflector oven, wannigans, packs with tump-straps—contribute to a wilderness-tripping aesthetic. A cooler for food storage and a solar shower may make your journey more pleasant, but be aware: *everything* will need to be carried during some parts of your trip.

Food

Food is, for obvious reasons, an important consideration when planning a Thru-Paddle on the NFCT. Fortunately, the Trail passes through, or near, forty-five communities, allowing frequent food resupplies. Some communities

Some call it gear, others call it stuff. Thru-Paddlers need to plan and pack it carefully. (Photo courtesy of Northstar Canoes)

support grocery stores while others may not even have a general store. It is usually possible to resupply every few days; however, the longest stretch of the NFCT with few amenities is 165 miles in Maine, from Jackman to the town of Allagash. Jackman is the last town with a grocery store before reaching Fort Kent.

Because of the number of portages along the route, it is advisable to keep food weight to a minimum. Buy less and buy often—shopping in local stores rather than relying on mail drops supports the local economy, saves money, allows more freedom in your itinerary, and increases freshness and variety.

THE END

Thru-Paddling is an individual experience. The unique set of water conditions you encounter have never, and will never, occur exactly alike again. The choices of daily mileages, campsites, whitewater lines, food and equipment, paddling partners, when to paddle or rest are yours and yours alone.

Whether you complete the NFCT as a Thru-Paddler on a single long journey or as a Section-Paddler experiencing the Trail little by little over many seasons, your journey will be like no one else's. The NFCT organization wants to hear about your experiences on the Trail and to celebrate your accomplishment. See the "Plan a Trip" section of the NFCT website for details about paddler recognition categories and the application form, and to find links to other Thru- and Section-Paddlers' blogs.

Suggested Trips

So much trail, so little time! Here are a few recommendations for trying out a paddle on Northern Forest Canoe Trail (NFCT) waters in each state or province. These itineraries are a good starting point for beginners, families interested in sampling several hours on a waterway, or those looking for overnight camping trips, as well as for those ready to tackle a larger adventure.

The suggested trips are limited to those with difficulty ratings of novice or moderate, and the info blocks include additional details that can enhance your visit to a particular Trail section. Use the online NFCT Trip Planner to view the route and landmarks as well as to find a comprehensive listing of available services (and contact information) and any changes to the Trail that may have occurred since this book was published. And no matter how long or short you plan to be out on the water, always let someone know where you are going and how long you expect to be gone, wear your PFD, and carry the Ten Essentials.

Generally speaking, expect to find higher water levels as well as more insects earlier in the season. Blackflies, those pesky defenders of wilderness, are present from ice-out to well into summer throughout most sections of the NFCT. Late summer and fall may offer more relief from biting insects, but expect more competition for popular campsites. Where possible, it's a good idea to reserve a site in advance or build a plan B into your float plan.

NEW YORK

Adirondack Adventure: Long Lake to Axton Landing

This trip takes you into the heart of New York State's Adirondack Park following the historic path of Iroquois trappers and their birch bark canoes. It offers a good multiday itinerary for those wanting to test their canoe-camping and portaging skills. Dozens of free water-access-only campsites and lean-tos can be found along the entire route.

High winds can be a hazard on any trip, especially on a large lake, so be prepared for that here too. But what is more likely to bump this trip up in difficulty is the 1-mile Raquette Falls Carry circumventing the falls. It includes

The Adirondacks offer a perfect introduction to NFCT waterways with remote rivers, mountain-ringed lakes, and plentiful free campsites (Photo by NFCT)

some hilly terrain and is rocky. Using portage carts (wheels) can be difficult on the rugged trail.

The trip starts at the state boat launch near the hamlet of Long Lake, where overnight parking is permitted. Most paddlers choose to spend the first night on the lake, heading into the wild Raquette River on the second day. Long Lake can be choppy, especially at its northern end near the river outlet. From there, paddlers head north into Raquette River, a remote, winding, slow-moving river with little to no shoreline development.

A well-signed mandatory portage warns paddlers of Raquette Falls. Although the portage is long, a nice swimming hole awaits you at the end of it. A lean-to as well as a beautiful dispersed camping area and a New York State Department of Environmental Conservation (NYSDEC) caretaker's cabin are also located here. Be sure to make time to visit the falls before returning to the river. A marked riverside trail leads through the pine forest where you can view several picturesque drops.

From Raquette Falls, the river continues to meander through silver maple and hemlock forests. Take out at Axton Landing or continue another 5 miles to end your trip at the Crusher boat launch. Overnight parking is permitted at both take-outs. This trip can even be extended another day, ending at the NYSDEC boat launch at Tupper Lake—however, overnight parking is not permitted there.

For more trip information, see Section 1 in the Map 2 chapter, New York.

Great Reasons to Take This Trip
- Remote paddling experience after leaving Long Lake
- Plentiful free campsites and lean-to options
- Picturesque Raquette Falls

TRIP DISTANCE: 21.7 miles (add another 0.5 mile if launching from the town beach)

TRIP DURATION: Allow 2–3 days

WATERBODY TYPE(S): 1 lake and 1 river (flows south to north to Stony Creek then east to west to Tupper Lake)

DIFFICULTY: Moderate

MAP: NFCT Map 2

PUT-IN: Long Lake boat launch, 88 Dock Rd., Long Lake. Improved boat launch. Overnight parking (use auxiliary lot). GPS: 43.978813°, −74.416154°; **Long Lake town beach,** 1258 Main St., Long Lake. Hand carry access. Overnight street parking. GPS: 43.974244°, −74.423943°

TAKE-OUT: Axton Landing. Gravel ramp at end of dirt road, with parking and primitive campsite up the hill. Overnight parking. GPS: 44.20354°, −74.326626°

HAZARDS: Late-morning and afternoon wind on Long Lake

PORTAGES (1): Raquette Falls Carry, 1 mile. This rutted, rocky portage is challenging with a wheeled cart. Expect to carry in places.

OTHER ACCESS: None until the end. See Extend Your Trip below.

BEST TIME TO GO: May through early October

CONTACT: Town of Long Lake Parks & Recreation; Tupper Lake; NYSDEC Region 5; NFCT Trip Planner

SERVICES: Restaurants, groceries, and lodging in Long Lake and Tupper Lake

CAMPING: Free primitive NYS DEC campsites and lean-tos are plentiful and available first come, first served.

CELL SERVICE: Dependent upon the carrier, service is unreliable on Long Lake and throughout much of this section.

EXTEND YOUR TRIP: Add 6 miles when you go to the **Crusher boat launch.** Hard-surface launching ramp with parking for 20 cars and trailers. Overnight parking. GPS: 44.239208°, −74.388628°; or add a total of 15 miles to the **Tupper Lake boat launch** on New York Route 30. No overnight parking. GPS: 44.196712°, −74.483716°

SEE AND DO MORE: Hike a section of the Northville–Placid Trail or visit the WILD Center in Tupper Lake.

Round the Mountain: Lower Saranac Lake to Lake Flower

This family-friendly (almost) loop begins and ends near the scenic village of Saranac Lake. It can be completed as a day trip or turned into an overnight adventure. The trip follows a portion of the same route used by race participants in the annual 'Round the Mountain Canoe & Kayak Race hosted by the Northern Forest Canoe Trail (NFCT) each May.

There are no portages, but you'll need to get back to your car at the end of your trip. Arrange for a shuttle, or walk or bike the 1.3-mile distance between the Ampersand Bay put-in and the Lake Flower take-out.

Highlights of this trip include landmark Bluff Island (known for cliff jumping) and passing through a set of historic hand-operated locks on the Saranac River. The fishing is excellent.

Saranac Lake Islands State Park offers dozens of water-access-only campsites, many of which are on islands, amidst pristine waters surrounded by the Adirondack High Peaks. Be sure to reserve your campsite. Popular sites book early. Boats can be rented and shuttles arranged in the village of Saranac Lake.

For more trip information, see Section 2 in the Map 2 chapter, New York.

Great Reasons to Take This Trip
* Charm of passing through an eighteenth-century hand-operated lock
* One of few NFCT trips that begins and ends (almost) at the same location

TRIP DISTANCE: 11 miles

TRIP DURATION: Allow 1–2 days

WATERBODY TYPE(S): 3 lakes, 2 ponds, 1 river (current flows west to east)

DIFFICULTY: Novice

MAP: NFCT Map 2

PUT-IN: Ampersand boat launch on Bayside Dr., Saranac Lake, with a small parking area. GPS: 44.325826°, −74.154389°

TAKE-OUT: NFCT kiosk on Kiwassa Rd., **Saranac Lake**. Overnight parking available at Dorsey Street parking lot or behind the police station at 3 Main St. GPS: 44.323832°, −74.131104°

HAZARDS: Afternoon wind and waves on the lakes

PORTAGES (1): 1.3-mile return by road to starting point. This can be driven by car as a shuttle.

OTHER ACCESS: Second Pond boat access (Saranac Lake Islands state campground headquarters) from New York Route 3. Overnight parking. GPS: 44.287367°, −74.184779°

TIME TO GO: April ice-out to November freeze-up

CONTACT: Adirondack Park Agency; New York State Department of Environmental Conservation (NYSDEC) Region 5; New York State Parks Reserve America; NFCT Trip Planner

SERVICES: Many services, including restaurants, lodging, and an outfitter in Saranac Lake

CAMPING: Saranac Lake Islands state campground (Lower Saranac Lake), fee and by reservation only. State park sites are dispersed throughout Lower Saranac Lake. Some free, first-come, first-served sites are available between Second Pond and the Lower Locks, and on Kiwassa Lake.

CELL SERVICE: Unreliable to nonexistent. Only Saranac Lake Village has coverage, dependent upon the carrier.

SEE AND DO MORE: Hike and bag one or more of the forty-six Adirondack High Peaks. Shop, dine, or sample craft beer in the village of Saranac Lake.

VERMONT

Missisquoi River Paddle

The number (and length) of portages, and the presence of occasional white-water, may push this itinerary beyond the comfort of a novice paddler. However, the Missisquoi River can be easily divided into shorter day trips that avoid many of the carries and most of the whitewater.

The appeal of completing this trip as an expedition is due in part to the numerous Vermont towns the Trail passes through as well as the location of well-positioned free, first-come, first-served campsites. Thanks to the cooperation of riverside landowners, paddlers are able to enjoy full access from the river's border crossing at East Richford to its outlet on Lake Champlain. Stopping at a village for a burger or a Creemee (Vermont's version of soft-serve ice cream) holds its own magnetism.

From Richford, you'll paddle a section of the Missisquoi that is designated a Wild and Scenic River, descending over ledges, through pastoral farm-lands, and within the shadow of Jay Peak. From Enosburg Falls to Swanton, a series of dams now tames the formerly feistier river, drowning gorges and rapids. The river is generally placid, and quiet impoundments are flanked

The Missisquoi River meanders its way through Vermont and Québec with easy options for either day or overnight trips. (Photo by Chris Gill)

by beeches, maples, cedars, and hemlocks. Marked and maintained portage trails have been established around all these human-designed obstacles but not around occasional ledges and other water hazards. Paddlers will need to either line, run, or avoid them by using local roads or the adjacent Missisquoi Valley Rail Trail (MVRT), a multi-use recreational trail extending from Richford to Sheldon Springs.

Because much of this section flows through agricultural lands, it is important that paddlers carry drinking and cooking water. It is not advisable to pump or filter water from this river.

This excursion can be extended by either beginning at the border or ending on Lake Champlain, or both. Above Richford, the Missisquoi flows more briskly over shallow riffles, around braided islands, and over Class II rapids. Below Swanton, the river slows into a waterfowl-rich delta.

For more trip information, see Sections 2 and 3 in the Map 4 chapter and Section 2 in the Map 5 chapter, Vermont.

Great Reasons to Take This Trip

- Multiple-day expedition following a generally placid river with well-placed, free campsites
- Trip traverses the entire Vermont NFCT section of the Missisquoi River

TRIP DISTANCE: 40 miles

TRIP DURATION: Allow 3–4 days

WATERBODY TYPE(S): 1 river (current flows east to west)

DIFFICULTY: Moderate (some segments within this trip are suitable for novices)

MAP: NFCT Maps 4 and 5

PUT-IN: Davis Park, below the rapids on River St. in Richford. Hand carry access. Overnight parking. GPS: 44.997901°, –72.676214°

TAKE-OUT: Above Swanton Dam by Vermont Route 78. Hand carry access. Overnight parking across the street at Marble Mill Park. GPS: 44.92001°, –73.127563°

HAZARDS: Magoon Ledges, Samsonville Ledges, Enosburg Ledges, Class II–III Abbey Rapids, and East Highgate Ledges; and all areas above and below dams

PORTAGES (3): Signed carries are established around all dams. Abbey Rapids is avoidable by using the MVRT as a portage option. See NFCT maps and the FarOut app for details.

OTHER ACCESS: See individual chapters earlier in this guidebook and the NFCT maps for more details about many additional access points.

BEST TIME TO GO: Spring and summer when water levels are highest. The river becomes scratchy in places, notably above Richford, in late summer and during periods of low water.

CONTACT: NFCT Trip Planner

SERVICES: Larger communities of Richford, Enosburg Falls, and Swanton offer lodging, restaurants, and groceries. Other services like

Creemee stands and convenience stores are also found along this section. There currently is no established shuttle service that will get you back to your car.

CAMPING: Free first-come, first-served NFCT primitive campsites: Coons, Leatherneck Landing, Believe It or Not, Doe, Brownway, Lawyer's Landing, Lussier, and Highgate

CELL SERVICE: Dependent upon area and carrier

EXTEND YOUR TRIP: This trip can be extended by beginning at the border behind the **United States Customs and Border Protection station**, 1683 Glen Sutton Rd., East Richford. Hand carry access. No overnight parking. GPS: 45.011145°, –72.588076°; or you can end at **Louie's Landing** in the Missisquoi National Wildlife Refuge on VT 78. Overnight parking. GPS: 44.958513°, –73.166566°; or end at **Sandy Point boat launch** (on the east side of the VT 78 bridge spanning the entrance to Missisquoi Bay). 72-hour parking. GPS: 44.970612°, –73.210439°

SEE AND DO MORE: Bike the MVRT and/or the Lamoille Valley Rail Trail (LVRT).

Wildlife-Rich Upper Clyde River Day Trip

In Vermont's Northeast Kingdom lies the village—and the lake—of Island Pond. Island Pond serves as the headwaters for the Clyde River, which flows 40 miles northwest to Lake Memphremagog. The area is rich in wildlife and is known for its abundant and diverse fisheries hosting trout, salmon, bass, and many other species. Island Pond and its environs make a perfect destination for anglers and paddlers in search of off-the-beaten-path lakes and running streams.

This day trip begins in the town of Island Pond. Put in either at the town park, entering the Clyde by paddling *under* Route 105 and a historic inn, or put in at an informal hand carry access behind the inn.

The Clyde originates as a shallow, narrow meandering stream, and this section holds two short sections of Class I–II water features. Expect to cross down trees and numerous beaver dams within the first 3 miles above the Five Mile Square boat access. If the water level is low enough, paddle through "The Tubes" and take out at the launch downstream of them. Five Mile Square Road is close enough to Island Pond, and the shoulder along Vermont Route 105 is wide enough that a bike could be staged and used for shuttling back to your car. However, this can be a busy highway with fast-moving vehicles.

Below Five Mile Square Road, you will enter the maze-like wetland known as a fen. Look for ospreys that nest in the area. The Clyde becomes more pondlike above Ten Mile Square Road where another public access is located.

Camping within this section is limited to the NFCT NorthWoods Landing, a small primitive campsite without any facilities, situated between Five Mile

Square and Ten Mile Square Roads. Lodging and additional campgrounds are available near the village of Island Pond.

Down trees, beaver dams, and the presence of whitewater above Five Mile Square Road pushes this trip more toward a moderate level of difficulty. Paddlers may also find the navigational complexity of the fen to be challenging. Service information for this itinerary is listed on the NFCT website. For more trip information, see Section 1 in the Map 6 chapter, Vermont.

Great Reasons to Take This Trip

- Small, intimate river with undeveloped shorelines and good opportunities to observe waterfowl and wildlife
- The fen, a unique bog community home to some rare plants
- Unusual experience of paddling under an inn and/or through huge culverts known as "The Tubes"

TRIP DISTANCE: 3 or 7.5 miles

TRIP DURATION: Allow a half to full day

WATERBODY TYPE(S): 1 river (current flows east to west)

DIFFICULTY: Novice to moderate

MAP: NFCT Map 6

PUT-IN: Lakeside Park in the village of Island Pond. Public dock and hand carry access. Overnight parking. GPS: 44.813713°, –71.879906°

TAKE-OUT(S): Five Mile Square Rd. ("The Tubes") on VT 105. Hand carry access. 72-hour parking. GPS: 44.801612°, –71.914849°; or **Ten Mile Square Rd.** adjacent to VT 105 bridge. Gravel boat ramp with 72-hour parking. GPS: 44.827662°, –71.973852°

HAZARDS: Class I–II short boulder garden and breached timber dam; down trees and numerous beaver dams above Five Mile Square Rd.

PORTAGES (0–2): None, but paddlers may choose to carry around the remnants of a breached timber dam. "The Tubes" may need to

be portaged in high water but only if continuing on to Ten Mile Square Rd.

OTHER ACCESS: None

BEST TIME TO GO: Early spring and summer when water levels are highest

CONTACT: Vermont Agency of Natural Resources; NorthWoods Stewardship Center; NFCT Trip Planner

SERVICES: Restaurants, lodging, and supplies in Island Pond

CAMPING: Private lakeside camping at Island Pond; Brighton State Park at nearby Spectacle Pond; fee-free NFCT NorthWoods Landing above Ten Mile Square Rd.

CELL SERVICE: Dependent upon carrier

SEE AND DO MORE: Hike the Bluff Mountain Community Trail in Island Pond with views of the Nulhegan basin and surrounding hills. Mountain bike or hike the Kingdom Trails. Sign up for a class or summer camp at the NorthWoods Stewardship Center.

QUÉBEC

North Branch Missisquoi River/Missisquoi River Day Trip

This calm, recreationally maintained river follows an ancient Abenaki waterway through hilly valleys. From the public boat launch located southwest of Mansonville (Potton Township), paddlers meander around North Branch Missisquoi oxbows flanked by silver maples before joining the main Missisquoi River channel near Highwater. The section offers plenty of beautiful places for swimming, fishing, and picnicking. Swiftwater near the put-in, a derelict bridge abutment responsible for a short Class I run (up to Class II in high water), and a section of up to Class I quickwater just before arriving at the takeout at Canoe & Co. provides the only action in this otherwise easy-flowing river. Trip durations range from 3 to 5 hours or longer. A passport and border crossing are necessary for visiting this section if not a Canadian citizen.

There is no public take-out at the Glen Sutton bridge. Plan on parking (for a small fee) at privately owned Canoe & Co. or booking a shuttle with them if using your own vessel. Talk with the outfitter about other put-in and take-out options for a shorter trip. Service information for this section is listed on the NFCT website.

For more trip information, see Section 1 in the Map 5 chapter, Québec.

Great Reasons to Take This Trip
- Liveries with boat rentals and shuttles at either end of this segment
- Village of Mansonville: A historic town with signed architectural walking tour and tempting restaurants

TRIP DISTANCE: Options between 7 and 15 km (4.4 to 9.3 miles)

TRIP DURATION: Allow a half to full day

WATERBODY TYPE(S): 1 river (current flows east to west)

DIFFICULTY: Novice

MAP: NFCT Map 5

PUT-IN: Mansonville launch on Québec Route 243. Hand carry. No overnight parking. Local liveries can provide shuttle assistance. GPS: 45.045146°, −72.396605°

TAKE-OUT: Canoe & Co. (private access), 1120 Chemin Burnett, Sutton. Small fee for parking. Hand carry. GPS: 45.041559°, −72.502106°

HAZARDS: Class I–II (old bridge at Ruiter Brook confluence)

PORTAGES (0): None

OTHER ACCESS: O'Kataventures, at the confluence of the North Branch Missisquoi, 2733 Chemin de la Vallée–Missisquoi, Mansonville. Private access with day-use fees. GPS: 45.031831°, −72.440772°

BEST TIME TO GO: May to October

CONTACT: NFCT Trip Planner

SERVICES: Restaurants, lodging, and supplies in Mansonville; local

liveries in Mansonville and Glen
Sutton (boat rentals, shuttle ser-
vices, camping)
CAMPING: Private campgrounds
CELL SERVICE: International rates

may apply
SEE AND DO MORE: Check out
Mansonville architectural walking
tour, featuring a unique round
barn. Hike or golf Owl's Head resort.

NEW HAMPSHIRE

Connecticut River Float

Bordered by agricultural fields and mountain views, this trip offers a leisurely float along a wide and gentle river with large sandy turns and plenty of places to stop for a picnic or a swim. The NFCT samples a mere 20 miles of the 407-mile Connecticut River, the longest river in New England. There are no portages and only a few short Class I rapids and quickwater (primarily in early spring) at the start where the Nulhegan River meets the Connecticut at Debanville Landing.

Farther downstream, the winding river has worn the banks into high, sandy cliffs where you may see the nesting holes of bank swallows. Sounds of nature may become more noticeable between Wheeler Stream and the circa 1885 Stratford–Maidstone Bridge, which the State of New Hampshire desig-nated as a "natural segment" and is the only portion of the entire NFCT where motorboats are prohibited. Lands around Maidstone have been protected by the Nature Conservancy. Waterfowl and other signs of wildlife throughout this section are abundant. Timbered steps leading from the river downstream of the Stratford–Maidstone Bridge, river-left, make for a good day trip stopping or starting point.

As you approach Groveton, signs of civilization become more obvious. If you arrive here on a weekend, you might hear—or want to visit—the nearby Riv-erside Speedway. Although the track itself cannot be seen from the river, the nearby fence and steep banks are a good landmark between the broad oxbows on the way to the Upper Ammonoosuc River, which enters from the left. Con-tinue following the Connecticut River current another few miles to the take-out, river-right, above the New Hampshire Route 102 bridge.

Overnight parking is available in Bloomfield. At Debanville's General Store, you can order pizza, buy a fishing license, or purchase a pair of Walking Boss suspenders, which are made in town and harken back to the region's logging days. Overnight parking is also permitted at the Stratford–Maidstone Bridge (also known as the Janice Peaslee Bridge) access point and in Guildhall, near the take-out.

A free, state-managed campsite is in the woods behind the NFCT kiosk, and any of three additional free, first-come, first-served campsites can turn a long day trip into an overnight adventure.

For more trip information, see Section 1 in the Map 7 chapter, New Hampshire.

Great Reasons to Take This Trip
- Easy beginner trip with several overnight camping options
- For railroad aficionados, historically significant examples of cut stone trusses, granite culverts, and other examples of architectural railroad craftsmanship

TRIP DISTANCE: 24.5 miles
TRIP DURATION: Allow 1–2 days
WATERBODY TYPE(S): 1 river (current flows north to south)
DIFFICULTY: Novice
MAP: NFCT Map 7
PUT-IN: Debanville Landing, at the confluence of Nulhegan and Connecticut Rivers in Bloomfield, Vermont. Take out by field. Overnight parking by NFCT kiosk on Vermont Route 102. GPS: 44.751425°, –71.632742°
TAKE-OUT: Guildhall, Vermont, above bridge, river-right. Hand carry access by trail to VT 102. Overnight parking available across from the county courthouse. GPS: 44.564802°, –71.558855°
HAZARDS: Class I–II waves (in high water) at the confluence with the Nulhegan
PORTAGES (0): None
OTHER ACCESS: North Stratford Municipal Park. Hand carry access. Overnight parking. GPS: 44.748039°, –71.628114°;
Stratford–Maidstone Bridge. Hand carry access. Overnight parking. GPS: 44.651925°, –71.56211°
BEST TIME TO GO: Spring through fall—water levels remain reliable throughout the paddling season, but bugs can be a nuisance in the shoreline campsites throughout summer.
CONTACT: Connecticut River Paddlers' Trail; Vermont River Conservancy; NFCT Trip Planner
SERVICES: General store with lunch counter in Bloomfield, Vermont; convenience store and restaurant in North Stratford, New Hampshire; grocery store, restaurants, and lodging in Groveton, New Hampshire
CAMPING: State-managed Belknap campsite; NFCT Maine Central RR Trestle and Samuel Benton campsites; Vermont River Conservancy Scott C. Devlin Memorial campsite
CELL SERVICE: Reliable for major providers
SEE AND DO MORE: Visit the Silvio O. Conte National Fish and Wildlife Refuge. Go hiking or look for moose from viewing platforms. Stay at the Nulhegan Hut, a unique timber-frame, off-the-grid cabin located on the East Branch Nulhegan River on Vermont River Conservancy land (by reservation only through the Vermont Huts Association).

Covered Bridges and the Upper Ammonoosuc River

Paddling this section of the river makes for a pleasant day outing, but can easily be turned into a nice first-time overnight canoe or kayak trip. Meander your way through lush riparian forests as you paddle downriver approximately 10 miles on the Upper Ammonoosuc River to Stark, New Hampshire. A highlight of this trip is charming Stark Village and its photogenic covered bridge that spans the river. The Upper "Ammo" is typically shallow and slow-moving until you approach the village. Numerous sandy oxbows offer tempting swim breaks.

The trip begins near a corner country store in West Milan, New Hampshire. The business owns the land where timbered steps and hand carry access lead to the river. Contact the store prior to arrival to arrange for parking. The NFCT first-come, first-served Cordwell campsite is only 2 miles from the put-in, so plan your time accordingly. The next day you will have an 8-mile paddle to the take-out, at the river access ramp and parking area above Stark Rapids.

Paddlers who are interested in testing their whitewater skills can run the next mile of Class I–II water when the river is up. Most of the stretch can be scouted from the New Hampshire Route 110 roadside. Arriving in the village of Stark, by water or by foot, adds another mile to your trip.

From flat to fast, the New Hampshire section of the NFCT is all about river paddling. (Photo by NFCT)

This trip can be further extended by paddling to Groveton; however, it then bumps this trip up beyond a novice rating. While none of the whitewater segments downstream of Stark Village is above Class II or technical, three portages, all of which circumnavigate dams within a short 1-mile section through the former industrial town, will make this trip more challenging.

Frizzell campsite appears a little more than a mile below the white covered bridge in Stark. From here the river begins to change in character and speed. Nash Stream enters, river-right, 0.3 mile above Emerson Road Bridge, creating a Class I–II run through a boulder field in high water. In low water, this segment is cobbled and the ride will be bumpy.

Each of the three dams in the Groveton area holds back water, turning the river in this area into a series of flatwater ponds. Red Dam is breached, and exposed rebar and other remnants could damage a hull. Carry around this hazard a short distance river-right. The portage around the dam at Brooklyn Street is wheelable following the road. Take out above the booms, and put in below the base of the dam, river-left. You'll paddle under a second covered bridge in the backwaters above Weston Dam.

The carry around Weston Dam is short, but turbulence at its base during high-water releases may make putting in here challenging or even dangerous. NFCT Normandeau campsite is another 0.4 mile downstream of the dam, where long-term paddler parking is permitted. If desired, you can easily end your trip at the Brooklyn Dam Carry take-out or above Weston Dam, where roadside access is present.

Great Reasons to Take This Trip

- The quaint village of Stark, with its white-steepled church, historic graveyard, and preserved covered bridge; paddle under and/or visit a second covered bridge in Groveton
- Well-spaced, free campsites within a remote-feeling river that is never far from civilization

TRIP DISTANCE: 10 or 11 miles (with options to extend your trip)	**TAKE-OUT: Stark access above the rapids.** Hand carry access. Parking permitted along Old Vermont Route 110 section. GPS: 44.610837°, –71.40064°
TRIP DURATION: Allow 1–2 days	
WATERBODY TYPE(S): 1 river (current flows north to south)	
DIFFICULTY: Novice to moderate	**HAZARDS:** Down trees may be present in constricted areas above Stark and around braided islands below Stark; below Stark access: Class I–II Stark Rapids, Class I Nash Stream boulder field, quickwater around braided islands
MAP: NFCT Map 7	
PUT-IN: Privately owned access **near corner country store at 1156 W. Milan Road.** Hand carry access. Overnight parking by permission only. GPS: 44.594791°, –71.301001°	

PORTAGES (0–4): None, if taking out above Stark; up to 4 carries if continuing through Groteton (Stark Rapids, Red Dam, Brooklyn Dam, and Weston Dam)
OTHER ACCESS: None above Stark; below Stark: Road access at or near each of the portages
BEST TIME TO GO: Spring and early summer are best. Water levels often drop later in the season.
CONTACT: NFCT Trip Planner
SERVICES: Groteton is the largest town with restaurants, a grocery store, lodging, laundry, and a library. There is a B&B in Stark and a general store with a deli in West Milan.

CAMPING: Free first-come, first-served NFCT Cordwell campsite above Stark; NFCT Frizzell and Normandeau campsites below Stark
CELL SERVICE: Dependent upon carrier or service
EXTEND YOUR TRIP: Go for a total of 20.6 miles by continuing on to NFCT Normandeau campsite in Groteton. Hand carry access. Long-term paddler parking permitted. GPS: 44.58996°, −71.520916°
SEE AND DO MORE: Bag a peak at the Percy Peaks. Hike the Cohos Trail.

MAINE

Rangeley Lakes Fishing and Camping Trip

With its largely timbered shorelines, open vistas, stunning mountain ranges, sandy beaches, and excellent fishing, it's easy to see why the Rangeley Lakes region is considered the "Jewel of the Western Maine Mountains." The region's natural wealth has attracted outdoor adventurers for generations.

Fishing is what helped put Rangeley on the map. It is here that modern fly-fishing was born, and people began flocking to the area when Carrie Stevens landed a world-record six-pound thirteen-ounce brook trout in Upper Dam using the Grey Ghost Streamer, a fly of her own design, in 1924.

The chain of lakes can be visited by canoe, kayak, sail or power boats, or even "Rangeley boats," unique wooden crafts explicitly built for local lake travel. The area also boasts several historic sporting camps, wilderness lodges, and cabins that encourage guests to settle into nature. These catered camps feature home-cooked meals and places to gather for sharing stories and maybe a beverage or two after a day of paddling or casting flies.

The easiest way to access remote Lower Richardson Lake is from the South Arm boat launch. From here you'll be heading north into Upper Richardson Lake, then portaging east into Mooselookmeguntic Lake following the Upper Dam Carry. The 0.2-mile unpaved road passes a few private camps and an artesian spring. A plaque honoring Carrie Stevens and her record-setting trout can also be viewed along the carry. Mooselookmeguntic Lake is the fourth-largest lake in Maine. Take care paddling on this expansive lake where high winds can quickly kick up big waves.

Powerboats and the occasional floatplane share these waters and campsites with nonmotorized vessels. Still, there is little shoreline development visible to take away the feeling of wilderness—particularly in the Richardsons. Rangeley Lake is the most developed lake of the four but home to Rangeley Lake State Park and several conserved parcels—including wildlife-rich South Bog.

Novice paddlers should stay close to shore and pay keen attention to weather conditions. Wind and waves are the biggest foes on these large lakes. The most challenging part of this trip, however, might be the logistics of transporting your gear and yourself 1.4 miles from Haines Landing on Mooselookmeguntic Lake to the hand carry access on Rangeley Lake. This is a 100 percent wheelable portage (unless you are attempting to move a ninety-pound cooler full of fish in your canoe). The portage route follows Carry Road (slightly uphill) through the village of Oquossoc, passing by a general store and several restaurants. However, if you don't relish the idea of a long portage, either return to your starting point or end your trip at Haines Landing. Shuttle services are available through local outfitters.

With the exception of two state-owned free campsites on Mooselookmeguntic, all campsites throughout this section charge a fee and must be reserved in advance of arrival. South Arm Campground manages sites on Upper and Lower Richardson Lakes. Cupsuptic Lake Park and Campground oversees remote water campsites north of Haines Landing, and the Stephen Phillips Memorial Preserve operates sites on Mooselookmeguntic Lake. You must book these water-access-only campsites through these different organizations. Camping on Rangeley Lake is available at Rangeley Lake State Park. Service information is listed on the NFCT website.

For more trip information, see Sections 1 and 2 in the Map 8 chapter, Maine.

Great Reasons to Take This Trip

- Superb fishing
- Scenic Maine wilderness almost as unchanged as visitors would have found it a century ago
- Available shuttle services

TRIP DISTANCE: Approximately 28 miles

TRIP DURATION: Allow 3 or more days (allow extra time for strong winds so you are not tempted to take chances keeping to a schedule)

WATERBODY TYPE(S): 4 lakes

DIFFICULTY: All skill levels can enjoy the beauty of this area

MAP: NFCT Map 8

PUT-IN: South Arm Campground boat launch, South Arm Rd., Andover. GPS: 44.752190°, –70.842923°

TAKE-OUT: Rangeley Town Cove Park, Park Rd., Rangeley. GPS: 44.964403°, –70.646042°

HAZARDS: Winds and high waves can keep you windbound

PORTAGES (2): Upper Dam Carry (Upper Richardson to Mooselook-megunntic), 0.2 mile; and **Carry Rd. Carry** (Haines Landing on Moosel-ookmegunntic to Rangeley Lake in Oquossoc), 1.4 miles; both wheelable

OTHER ACCESS: Cupsuptic River/Lake: State of Maine public boat launch off Maine Route 16. Improved access with parking. GPS: 45.01431°, –70.850017°; **Moose-lookmegunntic:** Haines Landing municipal boat launch at Carry Rd. GPS: 44.962336°, –70.794872°;

Rangeley Lake State Park: 1 State Park Rd., Rangeley. Overnight park-ing (day-use fee). GPS: 44.934203°, –70.706966°

BEST TIME TO GO: Ice-out to Octo-ber. Mid- to late summer offers best camping weather, but competition for campsites can be fierce.

CONTACT: Maine Bureau of Parks and Lands; Rangeley Lakes Heritage Trust; South Arm Camp-ground; Cupsuptic Lake Park and Campground; Stephen Philips Memorial Preserve; NFCT Trip Planner

SERVICES: Many lodging, restau-rants, shops, and other services are available in Oquossoc and Rangeley. An outfitter with shuttle services is located in Rangeley.

CAMPING: Numerous campsites throughout the Richardsons and Mooselookmegunntic. Must reserve specific sites in advance of arrival. State park campground on Rangeley Lake.

CELL SERVICE: Unreliable to non-existent until Rangeley

SEE AND DO MORE: Visit the Outdoor Heritage Museum in Oquossoc and the Maine Forestry Museum in Rangeley. Go moose watching and paddle in the watery fingers of the South Bog Con-servation Area. Drive the 35-mile Rangeley Lakes National Scenic Byway, stopping at the Height of Land overlook on ME 17 that offers spectacular views of the region and the Appalachian Trail. Hike the 2-mile Bald Mountain Trail to the open summit.

Flagstaff Lake Historical Trip

Just beyond the peak of Sugarloaf Mountain lies a magnificent valley to be dis-covered. Historic Flagstaff Lake, at nearly 20 miles long, wraps neatly around the base of the striking Bigelow Mountain Range. Paddling includes shallow seasonal water, marshes, and flatwater, plus amazing views of the mountains. All seven of the Bigelow summits are part of a 36,000-acre public reserve, and two of them are on the list of 4000-footers in Maine, making them sought after by peak-baggers.

One of the most unique stories in Maine history, the town of Flagstaff was established in 1775 by Benedict Arnold's forces on their way to Québec . . . and 175 years later it was flooded to make way for hydroelectricity production. Check out the Dead River Area Historical Society and see displays including memorabilia of the very towns you might paddle over. Paddlers looking to explore the lake can do so with a day trip or overnight camping trip. Since this is a lake trip with many camping options, it can be any distance you want. The approximate one-way distance from the Stratton boat launch on Maine Route 27 to School House Point campsite and the site of Old Flagstaff Village is 6.6 miles and 13.4 miles to the Round Barn campsites.

For more trip information, see Section 2 in the Map 9 chapter, Maine.

Great Reasons to Take This Trip
- Discovering the regional history behind Flagstaff Lake
- Beaches and beautiful campsites
- Quill Hill Conservancy panoramic vista between Rangeley and Stratton

TRIP DISTANCE: 10 or more miles
TRIP DURATION: Allow 1–3 days
WATERBODY TYPE(S): 1 lake
DIFFICULTY: All skill levels can enjoy the beauty of this area
MAP: NFCT Map 9
PUT-IN/TAKE-OUT: Stratton boat launch on ME 27. Improved launch with overnight parking. GPS: 45.151922°, –70.446872°
HAZARDS: Winds and high waves can keep you windbound
PORTAGES (0): None
OTHER ACCESS: Additional hand carry access points on southern and eastern shores from backcountry roads. See individual chapters earlier in this guidebook and the NFCT maps for more details.

BEST TIME TO GO: Ice-out through October
CONTACT: NFCT Trip Planner
SERVICES: Stratton and Eustis offer lodging, restaurants, general stores, and other services.
CAMPING: More than a dozen free first-come, first-served campsites. Sites accessible by road get more use than water-access only sites.
CELL SERVICE: Reliable, depending upon the carrier
SEE AND DO MORE: Hike the Bigelow section of the Appalachian Trail, which parallels Flagstaff Lake and offers two 4000-foot peak-bagger summits. Visit the Dead River Area Historical Society. Drive the Maine High Peaks Art & Heritage Loop.

The Allagash Wilderness Waterway: An Expedition
Ready to tackle a bigger adventure? Longtime favorite of youth camps and families alike, the Allagash Wilderness Waterway (AWW) threads together lakes, ponds, rivers, and streams with Indigenous names and stories, logging-era history, and environmentally significant wild places. This preeminent North American expedition canoe trip leads you through the heart of the Northern Forest wilderness on one of the first rivers designated in 1970 as part of the National Wild and Scenic River System. The waterway is surrounded by

For many, the Allagash Wilderness Waterway symbolizes the true meaning of wilderness travel. (Photo by Dean B. Bennett)

commercial forestland and other conservation lands, and it is a special place for many. For the Wabanaki who lived here for millennia before European settlers arrived, it is their ancestral homeland.

The waterways of the Allagash deliver a mostly placid, flatwater paddling experience. Like other bodies of open water, wind can still present an obstacle on larger Allagash lakes. Class II Chase Rapids provides the biggest whitewater challenge of the trip, but for a nominal fee, you can choose to either get shuttled around this section or have your gear shuttled to Bissonnette Bridge while you run the rapids in an empty boat. The river holds a few more areas of whitewater between Allagash Falls and the village of Allagash, but nothing higher than Class II and none are considered technical.

Certain rules apply regarding the size of watercraft permitted on the waterway and the use of motors. The put-in at Chamberlain Bridge (or other access points) is via private forest roads managed by North Maine Woods, Inc. A user fee (separate from the AWW camping fee) will be collected when you pass through one of these checkpoints.

Campsites are nonreservable, first come, first served, but a fee is charged for each night spent in the AWW. If you don't have time or the inclination to paddle the entire length of the AWW, shorter trips are possible. Shuttle services are available. For more trip planning needs specific to the AWW, contact Maine Bureau of Parks and Lands or the Allagash Wilderness Waterway Foundation (see Resources).

For more trip information, see Sections 3 and 4 in the Map 12 chapter plus Sections 1 and 2 in the Map 13 chapter, Maine.

Great Reasons to Take This Trip

- Dark night skies with a 180-degree view of the Milky Way and a better chance of seeing Northern Lights
- Logging-era remnants, including massive locomotive engines, tramways, and other mechanical artifacts, left behind in the forest
- Opportunity to see a lot of moose

TRIP DISTANCE: 92 miles

TRIP DURATION: Allow 7–10 days

WATERBODY TYPE(S): 6 lakes, 3 ponds, 1 river (current flows south to north)

DIFFICULTY: Moderate to expert

MAP: NFCT Maps 12 and 13

PUT-IN: Chamberlain Bridge Ranger Station on Telos Rd. Overnight parking. GPS: 46.169996°, –69.208433°

TAKE-OUT: White Birch Landing, immediately upstream of Casey Rapids, town of Allagash. Private boat launch. Overnight parking. Launch fees. GPS: 47.083110° –69.051295°

HAZARDS: Winds and high waves; Class II Chase Rapids, Class I McGargle Rocks, Class II Twin Brook Rapids, Class I Eliza Hole Rapids

PORTAGES (4): Chamberlain Lake to Eagle Lake via **Lock Dam Carry**, 0.1 mile (wheelable); or **Tramway Carry**, 0.5 mile (not easily wheeled);

Churchill Dam Carry, 0.1 mile (wheelable); **Long Lake Dam Carry**, 0.1 mile (not wheelable); **Allagash Falls Carry**, 0.25 mile (not easily wheeled)

OTHER ACCESS: Additional hand carry access points from backcountry roads are located at **Churchill Dam, American Realty Rd.** (the Thoroughfare), **Henderson Bridge** on Blanchette Rd., **Michaud Farm**, and **West Twin Brook**. See individual chapters earlier in this guidebook and the NFCT maps for more details.

BEST TIME TO GO: Summer through October; August to October is the best chance of seeing the Northern Lights; blackflies are out in force after ice-out

CONTACT: Maine Bureau of Parks and Lands; Allagash Wilderness Waterway Foundation; North Maine Woods; NFCT Trip Planner

SERVICES: Allagash village has a diner (closes by 3 p.m.) and limited lodging options but few other services. Area outfitters offer shuttle services by prior arrangement.

CAMPING: Dozens of first-come, first-served fee-based campsites. Pay at AWW Ranger Station at time of entry.

CELL SERVICE: Nonexistent until Allagash village

SHORTER TRIP OPTIONS: Decrease your time on the water by just going from Chamberlain Bridge to Churchill Dam (GPS: 46.493469°, –69.288763°), which is mostly lake paddling. Allow 3–4 days to paddle 30 miles; or plan on Umsaskis Lake Thoroughfare boat launch (GPS: 46.614113°, –69.39361°) to Allagash village, which is mostly river paddling. Allow 3–4 days to paddle 53 miles. Overnight parking permitted at all AWW boat launches.

SEE AND DO MORE: Visit the Churchill Depot History Center at Churchill Dam. Hike or paddle nearby Katahdin Woods and Waters National Monument. Summit Mount Katahdin from Baxter State Park.

Points of Interest

If overnight camping is not your thing, or if you are interested in combining sightseeing or other complementary activities with day trips, the NFCT offers visitors a wide range of opportunities. Many features found along the NFCT can be paired with your next adventure. Here are some highlights. See Resources or visit the online NFCT Trip Planner for more information and itineraries. (The maps and sections listed below reference chapters in this guide.)

SECTIONS WITH WATERSIDE LODGING

These sections of the Trail offer more services where you may be able to "base-camp" from a motel or even plan a trip paddling from inn to inn!

- Old Forge to Blue Mountain Lake, New York (Map 1, Sections 1 and 2)
- Lake Flower, Saranac Lake, New York (Map 2, Section 2)
- Lake Champlain Islands and Missisquoi Bay, Vermont—for experienced paddlers only (Map 4, Section 1)
- Island Pond, Vermont (Map 6, Section 1)
- Upper Ammonoosuc River, New Hampshire (Map 7, Section 2)
- Rangeley Lakes, Maine (Map 8, Sections 1 and 2)
- Greater Jackman Region, Maine (Map 10, Section 3)

PADDLING-HIKING COMBINATIONS

The NFCT is near—or in some places literally crosses paths with—premier hiking opportunities. Take a break from paddling or add in a few extra days to an itinerary sampling some of the water trail's land-based cousins.

- Long Lake and Northville–Placid Trail, New York (Map 2, Section 1)
- North Branch Missisquoi and Ruiter Valley Land Trust, Québec (Map 5, Section 1, Québec)
- Clyde and Nulhegan Rivers and Bluff Mountain Community Trail, Vermont (Map 6, Sections 1 and 4)
- Lake Memphremagog and Mont Owl's Head, Québec (Map 6, Section 2)
- Upper Ammonoosuc River and Cohos Trail, New Hampshire (Map 7, Section 2)
- Rangeley Lakes and Appalachian Trail, Maine (Map 8, Sections 1, 2, and 3)

- Flagstaff Lake and the Bigelow Range of the Appalachian Trail, Maine (Map 9, Section 2)
- Moosehead Lake and Mount Kineo, Maine (Map 11, Section 2)

PADDLING-BIKING COMBINATIONS
New York, Vermont, and Maine are home to former rail corridors that have been converted into multi-use trails, and several parallel—or are very close to—the NFCT. Explore adjacent regions by bike. Some sections of these recreational trails can even be used to create a paddle-pedal shuttle option!
- Adirondack Rail Trail, New York (Maps 1 and 2, all sections)
- Saranac River and Saranac River Trail Greenway, New York (Map 3, Section 4)
- Missisquoi River and Missisquoi Valley Rail Trail, Vermont (Map 4, Sections 2 and 3; Map 5, Section 2, Vermont)
- Missisquoi River and Lamoille Valley Rail Trail, Vermont (Map 4, Section 3)
- North Branch Missisquoi and Potton and Sutton Townships, Québec (Map 5, Section 1, Québec)
- Clyde River and Kingdom Trails, Vermont (off Map 6)
- St. John River and St. John Valley Heritage Trail, Maine (Map 13, Section 3)

AREA MUSEUMS AND ATTRACTIONS
Enhance your trip to the region by including time to visit one or more museums. Learn more about the natural environment and the preserved histories of the Northern Forest.
- Adirondack Experience, The Museum on Blue Mountain Lake, New York (Map 1)
- The WILD Center, Tupper Lake, New York (Map 2)
- ECHO Lake Aquarium and Science Center, Burlington, Vermont (off Map 4)
- The Berlin Falls House Museum Heritage Center, Berlin, New Hampshire (off Map 7)
- Outdoor Heritage Museum, Oquossoc, Maine (Map 8)
- Maine Forestry Museum, Rangeley, Maine (Map 8 or 9)
- Dead River Area Historical Society, Stratton, Maine (Map 9)
- Moosehead Marine Museum, Greenville, Maine (Map 11)
- Fort Kent Historic Site, Fort Kent, Maine (Map 13)

FISHING
The linked waterways of the NFCT offer fishing holes on big lakes, remote ponds, rushing rivers, and gentle streams. There are landlocked salmon,

small- and largemouth bass, lake trout, brook trout, bullhead, northern pike, and catfish waiting to be caught during an afternoon outing or on multiday fishing trips with a canoe or kayak. Fishing regulations vary and a valid license is required by state.

- Fulton Chain, New York (Map 1, all sections)
- Saranac River, New York (Map 3, all sections)
- Lake Memphremagog, Vermont and Québec (Map 6, Vermont, Section 3, and Québec, Section 2)
- Clyde River, Vermont (Map 6, all sections)
- Connecticut River, New Hampshire (Map 7, Section 1)
- Androscoggin River, New Hampshire (Map 7, Section 3)
- Rangeley Lakes, Maine (Map 8, all sections)
- Allagash Wilderness Waterway, Maine (Maps 12 and 13, all sections)

WILDLIFE VIEWING

The NFCT passes through three designated wildlife refuges as well as many remote backcountry sections, offering outstanding opportunities to view the region's iconic wildlife including moose, black bears, and beavers. Loons, ospreys, and bald eagles can all be encountered throughout the Trail. The region also includes important bird migration corridors and breeding areas.

- Missisquoi National Wildlife Refuge, Vermont (Map 4, Section 4)

There's no guarantee that you'll see a moose during your adventure. However, since Maine is home to the highest population of moose in the United States outside of Alaska, your chances there are good. (Photo by Clyde Smith)

- Nulhegan River and Silvio O. Conte National Fish and Wildlife Refuge, Vermont (Map 6, Section 4)
- Connecticut River, New Hampshire (Map 7, Section 1)
- Umbagog National Wildlife Refuge, New Hampshire (Map 7, Section 4)
- Allagash Wilderness Waterway, Maine (Map 12, all sections, and Map 13, Sections 1 and 2)

SECTIONS WITH WHITEWATER

Not all sections of the Trail are suitable for novice paddlers. Rapids and whitewater are present on many NFCT rivers. However, some sections are able to be paddled only when there is sufficient water, usually during the spring freshet and sometimes in the summer and fall, if there's been a lot of rain. Others hold water throughout the paddling season or because of scheduled dam releases. Refer to individual maps and sections for advice on a section's whitewater classification, when to visit, and recommended flow. **Note:** Rivers marked with an asterisk (*) are typically too low to paddle by midsummer.

- Saranac River, New York (Map 3, all sections)*
- Clyde River, Vermont—below Salem Lake (Map 5, Section 2, Vermont)*
- Missisquoi River, Vermont—short segments (Map 5, Sections 1 and 2 Vermont)
- Nulhegan River after Wenlock Crossing, Vermont (Map 6, Section 4)*
- Androscoggin River, New Hampshire (Map 7, Section 3)
- Rangeley River, Maine (Map 8, Section 1)
- Rapid River, Maine (Map 8, Section 3)
- South Branch Dead River, Maine (Map 9, Section 1)*
- Moose River, Maine (Map 10, Section 4)
- Allagash River, Maine (Map 12, Section 4 and Map 13, Section 2)
- St. John River, Maine (Map 13, Section 3)

Acknowledgments

The original publication of this guidebook was a coordinated collage of diverse voices, skilled hands, and a lot of passion—much like the Northern Forest Canoe Trail (NFCT) itself. This second edition relies on all the knowledge and information that went into the first edition and builds on over a decade of experience molding what has become a renowned paddling trail, a source of inspiration, and a community of paddlers. I join my predecessor, Kate Williams, in a deep bow of gratitude to a number of people for the talent and plain old hard work that went into the creation of this guidebook.

Inspired by historic travel routes, the NFCT crosses the ancestral lands of the Haudenosaunee and Wabanakiak ta Wabanakiak peoples, who are still important members of our communities. The NFCT seeks to honor and respect their homelands and the waterways that traverse them.

Thanks go to:

Ron Canter, Mike Krepner, and Randy Mardres for hatching the idea of the NFCT and logging the water and road miles to create the initial hand-drawn maps of the route.

Rob Center and Kay Henry for throwing their weight and energy into building the Trail into a mapped recreational resource with an organizational home.

Senators Patrick Leahy, Vermont, and Judd Gregg, New Hampshire, who should be cited among the Trail's founders for securing our key start-up funding, administered by the National Park Service.

Jen (Lamphere) Roberts, former NFCT trail director and editor, for staying with this guidebook project from start to finish and pouring her knowledge of and affection for both the Trail and the English language into its every page.

Beth Krusi, project manager, for coordinating many moving parts, sharing much-needed wisdom, and generally keeping us on track and of good perspective.

The team of writers, for their knowledge, their voices, their enthusiasm, and their graciousness.

The Mountaineers Books' Helen Cherullo, former publisher, and Kate Rogers, editor in chief, for their faith in this project and our organization, and for their partnership in the process of producing this book.

The land managers and landowners—big and small—and community, state, and regional partners who have granted permission, offered advice, shared experience, and generally made it possible for this public-access trail to exist and to thrive.

The NFCT staff and Board of Directors, especially the original Guidebook Committee, including Steve Gladstone, Alix Hopkins, Ron Canter, and Rob Center, for asking all of the right questions and having only the highest expectations. Stewardship Director Noah Pollock also contributed his considerable knowledge of the Trail to ensure accuracy, clarity, and relevance of information in subsequent reprints and the second edition.

This second edition would not have been possible without Katina Daanen. Since her first Thru-Paddle in 2011, her dedication to the Trail and her commitment to supporting the ongoing maintenance of all our resources have provided paddlers along our route with access to clear and accurate guidance on their adventure.

Finally, the paddlers who watched, waited, cheered, and ultimately paddled or aspire to paddle along the NFCT. We hope this book inspires and informs both novice and expert alike.

Karrie Thomas
Waitsfield, Vermont
NFCT Executive Director, 2014–present

Resources

MAPS AND ROUTE INFORMATION
Northern Forest Canoe Trail
  P.O. Box 565
  Waitsfield, VT 05673
  802-496-2285
  info@northernforestcanoetrail.org
  www.northernforestcanoetrail.org

FarOut App
www.faroutguides.com
In partnership with FarOut Guides, the NFCT also offers a downloadable app documenting the entire water trail. While the app alone won't replace the need to pack NFCT maps (devices can lose power or fall overboard), it is another tool to use on the water. The Trail is shown as a linear line displaying your current location and offers real-time updates reported by users in the NFCT paddling community. The GPS-enabled NFCT guide features over 1400 waypoints, site photos, and several base maps, which work online and can be downloaded for offline, out-of-service use.

The Northern Forest Canoe Trail Through-Paddler's Companion by Katina Daanen
This guidebook documents the NFCT in its entirety specifically for the expedition paddler who is following the water trail in a singular west-to-east direction. It provides information about the most challenging Trail segments, such as navigating more than 160 miles of upstream paddling, as well as detailed descriptions for every portage from the unique perspective and needs of a Thru-Paddler. The book also offers planning guidance for the Thru-Paddler including statistics about average trip durations, tips for daily mileage goals, and other important logistics associated with managing a long-distance paddling trip.

The *Companion* is available at the Northern Forest Canoe Trail online store or other online retailers.

NFCT MAP SERIES

Each NFCT map has specific information for that area, including contacts for campsite reservations, regulations regarding camping and fire permits, boating laws, emergency contact information, and more.

WATER GAUGES AND SCHEDULED DAM RELEASES

Water gauges provide a way to get a quick snapshot of what to expect on the water. The following sites enable you to check water levels before heading out on a trip.

US Geological Survey Real-Time Water Data

https://waterdata.usgs.gov/nwis/rt

Applicable Gauges

Raquette River at Piercefield, NY
Saranac River at Plattsburgh, NY
Missisquoi River at Swanton, VT
Missisquoi River near East Berkshire, VT
Missisquoi River near North Troy, VT
Clyde River at Newport, VT
Connecticut River at North Stratford, NH
Androscoggin River at Errol, NH
Spencer Stream near Grand Falls, ME
Allagash River near Allagash, ME
St. John River at Dickey, ME

American Whitewater National River Database

www.americanwhitewater.org/content/River/view/river-index

Applicable River Gauges

New York

- Raquette—Forked Lake state campground to Deerland
- Saranac—Union Falls to Silver Lake Road
- Saranac—Silver Lake Road to Redford
- Saranac—High Falls Gorge
- Saranac—Foot of Kent Falls to Lake Champlain

Vermont

- Missisquoi—East Richford to Lake Champlain
- Clyde—Five Mile Square Road to Clyde Road

New Hampshire

- Nulhegan—Hatchery to Connecticut River
- Androscoggin—Errol Rapids
- Androscoggin—Braggs Bay to Pontook
- Androscoggin—Pontook

LOOKING FOR SERVICE INFORMATION?

Visit the Northern Forest Canoe Trail (NFCT) website and online Trip Planner. A directory of services is located under the "Plan a Trip" link, and the interactive Trip Planner tool shows where services, campsites, and points of interest are located along the route. These resources contain the most recent service updates and changes.

Maine
- Rapid—Pond in the River to Lake Umbagog
- Dead, South Branch—Dallas School (Maine Route 16) to Langston Mill
- Dead, South Branch—Green Farm Branch to Flagstaff
- Dead—Spencer Falls to West Forks (below the NFCT but will indicate flow upstream)
- Spencer Stream—Logging Branch to Dead River
- Little Spencer Stream—Spencer Lake to Spencer Stream
- Moose—Long Pond to Brassua Lake
- Penobscot, West Branch—Seboomook Dam to Roll Dam campsite
- Allagash—Chamberlain Lake to Allagash Village
- Allagash Stream—Allagash Lake to Chamberlain Lake
- St. John—American Realty Road 71.8 miles to Allagash, 28 miles to Fort Kent

Note: Do not confuse the Upper Ammonoosuc River of the NFCT with the Ammonoosuc River. These are two separate, unconnected rivers in New Hampshire.

Scheduled Dam Release Information

Water release schedules and flow levels are posted by Brookfield Renewable online at the SafeWaters website. View water levels, flow rates, and safety information related to hydropower facilities located along the Trail. Searchable by state.

SafeWaters
Brookfield Renewable US
hotline: 844-430-FLOW (3569)
www.safewaters.com

The annual schedule of whitewater releases in New England is posted by the Boston Paddlers Appalachian Mountain Club.
www.amcbostonpaddlers.org/documents/river-releases

ORGANIZATIONS

There are a number of organizations that can be of use in planning and executing your Northern Forest trip, including waterway, trail, and paddling organizations; land and water management agencies and landowners; chambers of commerce and information centers; and cultural and historical organizations.

National Organizations
These organizations are relevant to all maps and regions.

American Canoe Association
P.O. Box 7996
Fredericksburg, VA 22401
540-907-4460
aca@americancanoe.org
www.americancanoe.org

American Rivers
1101 14th St. NW, Suite 1400
Washington, DC 20005
877-347-7550
feedback@americanrivers.org
www.americanrivers.org

American Whitewater
P.O. Box 1540
Cullowhee, NC 28723
866-262-8429
info@americanwhitewater.org
www.americanwhitewater.org

Clear Outside (by First Light Optics)
www.clearoutside.com/forecast

Leave No Trace
P.O. Box 997
Boulder, CO 80306
800-332-4100
info@lnt.org
www.lnt.org

US Coast Guard Boating Safety Division
1 Depot St.
Burlington, VT 05401
802-951-9760
www.uscgboating.org

US Fish and Wildlife Service
1849 C Street NW, Room 3349
Washington, DC 20240
800-344-WILD
www.fws.gov

Regional Organizations
The following organizations may be helpful if you are paddling only specific sections of the Trail. The relevant maps are listed parenthetically after the name of the organization. Note that the geographical reach of a few of the entities listed may extend beyond the state under which they are listed.

New York

Waterway, Trail, and Paddling Organizations
Adirondack Mountain Club (Maps 1–3)
P.O. Box 4390
Queensbury, NY 12804
516-523-3441
1002 Adirondack Loj Rd.
Lake Placid, NY 12946
518-523-3441
www.adk.org

The Adirondack Rail Trail (Maps 1 and 2)
info@adirondackrailtrail.org
www.adirondackrailtrail.org

Friends of Saranac River Trail (Map 3)
info@saranacrivertrail.org
www.saranacrivertrail.org

Land and Water Management Agencies and Landowners
New York State Adirondack Park
Agency (Maps 1–3)
P.O. Box 99
1133 New York Route 86
Ray Brook, NY 12977
518-891-4050
contact@apa.ny.gov
www.apa.ny.gov

New York State Department of
Environmental Conservation (Maps 1–3)
contact@dec.ny.gov
www.dec.ny.gov/about/558.html

Region 5
1115 New York Route 86
P.O. Box 296
Ray Brook, NY 12977-0296
518-897-1200

Region 6
317 Washington St.
Watertown, NY 13601-3787
315-785-2239

New York State Electric and Gas (Map 3)
4125 New York Route 22
Plattsburgh, NY 12901
custserv@nyseg.com
www.nyseg.com

New York State Parks (Maps 1 and 2)
www.parks.ny.gov/parks

Chambers of Commerce and Information Centers
The Adirondack Coast Visitors Bureau
(Maps 2 and 3)
P.O. Box 310
7061 US Route 9
Plattsburgh, NY 12901
518-563-1000
info@goadirondack.com
www.goadirondack.com

Inlet Information Office (Map 1)
160 New York Route 28
Arrowhead Park
Inlet, NY 13360
315-357-5501
info@inletny.com
www.inletny.com

Saranac Lake Area Chamber of
Commerce (Maps 2 and 3)
39 Main St.
Saranac Lake, NY 12983
518-891-1990
welcome@slareachamber.org
www.slareachamber.org

Town of Long Lake Parks & Recreation
(Maps 1 and 2)
1130 Deerland Rd.
Long Lake, NY 12847
518-624-3077
longlake@mylonglake.com
www.mylonglake.com

Town of Webb Visitor Information
Center (Map 1)
P.O. Box 68
3140 State Route 28
Old Forge, NY 13420-0068
315-369-6983
www.visitmyadirondacks.com
www.oldforgeny.com

Tupper Lake Chamber of Commerce
(Map 2)
   121 Park St.
   Tupper Lake, NY 12986
   518-523-2445
   info@tupperlake.com
   www.tupperlake.com

Cultural and Historical
Organizations
Adirondack Experience (Map 1)
   P.O. Box 99
   9097 New York Route 30
   Blue Mountain Lake, NY 12812-0099
   518-352-7311
   info@theadkx.org
   www.theadkx.org

Adirondack Interpretive Center at
Newcomb (Maps 2 and 3)
   5922 New York Route 28N
   Newcomb, NY 12852
   518-582-2000
   aic@esf.edu
   www.esf.edu/aic

Adirondack Park Visitor Interpretive
Center at Paul Smiths (Maps 2 and 3)
   8023 New York Route 30
   Paul Smiths, NY 12970
   518-327-6241
   vic@paulsmiths.edu
   www.adirondackvic.org

Battle of Plattsburgh Association,
War of 1812 Museum (Map 3)
   31 Washington Rd.
   Plattsburgh, NY 12903
   518-566-1814
   www.battleofplattsburgh.org

Clinton County Historical Association
(Map 3)
   98 Ohio Ave.
   Plattsburgh, NY 12903
   518-561-0340
   info@clintoncountyhistorical.org
   www.clintoncountyhistorical.org

Goodsell Museum (Map 1)
   P.O. Box 513
   Old Forge, NY 13420
   315-369-3838
   www.webbhistory.org

Great Camp Sagamore (Map 1)
   P.O. Box 40
   1105 Sagamore Rd.
   Raquette Lake, NY 13436
   315-354-5311
   info@greatcampsagamore.org
   www.sagamore.org

Six Nations Iroquois Cultural Center
(Map 3)
   1462 County Rd. 60
   Onchiota, NY 12989
   518-891-2299
   geninfo@6nicc.com
   www.6nicc.com

The WILD Center (Map 2)
   45 Museum Dr.
   Tupper Lake, NY 12986
   518-359-7800
   info@wildcenter.org
   www.wildcenter.org

Vermont

Waterway, Trail, and Paddling Organizations

Appalachian Trail Conservancy
New England Regional Office
(Maps 4–6)
P.O. Box 649
Hartford, VT 05047
802-281-5894
www.appalachiantrail.org

Green Mountain Club (Maps 4–6)
4711 Waterbury–Stowe Rd.
Waterbury Center, VT 05677
802-244-7037
gmc@greenmountainclub.org
www.greenmountainclub.org

Kingdom Trails Association (Map 6)
P.O. Box 204
478 Vermont Route 114
East Burke, VT 05832
802-626-0737
info@kingdomtrails.org
www.kingdomtrails.org

Lake Champlain Bikeways (Map 4)
c/o Local Motion Trailside Center
1 Steele St., #103
Burlington, VT 05401
802-861-2700
info@localmotion.org
www.localmotion.org

Lake Champlain Committee (Map 4)
208 Flynn Ave., Bldg. 3, Studio 3F
Burlington, VT 05401-8434
802-658-1414
lcc@lakechamplaincommittee.org
www.lakechamplaincommittee.org

Lamoille River Paddlers' Trail (Map 4)
www.lamoilleriverpaddlerstrail.org

Lamoille Valley Rail Trail (Map 4)
www.railtrails.vermont.gov

Missisquoi Valley Rail Trail
(Maps 4 and 5)
www.railtrails.vermont.gov

NorthWoods Stewardship Center
(Map 6)
154 Leadership Dr.
Island Pond, VT 05846
802-723-6551
info@northwoodscenter.org
www.northwoodscenter.org

Upper Missisquoi and Trout Rivers
(Map 5) Wild and Scenic Committee
www.umatrwildandscenic.org

Vermont Huts Association (Map 6)
802-798-3003
info@vermonthuts.org
www.vermonthuts.org

Land and Water Management Agencies and Landowners

Missisquoi National Wildlife Refuge
(Map 4)
29 Tabor Rd.
Swanton, VT 05488
802-868-4781
missisquoi@fws.gov
www.fws.gov/refuge/missisquoi

Missisquoi River Basin Association
(Maps 4 and 5)
2839 Vermont Route 105
East Berkshire, VT 05447
802-933-3645
www.mrbavt.com

Silvio O. Conte National Fish and Wildlife Refuge (Map 6)
Nulhegan Basin Division
5396 Vermont Route 105
Brunswick, VT 05905
802-962-5240
www.fws.gov/refuge/silvio-o-conte

Vermont Agency of Natural Resources (Maps 4–6)
1 National Life Dr., Davis 2
Montpelier, VT 05620-3901
802-828-1294
anr.info@vermont.gov
www.anr.vermont.gov

Vermont River Conservancy (Maps 6 and 7)
29 Main Street, Suite 11
Montpelier, VT 05602
802-229-0820
www.vermontriverconservancy.org

Vermont State Parks (Maps 4–6)
1 National Life Dr., Davis 2
Montpelier, VT 05620
888-409-7579
parks@vermont.gov
www.vtstateparks.com

Chambers of Commerce and Information Centers

Franklin County Regional Chamber of Commerce (Maps 4 and 5)
2 North Main St.
St. Albans, VT 05478
802-524-2444
info@fcrccvt.com
www.fcrccvt.com

Jay Peak Area Chamber of Commerce (Maps 5 and 6)
P.O. Box 218
Troy, VT 05868
802-988-4120
info@topofvt.com
www.topofvt.com

Lake Champlain Islands Economic Development Corporation (Map 4)
P.O. Box 213
North Hero, VT 05474
802-372-8400
director@champlainislands.com
www.champlainislands.com/region-index

Northeast Kingdom Travel and Tourism Association (Map 6)
466 Vermont Route 114
East Burke, VT 05832
802-626-8511
info@getnekedvt.com
www.northeastkingdom.com

Cultural and Historical Organizations

ECHO, Leahy Center for Lake Champlain (Map 4)
1 College St.
Burlington, VT 05401
802-864-1848
info@echovermont.org
www.echovermont.org

Lake Champlain Maritime Museum (Map 4)
4472 Basin Harbor Rd.
Vergennes, VT 05491
802-475-2022
info@lcmm.org
www.lcmm.org

Railroad Depot Museum (Map 4)
  58 South River St.
  Swanton, VT 05488
  802-868-5436
  www.swantonhistoricalsociety.org/
  museum

Québec

Waterway, Trail, and Paddling Organizations
Corridor Appalachien/Appalachian
Corridor (Map 5)
  466 rue Principale
  Eastman, QC, J0E 1P0
  Canada
  450-297-1145
  info@corridorappalachien.ca
  www.corridorappalachien.ca

North Missisquoi Valley (Map 5)
  info@missisquoinord.com
  www.missisquoinord.com

Land and Water Management Agencies and Landowners
Ruiter Valley Land Trust (Map 5)
  CP 893
  Potton, QC, J0E 1X0
  Canada
  info@valleeruiter.org
  www.valleeruiter.org

Chambers of Commerce and Information Centers
Potton Township Tourism Office (Map 5)
  Open May–October
  291 rue Principale
  Mansonville (Potton Township),
  QC J0E 1X0 Canada
  844-467-6886
  bureautouristique@potton.ca
  www.potton.ca

Tourism Eastern Townships (Tourisme
Cantons-de-l'Est) (Maps 5 and 6)
  20, Don–Bosco Sud
  Sherbrooke, QC J1L 1W4
  Canada
  800-355-5755
  info@atrce.com
  www.easterntownships.org

New Hampshire

Waterway, Trail, and Paddling Organizations
Appalachian Mountain Club (Map 7)
  10 City Square
  Boston, MA 02129
  800-372-1758
  amcinformation@outdoors.org
  www.outdoors.org

The Cohos Trail Association (Map 7)
  P.O. Box 82
  Lancaster, NH 03584
  cohos@cohostrail.org
  www.cohostrail.org

Connecticut River Paddlers' Trail
(Map 7)
  www.ctriver.org/our-work/ct-river-
  paddlers-trail/

Land and Water Management Agencies and Landowners
Connecticut River Joint Commissions
(Map 7)
  10 Water St., Suite 225
  Lebanon, NH 03766
  603-448-1680
  info@crjc.org
  www.crjc.org

New Hampshire Department of
Environmental Services (Map 7)
  29 Hazen Dr.
  Concord, NH 03302
  603-271-3503
  info@des.nh.gov
  www.des.nh.gov

New Hampshire Department of Natural
& Cultural Resources (Map 7)
  172 Pembroke Rd.
  Concord, NH 03301
  603-271-2411
  www.dncr.nh.gov

New Hampshire Fish and Game
Department (Map 7)
  Region 1 (North Country)
  629B Main St.
  Lancaster, NH 03584
  603-788-3164
  www.wildlife.nh.gov

New Hampshire State Parks (Map 7)
  172 Pembroke Rd.
  Concord, NH 03301
  603-271-3556
  nhstateparkscamping@dncr.nh.gov
  www.nhstateparks.org

Umbagog National Wildlife Refuge
(Maps 7 and 8)
  2756 Dam Rd.
  Errol, NH 03579
  603-482-3415
  www.fws.gov/refuge/umbagog

Chambers of Commerce and Information Centers
Androscoggin Valley Chamber of
Commerce (Map 7)
  961 Main St.
  Berlin, NH 03570
  603-752-6060
  www.androscogginvalleychamber.com

North Country Chamber of Commerce
(Map 7)
  100 Main St.
  Colebrook, NH 03576
  603-237-8939
  info@chamberofthenorthcountry.com
  www.chamberofthenorthcountry.com

Northern Gateway Regional Chamber
of Commerce (Map 7)
  P.O. Box 537
  Lancaster, NH 03584
  603-788-2530
  northerngatewaychamber@gmail.com
  www.northerngatewaychamber.org

Cultural and Historical Organizations
Berlin and Coös County Historical
Society (Map 7)
  603-752-4590
  info@berlinnhhistoricalsociety.org
  www.berlinnhhistoricalsociety.org

Maine

Waterway, Trail, and Paddling Organizations
Allagash Wilderness Waterway
Foundation (Maps 11–13)
  P.O. Box 10008
  Portland, ME 04104
  coordinator@awwf.org
  www.awwf.org

Appalachian Mountain Club
(Maps 8–13)
  10 City Square
  Boston, MA 02129
  800-372-1758
  amcinformation@outdoors.org
  www.outdoors.org

Maine Huts & Trails (Maps 9 and 10)
496C Main St.
Kingfield, ME 04947
207-265-2400
info@mainehuts.org
www.mainehuts.org

Maine Trail Finder (Maps 8–13)
www.mainetrailfinder.com

St. John Valley Heritage Trail (Map 13)
www.maine.gov/dacf/parks

Thoreau-Wabanaki Trail/Maine Woods
Forever (Maps 11 and 12)
P.O. Box 512
Oakland, ME 04963
info@mainewoodsforever.org
www.mainewoodsforever.org/
thoreau-wabanaki-trail

**Land and Water Management Agencies
and Landowners**
Maine Bureau of Parks and Lands
(Maps 8–13)
22 State House Station
18 Elkins Ln.
Augusta, ME 04333-0022
207-287-3821
www.maine.gov/dacf/parks

Maine Department of Inland Fisheries
& Wildlife (Maps 8–13)
41 State House Station
353 Water St.
Augusta, ME 04333-0041
207-287-8000
info.ifw@maine.gov
www.maine.gov/ifw

Maine Forest Service (Maps 8–13)
Department of Agriculture,
Conservation & Forestry
22 State House Station
18 Elkins Ln.
Augusta, ME 04333-0022
207-287-3200
www.maine.gov/dacf/mfs

North Maine Woods (Maps 11–13)
P.O. Box 425
92 Main St.
Ashland, ME 04732
207-435-6213
info@northmainewoods.org
www.northmainewoods.org

Rangeley Lakes Heritage Trust (Map 8)
2424 Main St.
Rangeley, ME 04970
207-864-7311
info@rlht.org
www.rlht.org

**Chambers of Commerce and
Information Centers**
Flagstaff Area Business Association
(Map 9)
1216 Carrabassett Dr.
Kingfield, ME 04947
207-235-6008
info@mainesnorthwestern
mountains.com
www.mainesnorthwesternmountains
.com

Franklin County Chamber of
Commerce (Maps 8 and 9)
P.O. Box 123
Farmington, ME 04938
207-778-4215
director@franklincountymaine.org
www.franklincountymaine.org

Greater Fort Kent Area Chamber of Commerce (Map 13)
  416 West Main St., Suite 101
  Fort Kent, ME 04743
  207-834-5354
  fortkentchamber@gmail.com
  www.fortkentchamber.com

Jackman–Moose River Region Chamber of Commerce (Map 10)
  536 Main St.
  P.O. Box 368
  Jackman, ME 04945
  207-668-5225
  www.jackmanmaine.org

Moosehead Lake Region Chamber of Commerce (Map 11)
  P.O. Box 581
  480 Moosehead Lake Rd.
  (Maine Route 15)
  Greenville, ME 04441-0581
  207-695-2702
  destinationmooseheadlake@gmail.com
  www.destinationmooseheadlake.com

Rangeley Lakes Chamber of Commerce (Map 8)
  P.O. Box 317
  Rangeley, ME 04970
  207-864-5571
  info@rangeleymaine.com
  www.rangeleymaine.com

Cultural and Historical Organizations

Acadian Archives/Archives Acadiennes (Map 13)
  University of Maine at Fort Kent
  23 University Dr.
  Fort Kent, ME 04743
  207-834-7535
  acadian@maine.edu
  www.umfk.edu/offices/archives

Dead River Area Historical Society (Map 9)
  P.O. Box 15
  Stratton, ME 04982
  207-246-2271

Fort Kent State Blockhouse Historic Site (Map 13)
  www.nps.gov/maac/planyourvisit/blockhouse.htm

Maine Forestry Museum (Maps 8 and 9)
  221 Stratton Rd./Maine Route 16
  Rangeley, ME 04970
  207-864-3939
  maineforestry@gmail.com
  www.maineforestrymuseum.org

Moosehead Historical Society & Museums (Map 11)
  P.O. Box 1116
  444 Pritham Ave.
  Greenville, ME 04441-1116
  207-695-2909
  director@mooseheadhistory.org
  www.mooseheadhistory.org

Moosehead Marine Museum (Map 11)
  12 Lily Bay Rd.
  Greenville, ME 04441
  207-695-2716
  info@katahdincruises.com
  www.katahdincruises.com/museum/

Outdoor Heritage Museum (Map 8)
  P.O. Box 521
  Rangeley, ME 04970
  207-864-3091
  info@outdoorheritagemuseum.org
  www.outdoorheritagemuseum.org

Index

About the Writers

This guidebook contains the work of eight writer-paddlers who have explored the Northern Forest Canoe Trail (NFCT) from one end to the other.

KATINA DAANEN,
SECOND EDITION NFCT GUIDEBOOK WRITER AND EDITOR

Katina first learned about the NFCT in 2010—the same year the official NFCT guidebook was first published—at Canoecopia, a three-day paddle sport show held annually in Madison, Wisconsin. She was immediately hooked on the idea of paddling across the Northeast and completed her first Thru-Paddle in 2011. Relying on paddler blogs that painted the day-to-day journey, she kept detailed records of her own trip with the idea of paying it forward to future adventurers. Katina's blog became the basis of what turned into a guidebook specific to the needs of Thru-Paddlers, *The Northern Forest Canoe Trail Through-Paddler's Companion*. She has returned many times to repaddle sections of the trail and completed her second Thru-Paddle trip, solo, in 2021.

JOHN THOMPSON, NEW YORK (SECTIONS 1 AND 2)

John is a trip leader who has taught flatwater, whitewater, and efficient-paddling classes. He completed the first of many 90-Miler Adirondack Canoe Classics beginning in 1986. As a member of the "Flotilla" that publicized the Savage River International Whitewater Races in 1989, he paddled 203 miles upstream from Washington, DC, to Cumberland, Maryland. In 1998, Ron Canter persuaded John to help promote, survey, mark, and provide annual maintenance for the NFCT. His fondest memories are of his many canoe trips in the Northern Forest.

RONALD CANTER, NEW YORK (SECTIONS 2 AND 3)

Ron is one of the Trail's founders and has been canoeing since he was a youth. He faults author Eric Morse for presenting the way of the voyageur so well in his book of fur trade routes in Canada. With several equally foolish friends, Ron decided to tackle a few weeklong canoe trips. There was a steep learning curve through mud and bugs and blisters, but he was hooked. Retracing ancient canoe trails has led Ron through the Northern Forest, onto the Canadian Shield, down east along the coast of Maine, and strangely, into the jungles of Central America. For Ron, rivers lead to some of the greatest places and memories. He considers no portage he's ever done to be too long—though a few came close.

THOMAS K. SLAYTON, VERMONT (SECTIONS 4–6)

Tom is a journalist with a strong interest in the environment and outdoor recreation. He served as editor-in-chief of *Vermont Life* magazine for twenty-one years and is a past president of the International Regional Magazine Association. His 2007 book, *Searching for Thoreau: On the Trails and Shores of Wild New England*, won the gold IPPY Award for creative nonfiction. Tom is the author of several other books and is a commentator for Vermont Public Radio. He has been awarded honorary doctorates of letters by the University of Vermont, Sterling College, and Southern Vermont College.

ROBERT HENDERSON, QUÉBEC (SECTIONS 5 AND 6)

Starting as a camper and canoe-tripping staff member at Camp Ahmek in Algonquin Park, Bob developed a lifelong interest in Canadian travel heritage and travel guiding. For many years he wrote regular travel features for *Kanawa* magazine and is the author of *Every Trail Has a Story: Heritage Travel in Canada*. He edited *Nature First: Outdoor Life the Friluftsliv Way* with Nils Vikander and *Pike's Portage: Stories of a Distinguished Place* with Morten Asfeldt. Bob holds a PhD from the University of Alberta for his work focused upon approaches to travel guiding.

LORI DUFF, NEW HAMPSHIRE (SECTION 7)

Lori's photography and journalism career began at the age of thirty after working for a park in Kentucky, apprenticing as an actress, and serving as a Peace Corps water and sanitation volunteer in Ivory Coast. She earned her BA at Indiana University and her MA at the University of Missouri. Lori was a contributor for the *Concord Monitor*, and her work has been honored by the New England Newspaper & Press Association, Pictures of the Year International, and the National Press Photographers Association. She was also awarded a Rotary Ambassadorial Scholarship that took her to Tanzania, where sadly, she was unable to bring her canoe.

DONNIE MULLEN, MAINE (SECTIONS 8–13)

In 2000, Donnie paddled the NFCT in his hand-built wood-and-canvas canoe, becoming the first modern paddler to cover the distance in a single trip. Inspired by this adventure, Donnie convinced his wife to join him a few years later on a canoe odyssey through the wilds of Québec and Labrador. A Maine native, Donnie was an instructor for Outward Bound before becoming a freelance writer and photographer. He has written for *Maine: Boats, Homes & Harbors*; *WoodenBoat*; *Down East*; and *College of the Atlantic* magazines.

NICOLE GROHOSKI, THRU-PADDLER'S OVERVIEW

Nicole was born and raised in Ellsworth, Maine. She graduated from Middlebury College, where she studied environmental studies and chemistry with a minor in math. Nicole is a geographic information system (GIS) specialist and cartographer who works for a small, Maine-based mapping company. She has bicycled across the United States and western Europe and in 2006, Nicole and friend Tommy Perkins Thru-Paddled the NFCT, the first to officially do so using the published map set.

ABOUT NORTHERN FOREST CANOE TRAIL

Incorporated in 2000, the Northern Forest Canoe Trail is a nonprofit organization and water trail connecting communities, history, and wildlands across the Northern Forest. We believe access to wild places improves people's lives, strengthens our communities, and increases our care for the natural world. Our vision is to provide an unrivaled network of paddling opportunities across the Northern Forest, inspiring ongoing experiences and stories, and enticing people to fall in love with the region. Their passion and commitment will contribute to the health of our communities, landscapes, and waterways. As an organization we promote and steward our water trail and support communities, waterways, and paddling across the Northern Forest.

Our community of paddlers, staff, directors, and partners upholds a commitment to these values:

HISTORY: We are inspired by the deep human history of the Northern Forest, by the Indigenous Peoples who established the routes we steward, and by those who continue to work and travel on the land to this day.

INCLUSION: We believe everyone should have access to the outdoors and feel welcome in the outdoor community.

CONNECTION: We create opportunities to connect people and the environment in order to protect the places and relationships that sustain us.

COLLABORATION: We are passionate about working with others and listening to and including the voices within and beyond our community.

COMMUNITY: We dedicate ourselves to work that strengthens and bridges communities across the Northern Forest and to building a community of paddlers invested in the region.

WILD PLACES: We are fueled by our love of wild places. Whether a park, forest, or wilderness river, these places are the reason for our work.

Northern Forest Canoe Trail
P.O. Box 565
Waitsfield, VT 05673
802-496-2285
info@northernforestcanoetrail.org
www.northernforestcanoetrail.org

The Northern Forest Canoe Trail is a mapped inland water trail tracing 740 miles of historic travel routes across New York, Vermont, Québec, New Hampshire, and Maine. NFCT connects people to the Trail's natural environment, human heritage, and contemporary communities by stewarding, promoting, and providing access to paddling experiences along this route.

MOUNTAINEERS BOOKS, including its two imprints, Skipstone and Braided River, is a leading publisher of quality outdoor recreation, sustainability, and conservation titles. As a 501(c)(3) nonprofit, we are committed to supporting the environmental and educational goals of our organization by providing expert information on human-powered adventure, sustainable practices at home and on the trail, and preservation of wilderness.

Our publications are made possible through the generosity of donors, and through sales of more than 700 titles on outdoor recreation, sustainable lifestyle, and conservation. To donate, purchase books, or learn more, visit us online:

MOUNTAINEERS BOOKS
1001 SW Klickitat Way, Suite 201 • Seattle, WA 98134
800-553-4453 • mbooks@mountaineersbooks.org • www.mountaineersbooks.org

An independent nonprofit publisher since 1960

 Mountaineers Books is proud to support the Leave No Trace Center for Outdoor Ethics, whose mission is to promote and inspire responsible outdoor recreation through education, research, and partnerships. The Leave No Trace program is focused specifically on human-powered (nonmotorized) recreation. For more information, visit www.lnt.org.

YOU MAY ALSO LIKE:

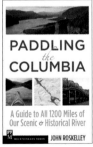

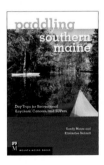